THE PAT BOONE FAN CLUB

D0289617

AMERICAN LIVES | SERIES EDITOR: TOBIAS WOLFF

The Pat Boone Fan Club

My Life as a White Anglo-Saxon Jew

SUE WILLIAM SILVERMAN

UNIVERSITY OF NEBRASKA PRESS

LINCOLN AND LONDON

Acknowledgments for the use of copyrighted
material appear on pages xi–xii, which constitute
an extension of the copyright page.
All rights reserved
Manufactured in the United States of America ∞

Library of Congress Cataloging-in-Publication Data
Silverman, Sue William.
The Pat Boone fan club: my life as a white Anglo-
Saxon Jew / Sue William Silverman.
pages cm.—(American lives)
ISBN 978-0-8032-6485-4 (pbk.: alk. paper)—
ISBN 978-0-8032-6498-4 (pdf)—ISBN 978-0-8032-
6499-1 (epub)—ISBN 978-0-8032-6500-4 (mobi)
1. Silverman, Sue William. 2. Jews—United States
—Biography. 3. Jewish women—United States
—Biography. 4. Jews—United States—Identity.
5. Jewish women—United States—Identity.
6. Boone, Pat—Appreciation. I. Title.
E184.37.S55A3 2014   973'.04924—dc23
2013034570

Designed and set in Scala and Scala Sans by
A. Shahan.

for Marc Sheehan, my Irish mensch

for Dr. Donald Moss who sees . . .
and who teaches me to see

Identity would seem to be the garment with
which one covers the nakedness of the self:
in which case, it is best that the garment
be loose, a little like the robes of the desert,
through which one's nakedness can always be
felt, and, sometimes, discerned. This trust
in one's nakedness is all that gives one the
power to change one's robes.

JAMES BALDWIN

Life is a tragedy when seen in close-up,
but a comedy in long-shot.

CHARLIE CHAPLIN

Take my hand and walk this land with me . . .

PAT BOONE, LYRICS TO "EXODUS"

Contents

Acknowledgments

I AM HONORED TO HAVE Kristen Elias Rowley as my editor at the University of Nebraska Press. I am also extremely grateful to Marguerite Boyles, Martyn Beeny, Kyle Simonsen, Andrea Shahan, Laura Wellington, Alison Rold, Emily Giller, Joy Margheim, and all the other talented people at the press.

A heartfelt thanks to Peggy Shumaker and Lee Martin for their support, friendship, and wisdom.

Profuse thanks to the faculty and students at Vermont College of Fine Arts who listened to me read much of this material in earlier drafts.

Several sections in this book, often in different forms, previously appeared in the following publications. Many thanks to the judges and editors who supported my work.

"The Pat Boone Fan Club." *Arts & Letters: Journal of Contemporary Culture* (Spring 2005). Also selected for the second edition of *The Touchstone Anthology of Contemporary Nonfiction: From 1970 to the Present* (Simon and Schuster, 2007).

"Galveston Island Breakdown: Some Directions." Winner, Brenda Euland Prose Prize, *Water˜Stone Review*, Fall 2006; judge: Nicholas DelBanco. Received special mention, Pushcart Prize xxxii: Best of the Small Presses, 2008.

"That Summer of War and Apricots." Winner, *Mid-American Review* essay contest, 2006; judge: Josip Novakovich.

"The Wandering Jew" (originally titled "Tramping the Land of Look Behind"). Winner, *Hotel Amerika* essay contest, Spring

2006. Received notable essay citation, *The Best American Essays*, 2006.

"I Was a Prisoner on the Satellite of Love." *River Teeth: A Journal of Nonfiction Narrative* (Spring 2006).

"Concerning Cardboard Ghosts, Rosaries, and the Thingness of Things." *Prairie Schooner* (Spring 2007).

"See the Difference." *Silence Kills: Speaking Out and Saving Lives*, ed. Lee Gutkind (Southern Methodist University Press, 2007). Nominated for a Pushcart Prize, 2007.

"Prepositioning John Travolta." *Ninth Letter* (Fall/Winter 2011–12). Nominated by the Pushcart Board of Contributing Editors for a Pushcart Prize, 2011.

Quotes in "I Was a Prisoner on the Satellite of Love" are from episodes of *Mystery Science Theater 3000*, created and produced by Best Brains, Inc., Eden Prairie MN.

The inspiration for "An Argument for the Existence of Free Will and/or Pat Boone's Induction into the Rock and Roll Hall of Fame" (a work of the imagination) is *Superman's Girlfriend, Lois Lane*, no. 9 (May 1959), National Comics Publications, Inc. Some quotes from Pat Boone are from Pat Boone's *America, 50 Years: A Pop Culture Journey through the Last Five Decades* (B&H Publishing Group, 2006).

This is a work of creative nonfiction. Since every experience has different points of view, some people might remember events differently. These, in compressed time and in nonchronological order, are my memories, recollected to the best of my ability. Some names and details have been changed to protect people's privacy.

THE PAT BOONE FAN CLUB

Friends, Christians, Lundsmen, Lend me your Souls (Lost or otherwise). I come not to Malign or Bury (nay Besmirch) my Fellows, but, like Wayward or Wandering Jews Everywhere, to Seek that which is most Holy: A Birthright. I Strayed Far from my Heritage, my People, and Now I ask you, Gentile And Jew Alike: *Am I Still a Jew? And if not, then What? Or Who?*

I Pray Thee, Dear Reader, whoever you are, do not avert your eyes as if I am Unclean or Traitorous based on the Title or Subtitle of this Unfortunate Saga. Show but a modicum of Pity. After being cast out from my Tribe, or so I felt (or was it Destiny? Fate?), I stumbled Hither and Yon—a one-Jew Diaspora.

I labored to discover Knowledge, Identity, Enlightenment, all Faithfully Rendered In this Document. I, Poor Pilgrim, Beseech Thee: Turn these Pages. Understand.

In short, Dear Reader, after Perusing my Tale of Farce and Woe, I Hope, most Fervently, to Hear You Call my Name in Welcome, offering Respite. For I Spent long Vagabond years as a Gefilte Fish Swimming Upstream with Nary a Fin . . . a Sorrowful, Utterly Lost and Sad Little Gefilte, far from her Glass Jar.

A Gefilte Without A School. A Gefilte Without a Home.

How Desperately I Swam against the Current (as have Not We All, Gentle Reader, whether Fish or Foul [sic]) Seeking a Place of Comfort to Rest my Weary Soul.

Your Most Humble Servant,
S.W.S.

The Pat Boone Fan Club

PAT BOONE DAZZLES ONTO THE STAGE of the Calvary Reformed church in Holland, Michigan. He wears white bucks, white pants, a white jacket with red- and blue-sequined stars emblazoned across the shoulders. I sit in the balcony, seats empty in the side sections. I'm here by chance, by luck. Kismet. A few weeks ago I happened to see his photograph in the local newspaper, the *Sentinel*, announcing the concert—part of Tulip Time Festival—only twenty minutes from my house. I stared at his photo in alluring black and white, just as, back in junior high school, I gazed at other photos of him. I ordered a ticket immediately.

This less-than-sold-out crowd enthusiastically claps after the opening number, his big hit "Love Letters in the Sand." But there are no whistles or shrieks from this mostly elderly, sedate, female audience. No dancing in the aisles, no mosh pit, no rushing the stage. If a fan swoons from her upholstered pew, it will more likely be from stroke than idolatry. The cool, unscented air in the auditorium feels polite as a Sunday worship service—rather than a Saturday-night-rock-and-roll-swaggering, Mick Jagger kind of concert.

Yet *I* am certainly worshipful. Of *him*. I am transfixed. Breathless . . . as if his photograph—that paper image—is conjured to life. I watch only him through binoculars, me in my own white jacket, as if I knew we'd match.

Pat Boone began as a '50s and '60s pop singer, though he has now aged into a Christian music icon favored by—I'm sure—Republicans. That I am a first-generation Russian American atheist liberal Democrat gives me no pause, not even as he per-

3

forms in this concrete megachurch weighted with massive cross-es. In fact, as I grew up these very symbols gave me comfort.

I'm not surprised he still affects me. During the days lead-ing up to tonight's concert, I plotted to meet him backstage. But in case I am too overwhelmed to speak, I've written a letter ex-plaining the reason for my devotion. To further prove my loyalty, I've retrieved, from an old scrapbook, my "SUE IS A MEMBER OF THE PAT BOONE FAN CLUB" card, printed on white stock. Surely the letter and card are all the credentials I'll need to be waved past security, to grant me access to Pat Boone. Tonight I'm de-termined to finally tell him what I failed to say last time we met, years ago, when I got his autograph after attending one of his live television shows. Time collapses as if, even now, it's not too late for him to save me from my Jewish family, save me from a childhood long ended.

I curled up on the baby-blue bedspread in my home in Glen Rock, New Jersey, a magnifying glass in my teenage hand. Slowly I scanned the glass across black-and-white photographs of Pat Boone in the latest issue of *Life* magazine. In one, he, his wife, Shirley, and their four young daughters perch on a tandem bicy-cle in front of their New Jersey home, not many miles from my own. I was particularly drawn to the whiteness in the photos. Pat Boone's white-white teeth beamed at me, his white bucks spot-less. I savored each cell of his being as I traced my finger across his magnified image. I believed I felt skin, the pale hairs on his forearms. Only a membrane of paper separated me from a slick fingernail, a perfectly shaped ear, the iris of his eye. Surely the wind gusted his hair, his family's hair, but in the photograph all movement was frozen, the bicycle wheels stationary, never to speed away from me. The family itself pedaled in tandem, legs pumping in perfect, still arcs. It was this crisp, clean, unchang-ing certainty that I craved.

The hands on his wristwatch were stopped at 3:40. I glanced at my own watch, almost 3:40. I didn't move, waiting for the minute hand to reach the eight, as if I could will time itself to stop, entranced by the notion that we would both endlessly exist in this same segment of time. For even as I tumbled inside the photograph, we remained static in this one moment, suspended at 3:40 . . .

. . . together. *I sit on the tandem bike directly behind him, leaning toward him. Now inside the black-and-white photo, I see lilacs, maple trees, shutters on windows. But I'm not distracted by scents or colors. I don't inhale the Ivory soap of his shirt, don't sense warm friction of rubber beneath the wheels of the bike, don't feel loss or know that seasons change. My ponytail, streaming behind my back, is frozen, captured with him and his family—now my consistent and constantly loving family.*

I fantasized living inside this black-and-white print, unreachable. This immaculate universe was safe, far away from my father's all-too-real hands, hands that hurt me at night.

Through my bedroom window, sun glinted off the glass I held inches from Pat Boone's face. Round magnifier. Beam of light. Halo. I placed my hand, fingers spread, beneath the glass, hovering just above the paper, as if glass, hand, photograph, *him*—all existed in disembodied, heavenly light.

The bus rumbled across the George Washington Bridge, over the Hudson River. I clutched a ticket to his television show in one hand, a copy of his book, *'Twixt Twelve and Twenty*, in the other. Silently, I sang the jingle "See the USA in Your Chevrolet," with which he closed his weekly program—a show I watched religiously on our black-and-white Zenith. Now, with the darkness of New Jersey behind me, the gleaming lights of Manhattan before me, I felt as if I myself were a photograph slowly developing into a new life. In just an hour I would see him in person. I wanted to be with him—be his wife, lover, daughter, houseguest, girlfriend, best friend, pet. Interchangeable. Any one of these relationships would do.

Sitting in the studio during the show, I waited for it to end. Mainly, I waited for the time when we would meet. Yes, I suppose I loved his voice, his music. At least, if asked, I would claim to love his songs. What else could I say, since there was no language at that moment to specify what I most needed from Pat Boone? How could I explain to him—to anybody—that if I held that magnifying glass over my skin, I would see my father's fingerprints? I would see skin stained with shame. I would see a girl who seemed marked by her very Jewishness. Since my Jewish father misloved me, what I needed in order to be saved was an audience with Pat Boone.

There in *that* audience, I was surrounded by teenage girls crying and screaming his name. But I was different from those fans. Surely he knew this, too, sensed my silent presence, the secret life we shared. Soon I no longer heard the girls, no longer noticed television cameras, cue cards, musicians. No longer even heard his voice or which song he sang. All I saw was his face suffused in a spotlight, one beam emanating as if from an otherwise darkened sky.

I queued up after the show, outside the stage door, with other fans. I waited with my Aqua Net flipped hair, Peter Pan collar, circle pin, penny loafers. The line inched forward, girls seeking autographs.

But when I reached him, I was too startled to speak. I faced him in living color. Pink shirt. Brown hair. Suede jacket. His tanned hands moved; his brown eyes actually blinked. I saw him *breathe*. I forgot my carefully rehearsed words: *Will you adopt me?*

Besides, if I spoke, I feared he wouldn't hear me. My voice would be too low, too dim, too insignificant, too tainted. He would know I was too distant to be saved. I felt as if I'd fallen so far from that photograph that my own image was out of focus. I was a blur, a smudged Jewish blur of a girl, mesmerized by a golden cross, an amulet on a chain around his neck. I continued to stand, unmoving, speechless, holding up the line.

"Is that for me?" he finally asked, smiling. He gestured toward the book. I held it out to him. He scrawled his name.

Later, alone in my bedroom, lying on my blue bedspread, I trailed a fingertip over his autograph. I spent days tracing and duplicating it. I forged the name "Pat Boone" on all my school notebooks using black India ink. I wrote his name on my white Keds with a ballpoint pen. At the Jersey shore I scrawled my own love letters in the sand. But I had missed my chance to speak to him. My plea for him to save me remained unspoken.

Now, watching him through binoculars in the Calvary Reformed church in Holland, Michigan, I again scan every cell of his face, his neck. I'm sure I distinguish individual molecules in his fingers, palms, hands, wrists. He wears a gold pinkie ring, a gold-link bracelet. And a watch! That watch? I wonder if it's the same 3:40 watch. In his presence I am once again tranced—almost as if, all this time, we've been together in a state of suspension.

He doesn't even appear to have aged—much. Boyish good looks, brown hair. Yet this grandfather sings his golden oldies, tributes to innocence and teenage love: "Bernadine," "Moody River," "Friendly Persuasion," "Tutti Frutti." His newer songs reflect God and patriotism. Well, he sings, after all, to a white Christian audience, mainly elderly church ladies with tight gray curls, pastel pantsuits, sensible shoes. I know I am the only one here who voted for President Clinton, who wears open-toed sandals, who isn't a true believer. But nothing deters me. I feel almost like that teenage girl yearning to be close to him. Closer.

He retrieves, from the piano, a bouquet of tulips wrapped in cellophane. He explains to the audience that at each concert he presents flowers to one young girl. He peers into the darkened auditorium, asking, half jokingly, whether any girls have actually attended the concert. "Has anyone brought their granddaughters?"

I glance around. In one section sits a tour group of older women all wearing jaunty red hats. At least twenty of these hats turn in unison, searching the audience. No one else moves. The row in front of me seems to be mother-and-daughter pairs, but most of the daughters wear bifocals, while some of the mothers, I noticed earlier, used canes to climb the stairs. After a moment of silence, Pat Boone, cajoling, lets us know he found one young girl at his earlier, four o'clock show. He lowers the microphone to his side, waiting.

Me. I want it to be me.

A girl, her neck bent, silky brown hair shading her face, finally walks forward from the rear of the auditorium. Pat Boone hurries down the few steps, greeting her before she reaches the stage. He holds out the flowers, but she doesn't seem to realize she's supposed to accept them.

"What's your name?" he asks.

"Amber." She wears ripped jeans and a faded sweatshirt.

"Here." Again he offers her the tulips. "These are for a lovely girl named Amber." This time she takes them.

Strains of "April Love" flow from the four-piece band. His arm encircles her waist. Facing her, he sings as if just to her, "April love is for the very young . . ." The spotlight darkens, an afterglow of sunset. The petals of the tulips, probably placed onstage hours earlier, droop.

After the song, Pat Boone beams at her and asks for a kiss. "On the cheek, of course." He laughs, reassuring the audience, as he points to the spot. The girl doesn't move. "Oh, please, just one little peck." His laugh dwindles to a smile.

I slide down in my seat. I lower the binoculars to my lap.

Kiss him, I want to whisper to the girl, not wanting to witness Pat Boone embarrassed or disappointed.

No, walk away from him. Because he's old enough to be your father, your grandfather.

Instead, he bends forward and brushes his lips on her cheek. She escapes down the aisle to her seat, the bouquet held awkwardly in her hand.

The lights onstage are extinguished. His voice needs to rest, perhaps. Images of Pat Boone in the Holy Land flash on two large video screens built into the wall behind the pulpit, while the real Pat Boone sits on a stool. The introduction to the theme song from *Exodus* soars across the hushed audience. Atop the desert fortress Masada—the last outpost of Jewish zealots who chose mass suicide rather than Roman capture—a much younger Pat Boone, in tan chinos, arms outstretched, sings, "So take my hand and walk this land with me," lyrics he, himself, wrote. Next the video pans to Israelis wearing kibbutz hats, orchards of fig trees, the Sea of Galilee, Bethlehem, the Old City in Jerusalem. The Via Dolorosa. The Wailing Wall. The Dead Sea.

"Until I die, this land is mine."

A final aerial shot circles a sweatless and crisp Pat Boone on Masada. Desert sand swelters in the distance.

This land is mine . . .

For the first time I wonder what he means by these words he wrote. Does he mean, literally, he thinks the Holy Land is his, that it belongs to Christianity? Or perhaps, is he momentarily impersonating an Israeli, a Zionist, a Jew? Or maybe this appropriation is just a state of mind.

Pat Boone, Pat Boone. Who are you? I always thought I knew.

The lights flash on. Pat Boone smiles. The band hits the chords as he proclaims we'll all have "A Wonderful Time up There," a song with which I'm familiar.

I've always been more attuned to Christian songs than those of my own religion. I frequented churches over the years, immersing myself in hymns and votive candles. Once I even owned a garnet rosary, magically believing this Catholic amulet offered luck and protection. At only one period in my life, in elementary school, when I lived with my family on the island of St. Thomas, in the West Indies, did I periodically attend Jewish services.

We drove up Synagogue Hill some Saturday mornings, parking by the wrought-iron gate leading to the temple. We entered the arched stucco doorway, where my father donned a yarmulke. The air cooled, shaded from tropical sun. In my best madras dress, I followed my parents down the aisle, the floor thick with sand. My feet, in buffalo-hide sandals, etched small imprints behind the tracks left by my father's heavy black shoes. I sat between my parents on one of the benches. The rabbi, standing before the mahogany ark containing the six Torahs, began to pray. I slid from the bench to the sandy floor.

The sand was symbolic in this nineteenth-century synagogue, founded by Sephardic Jews from Spain. During the Spanish Inquisition, Jews, forced to worship in secret, met in cellars where they poured sand on floors to muffle footsteps, mute the sound of prayers. This was almost all I knew of Judaism except stories my mother told me about the Holocaust when bad things happened to Jews—even little Jewish girls.

I sprinkled sand over myself throughout the service, as if at the beach. I trailed it down my bare calves. I slid off my sandals, submerging my toes beneath grains of coral. Lines of sand streaked the sweaty crooks of my elbows. Small mounds cupped my knees. I trickled it on my head until it caught in the weave of my braids. I leaned against one of the cool, lime-whitewashed pillars, smudging my dress. I traced my initials in the sand. No one in the congregation, not even my parents, ever seemed to notice. Perhaps they were too engrossed by readings from the Torah to see me . . . while, to me, none of *their* prayerful chants were as lovely as sand. Wands of light beamed through arched windows, glinting off flecks of mica, off me. I felt as if I, myself, could become one with whitewash, with sand, with light. Then, later that night, home in bed, maybe my father wouldn't find me, wouldn't be able to see or distinguish me. Maybe if I poured enough sand over my body I could discover how to hide all little Jewish girls, make us invisible. Instead, it seemed to be my own father's footsteps that were muffled, for no one in the congregation ever heard or saw him. Not as he really was.

After the concert, I slowly walk through the church lobby, exhausted. I stop at the less-than-busy sales booth to buy a CD and ask whether Pat Boone will be signing autographs. No one knows. I had assumed a throng of grandmothers would line up for autographs and snapshots. A gray-haired man limps past, the word "Security" stenciled on his black t-shirt. The church ladies stream out the door, not seeming to expect anything more of the evening.

I could follow them.

But at the far corner of the lobby is a hallway leading to the back of the auditorium, behind the stage. No one guards the entrance. I turn down its plush, blue-carpeted stillness. My footsteps are silent. It is a hush that might precede a worship service. Solemn, scentless air. Dim sconces line the walls. I am alone, gripping his CD and the letter I wrote to him.

Two wide doors, shut, appear at the end of the corridor. I assume they're locked, but when I try the knob it turns. Another hallway. I pass a second t-shirted guard, this one holding a silent walkie-talkie, his ear plugged with a hearing aid. I worry he'll stop me. But my straight, solid footsteps, plus the determined look on my face, grant me entrance. I must act as if I belong here, as if I know what I'm doing.

I *do* belong here. I *do* know what I'm doing.

Beyond another set of doors I reach a small group wearing Dutch costumes, including the mayor and his wife. They appeared onstage earlier, in wooden clogs, to thank Pat Boone for celebrating the Tulip Time Festival. Beside them stands another security guard, this one a teenage boy, murmuring into his walkie-talkie. I approach, wanting to ask him where I might find Pat Boone. I decide to throw myself on his mercy. I'm prepared to beg, plead, cry. I will say I've been waiting my whole life. I will say the Voice of God Himself *told* me to speak to Pat Boone.

The guard continues to mumble into his walkie-talkie. I wait for him to finish, until anxiety floods me. Suppose I miss Pat Boone? He might be preparing to leave the building right this minute. He'll disappear before I find him.

Then, as if pulled by unseen forces, I turn away from the guard. I retrace my footsteps back through the set of doors.

I glimpse a white shirt. The back of a man's head. Brown hair. *Him.*

He and another man are just opening a door farther down the corridor.

I yell, "Mr. Boone. Pat Boone."

I rush after him, grabbing the door about to shut behind him. We stand in a small foyer just behind the stage. The other man, clearly not understanding the force of my need, tries to shoo me away. I ignore him, pleading, "Mr. Boone. I have to speak to you. Just for a minute. I've been waiting. Pat Boone."

I push past the assistant until I stand right in front of Pat Boone. His red- and blue-sequined jacket is off. He wears his white shirt, white pants, white shoes. His face, still in makeup, reveals few wrinkles. His eyes are almost expressionless. It's as if his whole life all he's practiced is his public smile, while the rest of his face is frozen—but familiar to me—the way he looks in photographs. There, as he smiles at me, albeit tentatively, are his white-white teeth.

My words are garbled, rushed, confused. I don't know when I'll be ordered to leave, when I'll be removed. So much to explain. I hardly know where to start. I tell him how much I loved that one particular photograph in *Life* magazine.

"Oh, yes, that tandem bicycle," he says. "I remember it."

"You saved my life," I say.

I am telling him about my father, what happened with my father, that it was *he*, Pat Boone, just knowing he existed kept me going, just seeing his photograph helped me stay alive . . . that he represented . . . what word do I use? "Safety"? "Holiness"? "Purity"?

He has taken a step back, away from me. His smile may have dimmed by one decibel. Am I acting like a crazy woman? Am I the first woman who ever pursued him to confess that her father once hurt her and that he, Pat Boone, represented *hope*? Just thinking that one day he might . . .

"Well I'm glad to know that I did something good," he says. "That I helped someone."

"You *did*," I say. "You were everything. Your family. Your daughters."

"I guess these things happen a lot," he says. "To children. It's terrible."

"Here." I give him the letter. "This will explain how I felt."

He takes the letter, folded in an envelope. That hand—those clean fingers I studied by the hour.

"I'll write back to you," he says. "After I read it."

My audience with him is over. "Thank you," I whisper, turning to leave.

I pause in the parking lot in the damp spring night. The massive walls of the church loom over me. Busloads of grandmothers rumble from the lot.

I was too overwhelmed to tell him about the magnifying glass or his wristwatch. Nor did I say *I want you to adopt me*—the important thing I neglected to say last time—the one thing I've most wanted. Of course, even *I* know how crazy that would sound. Besides, is it still true?

I get in my car but continue to watch the church. Maybe I'll catch one last glimpse of him. Him. *Did* he help sustain me all those years? *Did* he offer hope?

Yes. His image. His milky-white image. That sterile pose. I conjured him into the man I needed him to be: a safe father.

By my believing in that constant image, he *did* save me, without my being adopted, without my even asking.

At the end of the concert, the mayor of Holland and his wife came onstage to present Pat Boone with a special pair of wooden clogs painted to resemble his trademark bucks. Again, I had to lower the binoculars, embarrassed for him, unable to watch, just as when he gave the tulips to that young girl.

I wonder if anyone else in the audience felt uncomfortable when this father, this grandfather, tried to coerce a kiss from that adolescent girl? Or did anyone notice her embarrassment, her shame? No, that's not a thought that would trouble any of Pat Boone's fans in Calvary. But Calvary doesn't exist for me, cannot be made to exist for me—even by Pat Boone.

Pat Boone! Those two short syllables stretch the length of my life. So, regardless of religion or illusion, his love letters offered me improbable safety—grooved in vinyl, etched in sand.

The Wandering Jew

MY FAMILY AND I LIVE ON the island of St. Thomas for over a year before I notice the tramp, on Dronningens Gade. He walks along unaware of tourists veering to the other side of the street, away from this man weighted in burlap crocus sacks stitched into layers of clothes—pants, shirts, jackets, cap—despite tropical heat. Only his feet are bare. He sounds a metal triangle the exact moment his right heel strikes the ground. While he's not blind, his gaze seems distant, or as if he's more at home wandering paths through forests, fields, and mountains. I watch him from in front of the Apollo Theatre, my destination this day after school. I plan to see a movie, as I frequently do, while waiting for my father to leave the West Indies Bank and Trust Company, where he is president, to drive me up Blackbeard's Hill, home.

I don't follow the tramp, this first time I see him. I only watch. He passes Maison Danoise, Little Switzerland, Riise's rum warehouse, Katzin's Drug Store, before turning the corner toward Market Square.

Even after he disappears, I gaze at the corner as if he might reappear, like an apparition. Faintly, I still hear the silver pitch of the triangle. I imagine sun-sparked Caribbean water—as if a sound can be seen.

The next day at the Antilles School, high up a mountain, I stare out paneless windows. I don't hear Miss Duvall conjugate French verbs. I don't watch Mr. Waggoner chalk sums on the blackboard. My mates' voices, chanting answers, seem remote. Far below, white sails gust the U-shaped harbor, the tessellated azure, aqua, viridian sea. Pastel houses dot green volcanic mountains. Daydreaming, I re-create the scene when the tramp turned the corner . . . see him again *before* he turned the corner. I want to know who he is, where he lives, where he goes, where he is now. As if he offers a secret message, I want to hear his triangle, follow his bare feet, know what he sees in his distant gaze. Yesterday afternoon, while watching a film about Martians landing on Earth, I couldn't even pretend to be scared. Rather, *his* image continuously reels.

A week later, again in front of the theater, I finally hear the ping of metal. I look toward Emancipation Park. The sound sharpens. I slip the coins meant for the purchase of a movie ticket into my pocket. I step back under the canopy of the marquee. I don't yet want him aware of me. When he passes, it's as if his presence deepens the shade in which I stand. Not as a bad omen, as in movies, foreshadowing a car crash or the arrival of a monster. Rather, his shadowed scent is of mangrove swamps, is the core of a calabash, rain-rubbed earth after a tropical storm. As I take my first step after him, this scent is what I seem to follow.

He pays no attention to me. We continue along the main street past duty-free shops, tourists giving him a wide berth, and now me, as well. Again he turns toward Market Square. Here in the crowded market, I assume no one will notice me, even though I am a white girl trailing after him. I dawdle past booths of sugarcane, myrtle, Bombay mangoes, squawking guinea fowl. Men sit outside snackettes drinking small glasses of white rum. I pause beside a donkey to stroke his mangy fur, still aware of the man's burlap-sack back. Even above shouts of women in headties selling guava ices, I hear the strokes of his triangle.

He leaves the market, continuing along the marl alleys of shantytown. Here I will be noticed, in this place my parents forbid me to enter. I follow anyway, past shacks with corrugated tin roofs, walls constructed of newspapers, egg cartons, rusty biscuit tins. A woman watches me as she cups rainwater from a kerosene drum. Another woman, sweeping her dirt yard with a palm frond, pauses. I don't know if I should smile, explain my presence. I do nothing. It's not as if I'm scared to be here, not at all, and I don't understand my parents' warning. Rather, I worry that, because of my skin color, I am the one to cause concern even though I'm young. I hunch my shoulders as if this can make me seem even smaller, as if to say, *I'm only a little girl who won't cause trouble.* I shuffle as quietly as possible in my buffalo-hide sandals, my toes now dusty with limestone soil. The man never slows his gait.

Once we leave shantytown, we are in solitude. We are at the point on the island where streets lead to alleys, alleys lead to fields of fever grass, fields flow up volcanic mountains or meander into donkey trails and goat paths, here, where streets aren't streets at all but muddy footprints leading into mangrove swamps, into forests of mimosa, mampoo, coconut palm.

He enters the woods. Reluctantly I pause just inside the entrance. If I don't meet my father at the appointed time, he'll be angry. Grasses sway as the tramp follows the trail, soon disappearing. Now, the ring of his triangle is the chirp of banana-quits and scarlet tanagers. Even though the island is small, finite, *this* place seems like an unearthly, overgrown, magical garden where cool trade winds sough flame trees, where sphagnum moss thrives, where phalaropes sleep. I clink my movie coins together, to mimic his sound.

Around this same time, I first hear the story of the Pied Piper, probably at school, told as a caution, a warning: *he leads children away from their parents.* But I love the word "pied." At first I imagine the piper as a sort of baker with a kitchen full of pies—a dessert I prefer to cookies or cake. When I understand that the word means someone dressed in patchwork rags, I of course think of the tramp. Does this story stay with me because I am already following him—following the sound of his triangle—even as I know that, unlike the piper, the tramp is perfectly safe?

I also hear stories about ancient people wandering in faraway deserts—or about others being led to gas chambers. All stories seem equally real and unreal, true and untrue, at the same time. I don't quite understand why gas would be in a chamber. After all, we get gas for our car at the Esso Service Center, located at the entrance to the airport. As the attendant pumps it, I love to watch British West Indian Airways or Caribair planes soaring toward Antigua, St. Kitts, San Juan. Sometimes I want to be aboard in order to explore distant places. Other times I don't, knowing I'd miss my mates, my ballet lessons, and now, the tramp.

In some of these stories, following seems to be a good thing. In others, not. I could ask my parents or teachers about this, but I don't.

The following Sunday evening, as usual, my parents drive my older sister and me to the Virgin Isle Hotel. It caps one of the mountaintops like a snow peak. We arrive when the sun, crimson as a hibiscus, sizzles the horizon, sinking below sea for the night. Foam encircles the island like fiery opals, as if you might scorch your feet if you stray from shore. Inside the hotel, blazing with light, we cross the marble lobby to the dining room. As always, we sit next to the dance floor, close to tables where my mates from school sit with their parents, intermingled with tourists. We eat roast beef and baked Alaska. All evening parents sip planter's punches or grenadine and rum in frosty glasses, rims outlined in rose-colored sugar. Flames of white tapers shiver in winds gently blowing through floor-to-ceiling windows. Panmen on the stage *plonk* calypso rhythms. Men swirl across the dance floor in white linen dinner jackets trailing the scent of bay rum aftershave, of Bances Aristocratos, dark vuelta cigars. They dance with wives whose sequined gowns sparkle, whose silk guipure skirts whisper, whose Maltese shawls smell of Chanel No. 5.

Vicki, a friend from school, eats dinner with her parents and brother a few tables away. Even from here I notice a small bruise by her left eye. I know her father hits her—though we never speak of it. Here where we live, where we dance, where we eat—isolated atop mountains or behind *chevaux-de-frise*, high stucco walls strung with tigerwire—we *shall* be safe. Perfect. In our wealth. In our whiteness. The waiters and waitresses, as well as the panmen, are black.

After dinner, Vicki and I stroll outside to the upper terrace. We stand by the wrought-iron railing. On the lower terrace, the lit swimming pool ripples turquoise. *Labelles*, fireflies, sparkle like stardust. Pinpricks of light pulse dark mountainsides. Lower, at the base of the mountain, a cruise ship in the harbor, strung with colored bulbs, glitters like bijoux. Lights define Charlotte Amalie, the capital, while lamps in Emancipation Park outline paths among lignum vitae trees. Yes, it is perfect. We are perfect, aren't we?

How can one small bruise by a girl's eye mar the visage of a colorful, tropical island?

Only the fields and forests beyond shantytown, where the tramp led me, are dark, pristine, original—not lit by artificial light.

When we first arrived on the island from Washington DC, where my father had worked for the Department of the Interior, a demonstration was organized by islanders who thought my father's bank was only for his own gain. They believed that if they opened accounts, he would steal their money, like a pirate. The crowd, carrying torches and drums, marched from Market Square to Emancipation Park to burn my father in effigy. For safety, my sister and I were sequestered in Riise's rum warehouse behind brick-and-stucco walls originally built by Danish colonialists to withstand pirate attacks, fires, and hurricanes. I watched the flames through an iron keyhole. I felt a vibration of drums against my forehead. As the hour grew late I became dizzy with the scent of rum, dizzy with shouts echoing against brick. My senses were dulled from having lived in cool, white-marbled

Washington DC. New to the island, I felt bewildered by the pungency of wild fruit, the susurrus of waves, the heat. That night in the warehouse, I felt confused by people as well. I felt trapped, as if I might never escape.

Later, order was restored. The crowd, reassured by my father, dispersed. My sister and I, freed from the warehouse, returned to our home across the street from Blackbeard's Castle.

Except my mother didn't want this island to be our home. After the demonstration, she pleaded with my father to leave, take us back to our real home in the States. Although he'd calmly talked to the crowd in order to quiet them, now he yelled at my mother, accusing her of not supporting him, not standing by his side. My sister and I said nothing, but he raged at us as well. My sister turned from him, stalking from the room, followed by my mother, who rushed to the bathroom, crying.

I tried to pass him to escape to my bedroom. He blocked the doorway. *Please,* I thought, *move.* He didn't. He held me. His arms, tight around me, felt more like a throttle than a hug, gripping me, in a way that wasn't love.

He released me when he heard my mother returning. I rushed to my room and opened the shutters overlooking the verandah. Across the valley rose Synagogue Hill, the synagogue itself invisible from here. Sky and sea merged at night, as though you could walk right off the island toward the horizon. If only you knew how.

Now, as I stand beside Vicki on the hotel terrace, with the island below us, my gaze follows the route the demonstrators marched that night from Market Square to Emancipation Park. I wonder if the tramp marched with them.

"Have you ever seen that man?" I describe him and his triangle.

"Sure," she says, "the loco-crazy man."

I turn to look at her. Here on the terrace, in the rippled light reflected from the swimming pool, her face seems paler, the bruise below her eye darker. "But he never bothers anyone, does he?"

Vicki shrugs. "We're supposed to stay away from him. My father said."

Once, on a Saturday, Vicki and I went swimming at Magens Bay, instructed by her parents to be back no later than four. But we lost track of time so didn't return until after five, drowsy with sun, our lips stained from sea grapes. As soon as we reached her house, her father slapped her. I sucked in my breath and, without thinking, said, "Wait." I stepped back, fearing he might hit me, too, her father angry we'd stayed late on a public beach where someone might hurt us.

The next evening I visit Sylvanita, our cook, who lives in a cabin behind our house, almost hidden among woman's-tongue trees. She never invites me inside, so I stand on her stoop, asking her about the tramp: *Do you know him? Why does he ring the triangle?*

She doesn't answer directly. Instead she explains that, decades ago, some slaves, forced to the island from Africa, fled their masters. They hid in rain forests. Many of their descendants remain, some still wandering these forests, named, by the slaves, the Land of Look Behind. They also renamed themselves Maroons.

She disappears for a moment, telling me to wait. From inside, I smell mango leaves, burning, to discourage mosquitoes. She returns and shows me a freedom paper, once belonging to her ancestor, carefully wrapped in unbleached muslin.

One afternoon I see the movie *Limelight*, starring Charlie Chaplin, preceded by one of his "Little Tramp" shorts, *The Vagabond*. *Limelight* is about a once-famous clown in London, now poor and forgotten, who saves a young ballerina, Thereza, who is about to commit suicide because she suffers hysterical paralysis. She can neither walk nor dance. In *The Vagabond* Chaplin's tramp character rescues a young woman who, kidnapped, is mistreated and whipped by her captor.

After I see the movie, I am virtually mute for days. I stay home sick from school. I refuse to eat. I refuse to get out of bed. Only he can soothe me, Chaplin, *this* tramp, helping young ballerinas dance. He comforts girls who are lost, lonely, confused, paralyzed, trapped. He leads them away from harm, saving them.

I must see *Limelight* again. I finally leave my house to walk down the mountain to town. But when I reach the theater, the movie is no longer playing. It was scheduled for only one show. *But where has it gone?* I ask. *To St. Croix*, I'm told. Another film is advertised on the marquee. I stare at movie posters tacked in glass cases as if I can will *Limelight* back into being, can conjure Charlie Chaplin to stand here before me. I want to run away with him, follow him, be a tramp with him. At the same time I want to save him from his "trampness" by giving him all that I have. I will draw a rainwater bath for him, sprinkled with bay leaves. I will feed him roast chicken and guava jelly for dinner.

But meshed with this love is loss. In *Limelight* Chaplin's character dies. He leaves both Thereza and me behind. She dances alone on the stage. I stand here on the sidewalk outside the theater, unmoving, unsure where to go. This loss is almost too terrible to bear.

Since we first moved to the island, I have taken ballet lessons from Madame Caron at the Virgin Isle Hotel. She is the mother of French actress Leslie Caron, star of *Gigi*. I've never seen Leslie Caron in person, but her brother sometimes visits the island. The other girls and I, while practicing pliés and arabesques, watch for him outside the hotel windows. He struts around the swimming pool in a French-cut bathing suit, a Gaulois Disc Blue aslant between his lips. We girls dance as if for him, hoping to be noticed.

Today, however, after seeing *Limelight*, I don't watch for him. Nor am I able to chatter with Vicki and my friends as we change into Danskin leotards and pink tutus. I sit on the floor in the dressing room, my Selva ballet slippers in my hands. I mold the rabbit fur into the toes, then slide my feet inside the soft cushions. I crisscross the pink satin ribbons up my ankles and calves.

Once I'm ready to dance, I feel transported to London. The scent of trade winds ebbs as I inhale a cold, damp winter. As all the girls trail down the corridor to the hotel ballroom, I, Thereza, enter the stage of the Empire Theatre. Charlie Chaplin waits for me in the wings. My adult eyes are lined with mascara and kohl, my cheeks and mouth rouged.

The orchestra tunes in the pit.

One night a few months later, my father out of town, I'm awakened by a loud rapping on the shutters. It is Vicki and her mother, who carries Vicki's younger brother. Vicki and her mother are bruised, their clothes ripped. When her husband fell asleep, Vicki's mother grabbed all the money in his wallet. They fled here on foot.

My mother settles them in the kitchen, pouring cold sodas. Vicki stares at the fizz of 7-Up in her glass. *We have to leave,* Vicki's mother whispers, as if her husband can hear. But she needs more money. She needs clothes for her children. Cold-weather clothes. She worries if she waits for the 8:40 a.m. flight to San Juan, her husband will be awake, looking for her. Now, tonight, she needs a boat to carry them away to Puerto Rico, the first stop on their journey home.

My mother directs my sister and me to the storage closet where our stateside clothes are packed in mothballs. When I pry open the box marked with my name, I'm surprised to see my blue sweater, my yellow-quilted skirt, my winter shoes. It's as if these clothes have been slumbering but now are startled awake.

My mother snaps open a set of leather luggage, filling it with clothes, shoes, blankets. She empties purses, gathering as much money as she can find. I crack open my piggy bank with a coral rock I once found at the beach. I wrap nickels and pennies, as well as my one silver dollar, into my best lace hankie. I tie the corners in knots. I'm too shy to hand it to Vicki, so I tuck it into a parcel for her to discover later.

We finish packing, and my mother wakes Sylvanita, whose cousin lives on a skiff in the harbor. I've never seen my mother so energized, so focused. I wonder if she ever thinks about grabbing her own children and fleeing?

My mother piles us all into the car even though she's scared to navigate narrow mountain roads, especially at night. She drives about five miles an hour, and I can tell Vicki's mother wishes she'd hurry, though she says nothing.

We park close to the harbor, by the Grand Hotel. Vicki's mother carries her son, while the rest of us grab the luggage. Our footsteps are the only sound except for boats knocking the dock in the small swell of waves. When we reach Sylvanita's cousin's skiff, she motions us to wait and climbs aboard. We hear her murmuring. Vicki stares out across the sea, her back to the island, her hands tight fists.

Sylvanita calls us to load everything onto the boat, hurry. My mother places all her remaining money in the cousin's hand.

We stand on shore watching the boat glide across the water into the night.

Goodbye, I think. *Goodbye Vicki, goodbye winter shoes, goodbye silver dollar, goodbye lace hankie.*

Several weeks later I awake early and slip from the house before my family is up. I walk toward town. Across the island, curds of mist hover mid-mountain, mountaintops floating free of the earth. Clouds of ibises rise like ghosts, winging from trees. Mica glints off the mound of yellow bauxite down by the harbor. In the distance, a pontoon plane passes Hassel Island.

I sit in Emancipation Park, waiting for my ragged savior.

Again, he and I are at the end of the street, the end of pavement, the end of marl alleys that ebb into fields of fever grass.

I know this is the place where I should stop, turn around, go back. I don't. Despite stories I've heard, this place seems the opposite of dangerous. Nor do I worry about getting caught. Surely no one sees him, or me. Maybe that glimpse of red—really my French madras shorts—is a scarlet tanager or a flower, some observer might think. I am determined to follow wherever he might lead me.

I walk deep into the forest trailing the tramp in all his clothes, layered, perhaps, to protect him from the wildness of the island. He reminds me of a mampoo tree, which hoards water in its trunk, safe from drought. So maybe the tramp is able to wander long distances without need of refreshment.

We pass remains of stone windmills, once used to grind sugarcane, and chimneys of abandoned sugar mills. Antillean euphonias and indigo buntings dart among leaves. Cerise bougainvillea and blue-white tree orchids tumble, seemingly from the sky. Divi-divi, shaddock, lantana trees shadow the donkey path. The air hums with tree frogs and crac-cracs. Sweat drips down my arms, while sticker weeds catch my bare legs. I don't care.

One moment I'm following him. The next, the tramp disappears from sight as if he's a spirit dispersed into mist. I no longer hear his triangle.

Still I continue on until I reach the mangrove swamp. Here, even the path ends. And while I know the swamp is a maze of red, black, and white mangroves—and that if you know how to recognize each you can find your way out—I'm not sure I do. Instead, I sit by the edge, my back in sunlight, my face in shade. I kick off my sandals, pushing my toes into cool, brackish tannin.

One winter night at college in Boston, years later, I attend Charlie Chaplin's movie *City Lights*, showing at an art cinema on Exeter Street. In it, the Little Tramp, penniless, tries to save a blind girl. He wants either to earn or steal enough money for an operation, so she can see.

After the movie I sit in the Hayes-Bickford Cafeteria with a cup of tea, watching ancient homeless men sip cold coffee, their clothes creased with dirt. Their hands shake. They smell of exile, of the hour just before dawn. . . .

The Caribbean tramp, his feet bare, is here with me as well. I don't know how he discovered this place first, but clearly he has. He will always be ahead of me, compelling as an oasis mirage that only I can see.

Charlie Chaplin also sits across from me, in his battered hat, his tattered jacket, his oversized shoes, toes pointing in opposite directions.

Back then, I simply had no choice but to love Charlie Chaplin—who was both the promise and the essence of that year—the year of tramps and triangles, tales and movies, ballet and Leslie Caron's mother, a mountaintop hotel, Vicki fleeing. In the confluence of island isolation and restless movement, I wanted, more than anything, to be the ballerina Charlie Chaplin noticed, the girl he taught to dance, the young girl he saved. Instead, I learned how to walk, not exactly *upon* water, but beyond, to where I both lead and am led . . . wandering with mystics and seers, seeking—not the meaning of life but the meaning of *my* life—as I look forward, as I glance back.

The Mercurialist

EVENINGS, AS A LITTLE GIRL, RESTLESS and sweaty, I wander across the verandah of our house, past the metal cistern, to visit Sylvanita. Sometimes we sit on her stoop in silence, slapping at mosquitoes. Other times she fetches her vial of mercury, pouring a puddle into my hand. My skin cools, even in West Indies heat. I press a fingertip against the plump, wobbly surface. I swirl it, small dimes segmenting from the quarter coined in my palm. Or maybe it looks like stars shooting off from a galaxy. I twist my wrist. Oblong shapes shiver toward the cracks between my fingers, seeking escape, until they portage back to safe harbor, anchored in my hand.

I return it to the vial.

Sylvanita grips my hand to study the palm lines where slivers of mercury remain. Her chiromancy itself seems to arise from trade winds, or from the rattle of woman's-tongue pods, swaying from tree limbs: If mercury trails my life line, I will live to be an ancient woman. If, on another evening, bubbles cling to my love line, I will be rich in romance. I imagine my pockets overflowing with Mercury-head dimes when wealth is promised. All her predictions strike my heart with such vivid lightning and longing that I am drawn again and again to this depthless pool of knowledge.

Other times, maybe the air is too dark, too hot—or maybe too many bat wings flutter spirits from flame trees—but I am reluctant to relinquish the mercury. Its denseness weights me to this island cuffed in foamy lace, while at the same time I feel almost light-headed. The surface of mercury blues as if steeped in the nighttime Caribbean Sea. I dribble it from palm to palm, back and forth, absorbing its properties, as if it seeps beneath the membrane of skin.

"G'won, swallow it," Sylvanita whispers, as if she reads my mind. She motions her own palm toward her mouth.

I never do, although I can't imagine the harm in more completely knowing my shimmery, mercurial, otherwise-unknowable future.

I, Your Most Humble Servant, Have Returned! As if from the Dead? Do You, Lundsmen and Goy alike, Wonder Where I, Your Diligent Scribe, Sought Shelter Lo these Many Years as if Time itself Travels forward And back . . . from Pat Boone Concerts in twenty-first-century Michigan to twentieth-century Nights Dark with (un)Holy Mysticism, where I followed a Tramp as if he could be the Savior to Lead me from the Wilderness . . . and where I Studied, as it were, the Powers and Properties of Mercury to Unravel the Mysteries of the Holiest of Grails. Or at least Shape The Future.

Okay, I confess: the jig is up. You suspect, of course, by now, that I'm *not* exactly a scribe, seventeenth century or otherwise.

You might recall, from my earlier epistle, I am, in my heart of souls, but a humble gefilte fish, long out of water.

As my tale continues, my father next uproots our family from St. Thomas. No, I don't flee the island like Vicki, though I should have. Instead, imagine a family of gefilte fish hunkering on the tarmac in sweltering tropical sun waiting to board a Caribair flight to San Juan before transferring to Pan Am flight #612 (I made up the flight number, having no idea what it actually was) to Idlewild Airport in New York. In the dead of winter. No shawl to cover my shivering gefilte shoulders. . . . Oh, but wait: gefilte fish don't have shoulders!

Before you know it, my family and I move into a suburban ranch house in Glen Rock, New Jersey. I enroll in junior high school, *where everyone is Christian*. Which of course is a mild exaggeration. Surely there are one or two other Jews. But not many. So I spend hours before the mirror yearning to witness my Christian transformation, hoping for my Jewish features to turn gentile.

I want to fit in.

That's it, isn't it? The crux of the problem: I don't want to see myself as a round, pasty-looking gefilte fish.

But surely a gefilte fish, as luck would have it, contains the natural properties of a chameleon—like the lizards on St. Thomas—to change appearance.

A Chameleon! A Jew for All Seasons. Or none?

This gefilte, in short, over the course of this long journey, rushes here and there, helter-skelter, donning numerous masks, camou- ⌐
flaging herself (sometimes more successfully than others) into new habitats and surroundings, seeking her place in the world.

Because, at the root of it all, this little gefilte is scared to be Jewish. Even though of course I know I *am* Jewish . . . or as Jewish as a gefilte fish is Jewish.

Hold your boos, hisses, and sneers. Yes, I'm talking to you. Don't throw any accusations of anti-Semitism and/or self-loathing my way. No, nope, don't even think of it.

I ask you: Would *you* want to be Jewish if your Jewish father is a bad man? A bad, bad man? (Here, imagine a school of gefilte fish, headless heads shaking *no, no, no.*) Wouldn't you, instead, want to be Christian if you believe Pat Boone is a good man, a good, good man? (Here, imagine gefilte fish, a whole jar of them, nodding *yes, yes, yes.*)

And since I'm convinced that all the Christian boys and girls in Glen Rock, New Jersey, represent some Mythical Ideal—right now, at this stage of the journey—I want to be them, or be adopted by them (just like I wanted to be adopted by the tramp or by Pat Boone), brought in from the cold, into *their* fold.

Will I be successful?

Well, unless you think that the problems of one small gefilte don't amount to a ball of matzohs, then we've got our work cut out for us. . . .

Especially since I want to be Christian even though I don't exactly believe in God. Only Pat Boone.

 S.W.S.

The Endless Possibilities of Youth

There's always something about that first love.

NATALIE WOOD

Suicide as Just One Possibility

I HAPPEN TO SEE A GIRLFRIEND from high school in the rotunda of the Capitol who tells me that, shortly after graduation, Lynn committed suicide. Hearing Lynn's name I also think of Christopher, my (our) ex-boyfriend. During much of junior and senior high schools, he arced between us—two rail-thin girls, one Christian, one Jewish—like an electrical charge between positive and negative poles. Now, after work, I catch a DC Transit bus outside the Longworth House Office Building where I'm a legislative aide. I sway in the crowded aisle, forward and back, gripping the metal handlebar. Christopher might not even recognize me now in a minidress and leather sandals, much like other hippies, so different from the primly starched shirtwaists Lynn and I both favored in our suburban high school.

Steamy air, gray with city grit, obscures white government façades. Even my face, glimpsed in the smudged windows of the bus, darkens with every block, the way I appeared to myself in high school. Then, afternoons, I leaned close to the bathroom mirror. I wanted to mystically command Lynn's sleek ponytail and pale, snub nose to reflect back . . . to *be* me, mine. But my frizzy hair, my intractable Jewish appearance, remained. Only when Christopher smiled at me, I no longer felt gloomy, an alien Jew adrift in the tidy Christian world of Glen Rock.

I *was* alien back then, for I wasn't a denizen of my own home, either. I always awoke to the arthritic shuffling of my Russian grandmother in her terrycloth slippers. Unable to live alone in her own apartment, she invaded my family with a black babushka, rolled wool stockings, a gnarled Yiddish tongue. She even cleared her throat in Yiddish. She skulked suburban streets as if still fleeing pogroms, even though she'd immigrated to America decades earlier. Or she prowled our neighborhood trailing the scent of boiled cabbage as if *she*, now the pursuer, hoped to capture *me*, save me from the Christians whom I emulated and desired.

From the balcony of my high-rise apartment, I watch the oval dome of the Capitol gleaming white and familiar, like the moon. My family left Washington DC years ago, but now, a recent college graduate, I'm drawn back to my birthplace: the Lincoln Memorial, the Washington Monument, the White House, the ellipse, the rectangular reflecting pool, columns, domes, pentagons, ovals. It's a city built upon the irrefutable, reassuring logic of geometry.

But tonight the marble seems too cool, the breeze off the Potomac moist. A thin chill shivers from my palms up to my scalp. Brain freeze, like that sharp yet numbing pain in my temples when I once sucked on Kool-Aid ice cubes on summer afternoons.

As if my brain *is* frozen, I now can't remember my girlfriend's exact words: did she say that Lynn "killed herself" or did she say "committed suicide"? The words "committed suicide" sound more exact, each letter chiseled in stone. No margin for error. No different ending.

You walk into your garage. You close the car door. You turn the key. Exhaust billows.

No going back.

The Love Triangle as a Problem of
High School Geometry

Mornings, when I arrive at school, I go into the girls' room and bolt the stall. I unhook the Star of David from the gold chain around my neck. I slip the black-and-white saddle shoe off my left foot, dropping this present from my grandmother inside it. I retie the lace, taut, double knotting it.

Later, in class, I grip my pencil, ruler, and protractor to draw circles and parallelograms on a piece of graph paper. Equilateral, isosceles, obtuse triangles. Here in geometry I'm able to prove, at least on paper, that *if* I am point B on a scalene triangle and Lynn point C, then I am the one who stands closer to Christopher, at point A. And *if* I stand closer to Christopher (the antecedent), *then* that means he loves me (the consequent).

Or: *If* Christopher smiles at me even once during the day *then* he loves me—not Lynn.

But suppose this geometric proof of love is merely a postulate? For *if* Christopher smiles at Lynn *then* _____.

I don't want to fill in the blank.

Memorize the following equation as if it's hard evidence: Lynn hates me as much as I hate her. This hate = the amount we both love Christopher.

Without turning around, I sense Lynn a few rows behind me wearing the pink dress she sewed in home-economics class. Her stare needles my back.

Lynn, Christopher, me. Really, we're an equilateral triangle: Lynn and I, equal sides, lean inward, reaching up toward Christopher at the apex.

Glen Rock as an Outpost
of the Cold War

Next class, English, I watch the backs of Christopher's wrists through lowered lashes. The winter sun, slanting through the row of rectangular windows, casts the wispy hairs in platinum light. Last autumn, the sun tinged them a reddish yellow. By June (I know I'll still be spying on him), after weeks of baseball, they'll deepen to gold. I rest my chin in my palm, canting toward him, inhaling his scent of Ivory soap and Juicy Fruit gum. The overlap of his front teeth, this one small flaw, makes me want to kiss him, though he's never even held my hand. I, with my darkness, feel almost inchoate in the presence of such incandescence.

Even the blunt shape of his hands appears all-American: exotically ordinary. Neither overly strong nor frail. His palms seem as at ease guiding a girl across a dance floor as pinning a wrestling opponent to the mat. His nails are neat, the lunulas pale as the tip of a day moon rising in a young summer sky. I long to touch his fingers, his wrists, those nails. I long for his sun-warm hand to lead me down Rock Road past Kilroy's Wonder Market, People's Bank, Mandee's Dress Shoppe . . . the Nabisco plant on the edge of town exhaling the scent of pure vanilla.

I pay scant attention to the teacher, Miss P. Five days a week her vague voice instructs on themes, plots, similes. We read boring short stories, one about a child who eats too many pancakes. These stories teach me nothing of boys, of love, of triangles—or how aliens meld into an all-American life. During class, my gaze strays from Christopher only when I press the nib of my fountain pen to my gray cloth notebook. In cursive I write *Christopher, Christopher, Christopher* across the front, the back, the spine. I dot each letter "i" with a ♥. Ink from the letters bleeds into the fabric.

But now, with only minutes left of class, the light suddenly darkens. The pale hairs on Christopher's wrists become invisible—or the same color as his skin—as if it's possible to be bleached by an absence of sunlight. The once-glittery day grows mute, clammy. I stir in my seat, Christopher's spell broken.

I glance around. My classmates' faces remain turned toward Miss P., paying attention. Am I the only one to notice the windows darken, implacable as lead?

Then, with no warning, the words "iron curtain" invade my consciousness with such force I'm stunned, motionless in my chair. The four stony syllables thud the base of my brain. My breath feels shallow, tight.

Even in school, beside Christopher, I'm subverted by a foreign power, my Russian grandmother. The icy hem of Siberian winters clings to her skirt. She casts Old World spells scented with wood smoke, wrenched from crooked alleys of shtetls, to shadow the golden streets of my new world. Her unblinking evil eye is a searchlight. I am x-rayed in its glare.

The Star of David sears the sole of my left foot.

Sock Hop as Wish Fulfillment

At the Paradise of Hearts dance, after I watch Christopher for more than an hour, he invites me to dance. That hand with the warm palm holds mine as the DJ plays "Blue Moon" by the Marcels. I wear a sweater with fringes that (I realize too late) resemble tzitzits, ceremonial fringes on Jewish shawls. I'm reassured, however, when a swirling light casts into relief the filaments of hair on Christopher's wrists, as if I, too, am now warmed in this glow. Except why, then, doesn't Christopher hold me close enough to hear his heart beneath his cotton shirt?

Valentines and paper roses adorn the school cafeteria, in whose blossoming Christopher next asks Lynn to dance. He holds *her* tight. Tighter. His cheek brushes hers. Her shiny ponytail sways on her shoulders. Her crisp poodle skirt floats around her knees. Her snip of a nose wrinkles when she smiles. I glare, willing her nose to grow, her shoulders to droop, her cheeks to lose their bloom.

At the end of the evening, girls cluster outside the school entrance waiting for parents to pick us up. I huddle with my friends, Lynn with hers. She and I pretend to ignore each other. We rarely speak—though I think about her constantly. My father's car stops beside the curb just behind her father's. As

Lynn opens the door, the dome light shadows rather than brightens her father's features. His sharp "get in" sounds like pebbles pitched against glass. Lynn and I close our doors. My father says I should have called earlier for him to bring me home. I lower the window of his black Fleetwood Cadillac, smoky from cigarettes. I feel his gaze on me in the rearview mirror. Headlights from a car behind us glint on his glasses. We slowly follow Lynn's car along the driveway and onto Harristown Road, as if we're in a procession.

Suburban Glen Rock as Refuge from the Shtetl

The Christian street I live on, Lowell Road, is elliptical, a perfect oval. Evenings, after dinner, I ride my bicycle around and around, glimpsing inside houses, all the parted curtains. Each picture window frames a still-life living room, a painting of modern Danish furniture adorning a background of wall-to-wall Euclidean carpet. Lamplight etches damp weedless lawns, reflecting exact rhombuses. Moths beat wire-mesh screens, this golden perfection irresistible. Pedaling past neighbors' houses, my heart quickens, too.

Later, inside, I stand by my bedroom window, a finger denting parallel slats in the venetian blinds, intersecting sight. If only I could conjure Christopher in his father's red Rambler, tires swishing to a stop in front of my house. But the only sound is the scuff of my grandmother's dirty terrycloth slippers, so frayed I imagine her wearing them in the shtetl, on the boat as she sails toward Ellis Island, all along the Lower East Side, tramping across the George Washington Bridge and into my teenage life.

As Technicolor Heartthrobs Take Suburbia by Storm

Christopher and I watch teenage movies such as *A Summer Place*. At the second-run, drive-in theater, as Molly (Sandra Dee) and Johnny (Troy Donahue) fall in love, I snuggle beside Christopher in my floral dress, our clothes damp against the seat of his father's Rambler.

The camera pans in for a close-up of Johnny and Molly alone in a lighthouse.

Molly: "We've got to be good, Johnny."

Johnny: "Good. Is it that easy to be good?"

Molly: "Have you been bad, Johnny? Have you been bad with other girls?"

She whispers the word "bad" with longing that swells from the base of her throat.

If "bad" is "good," is "good" "bad"? How to prove the theorem? How to decipher who Christopher wants me to be? *Christopher, would you be bad with me, kiss me—do more with me—if I didn't look Jewish, if I resembled Lynn or Sandra Dee?*

When I audition for my high school play, everyone thinks I'm perfect for the role and laughs at the right lines. Well, everyone thinks I'm perfect but the drama coach, Miss M. I don't get the part. Miss M., also my Spanish teacher, worships General Francisco Franco, who supported the Fascists during World War II. She brings photos of him to class. I squint, not wanting to see, willing the images to burn to vapor on a white-hot Iberian breeze. My mother says I didn't get the part because I'm Jewish.

Now, disembodied voices crackle from the speaker box hooked on the car window. When I lean my head against Christopher's shoulder, the movie sounds garbled, as if they're speaking a foreign language.

Big-Time Wrestling as Metaphor
for the Vicissitudes of Love

I sit in the bleachers, hands folded, watching Christopher wrestle. He's captain of the team, and I long to wear his letter sweater. Sweat drips from Christopher onto the square red mat, a white circle in the center. His skin glistens. I don't want him to get pinned. Halfway through, when I think he might lose, my shoulders feel narrow, drawn. I focus on my kneecaps, pale between kneesocks and a plaid kilt.

Earlier, while dressing, I was sure he'd love my pearly nail polish and pink-bubblegum lipstick. With religious fervor, I shined the copper pennies wedged in the leather slots of my loafers. If only he'll glance up in the stands, notice the lipstick, the Lincoln-head pennies.

I nervously scrape the polish from my nails before the match is over. Luminescent chips fleck my skirt.

Christopher drives me home. His good-night kiss brushes my lips, feathery, quick. After settling in the den of my split-level ranch house, I watch professional wrestling on our black-and-white Zenith. My grandmother hunches beside me. The Crusher. Black Jack Mulligan. Mad Dog Vachon. Killer Kowalski. Nothing like Christopher's orderly high school wrestling. Nothing like the gentle—"good"—way he hugs me, either.

"No Jews are such *meshuganahs*," she says. In this, at least, my grandmother and I agree as we watch gentile wrestlers slam off the ropes or plummet onto the mat.

Anna Karenina as Teenage Role Model

Saturdays, I ride the bus to the bookstore in Ridgewood to buy mounds of novels. The wooden floor smells raw, like a forest, in the damp morning air. I climb the rungs of the ladder on runners that glide past the floor-to-ceiling shelves. The words in all the books seem muffled, tightly packed together. Which ones most want to be released, read? In which ones will I discover the meaning of teenage life?

I ease a spine from the shelf and ruffle the pages. Words seem to spill everywhere. I must gather them. Believe every word I read. I leaf through *Anna Karenina* and *Madame Bovary*. Surely these women will teach me of love and all its triangles. Anna/Alexei/Vronsky. Emma/Charles/Rodolphe.

I also slide from the shelves *Crime and Punishment, War and Peace, The Brothers Karamazov*. Russian novels! I consider slipping them back in their empty niches. After all, no Russian novels are assigned in high school. None of my friends read them. Maybe I should only read American books instructing me how to be like Lynn?

Oh, but the passion of thousands of pages of operatic Russian intrigue! Grand gestures! The cashier puts the books in a sack. I keep my reading habits a secret.

I place my dollar bills on the counter and notice the Great Seal on the backs. Is the eye atop the pyramid God's? Is it my grandmother's? Has she been watching me, commanding my hand along the bookshelves to Russian titles? Both?

Failure as an Art Form

Don't know much about history . . .
But I do know that I love you . . .

Answering SAT questions, I grip my no. 2 yellow pencil, guessing wildly.

Choose the word or set of words that, when inserted in the sentence, best fits the meaning of the sentence as a whole.

The scientist ascribed the _____ of the park's remaining trees to the _____ of the same termite species that had damaged homes throughout the city.

A) ○ decimation . . prevalence
B) ○ survival . . presence
C) ○ growth . . mutation
D) ○ reduction . . disappearance
E) ○ study . . hatching

All the empty circles float across the page: a constellation of possibility. I *could* choose answer A. Except I love the idea of a "scientist ascribing the *growth* of the park's remaining trees to the *mutation* of the same termite species that had damaged homes throughout the city."

Mutation. My tongue clicks each consonant with satisfaction. Can I mutate from Russian to American? From Jew to Christian? Am I

A) ○ Anna Karenina?
B) ○ Sandra Dee?
C) ○ Both A & B?
D) ○ None of the above?

If Lynn didn't exist, I myself could fill in the blank of her absence.

Rapunzel as Teenage Role Model

I weave a chain of chewing-gum wrappers, folding the paper lengthwise, bending it in half, in half again. I slide the end of the next wrapper sideways inside the bend, linking them. I save my allowance for Juicy Fruit, Big Red, Adam's Clove, Beech-Nut, Black Jack, Doublemint, Clark's Teaberry, Beeman's, Fruit Stripe, Wrigley's Spearmint. Discarded foil, silver as coins, cascades to my feet.

I coil the gum-wrapper chain around the three-bulb lamp in my bedroom. I wind it over browned gardenia corsages, plastic Hawaiian leis, strands of pop-it beads. I will add to it until the chain reaches six feet. Longer. It will hang sturdy as rope, a braid of straight-straight hair—more valuable than rubles or gold.

Glen Rock Slumbers as
West Side Story Rumbles

Christopher holds my hand in the darkened theater. I breathe in unison with him, his shoulders' slight rise and fall. Along with Maria (Natalie Wood), I long for Tony as much as I yearn for Christopher. My breath pauses only when Puerto Rican Maria sings "I Feel Pretty." *Can* you be pretty, even without all-American skin and hair?

Natalie Wood, born Natalia Nikolaevna Zakharenko, is the child of Russian immigrants, Nikolai and Maria. Therefore, she is a Russian born in San Francisco impersonating a Puerto Rican who wants to be like the white American girls.

Years later, Russian string instruments play at her funeral.

Glen Rock as Teenage Exploitation Film

We play spin the bottle in rec-room basements, empty Coke bottles willed to revolve toward Christopher. Forty-fives plop on turntables: "I Love How You Love Me." Or give me just "One Last Kiss."

Kiss me, Christopher . . . in this whoosh of green glass whirling, clacking in concentric circles around the linoleum floor. Except tonight Christopher doesn't look my way. He watches Lynn. So I feel like a "Poor Little Fool," just as the lyrics say.

Later in the evening, Coke spins into Rheingold, boys arrive in black leather with Chesterfield cigarettes and fake IDs. Lights dim. Bottles ricochet out of orbit. Sprawled on furniture, we look like refuse washed up on a foreign shore: jumbled arms, legs, and torsos. Christopher kisses Lynn. I kiss a different boy.

My parents go out of town for the weekend, taking my grandmother with them. I mold my hair into a perfect flip, rigid with Aqua Net hairspray. Without my grandmother's gnarled and wrinkled presence, the strands relax their frizz and straighten. With the scroll of pearly lipstick, the matte of pale powder, I emerge as if from a genie's bottle in a different, exotic form: pure, unadulterated suburban teenager. One, moreover, with her mother's car, which she uses to lure her would-be boyfriend.

Christopher hotwires the Plymouth and drives us to Century Road, a few miles out of town. We join other kids also in parents' cars. Lighting cigarettes, our wrists torque matches into flame. We drag race, headlights like movie projectors tunneling night.

Our energy unsettles Glen Rock. Drag racing itself transports us to something more, different, better. When the race ends, I don't know who, if anyone, wins. We are dazed by speed, having reached the end of Century Road, our destination, so quickly. A residue of cigarette smoke and exhaust fumes lingers.

Glen Rock as a Lost Chapter from Vladimir Nabokov's Famous Novel *Lolita*

This is a secret: Lynn's father is Humbert Humbert. So is mine. Intersecting triangles of daughters, fathers, mothers. But these secrets are nighttime shadows slinking like black cats through suburban yards. Hope flattens, thin as bedsheets. Streetlamps blacken with gnats. The moon pauses behind a cloud.

The breeze stalls. Night insects rub their legs. Skin bruises in constant friction. Only fireflies—following their globe-lit path away from czars—flee.

Glen Rock as Illusion

Summers, I taste time as it rises slow and yellow from morning skies. I watch for Christopher at the turquoise-tinted swimming pool, even though he doesn't always watch me. We high school girls clump at one end of the patio area, boys the other. We slather Coppertone on wintry skin. We lie on our stomachs. We flip onto our backs. We wish on four-leaf clovers and shooting stars. We are stunned by warmth, thick and sweet with humidity, greening trees the color of Glen Rock grass. Chlorine seeds the air until I seem to swallow it. And when rain comes, it moistens summer and hydrangeas with possibility.

No one can prove we aren't more than we seem.

Raskolnikov's Ax as an Appropriate Tool
to Nail a Mezuzah to the Door

My grandmother positions a mezuzah on the doorpost. "That will only *help* czars—Nazis—whoever, find you," I say. "*Pass over*," she hisses, believing the mezuzah will protect her from all future pogroms.

She gets the hammer and tape measure. I stand outside on the front stoop trying to hide her from neighbors. I turn my transistor radio full volume as the crack of the hammer splinters the usual silence of the neighborhood. With steely fingers, she nails the gold-plated sphere one-third down the frame, slanting inward. By tradition, it's positioned at an angle because rabbis couldn't decide between horizontal and vertical.

"*Barukh atah Adonai, Elohaynu, melekh ha-olam*," my grandmother intones. Why can't we simply recite "Our Father who art in heaven"? Straightforward. You know where *He* is, where you are. Hebrew words slosh together, soupy, indecipherable on the tongue.

Later, I find my grandmother asleep in the den, sitting straight up, the television tuned to *I Love Lucy*. Even though her eyes are closed, I feel her watching me. Her lids tremble. Her snores could wake the dead.

I consider Raskolnikov bludgeoning the ancient pawnbroker with the blunt side of an ax. I stare at my grandmother. She's not frail. Her solid peasant Russian frame could nail me to the door.

My grandmother lives several more years, though I don't remember exactly when she dies. Perhaps it's around the same time as Lynn. I don't remember who calls to tell me of my grandmother's death, if the caller is sad, or whether I'm relieved. I don't attend the funeral, probably don't consider it. Nor do I know where it's held or where she's buried. I never visit the gravesite. My desire not to be my grandmother's granddaughter remains.

In the many houses in which I live after leaving Glen Rock, no mezuzah is ever displayed.

Shakespeare as Oracle

In English class, toward the end of the year, I barely pay attention to the discussion of feuds and warring families in *Romeo and Juliet*. I'm more conscious of Christopher, golden from baseball practice. At least, I barely pay attention until I hear the phrase "star-crossed lovers." I suck in my breath. When Miss P. explains "irony"—Juliet swallowing a secret potion to feign death—I feel a tap on my shoulder. I turn around. A girl, seated behind me, slips me a note. She nods her head toward the back of the room, indicating the note traveled up the row from Lynn. It's folded into a neat square, my name printed on the outside.

I no longer remember what Lynn wrote in the note. Did she ask if I liked the play? If I had a date for the senior prom? Was I upset Christopher hadn't invited me—though he hadn't invited her either? Did Lynn want to know what I ate for dinner, if I wanted to go to the drugstore after school for a Coke? Or did she ask me about Juliet? Did she wonder if I thought love worth dying for? What would *I* do for love?

If only, now, I could peel back the corners again, open the note as if it is origami, a delicate paper swan to unfold. Peer inside at its secrets. Read it like prophecy.

Lynn as Natalia Nikolaevna Zakharenko

At the senior prom, Christopher dances with his date, a girl from Ridgewood. Lynn's lashes lower as she hugs her fiancé, a boy from a different town. A ring with a tiny diamond encircles her finger. For a precarious moment the metal glows platinum, the gem sparkling prisms, before the decorated cafeteria darkens. I dance with a boy, a pale facsimile of Christopher.

No more geometry class. No teacher erasing triangles at the end of the hour, chalk evanescing in a cloud of dust, like smoke.

Yet now, on the threshold of the future, the particles of chalk seem trapped—yet oddly unsettled—as if forever humming in a shaft of sun angling through a window, or in my mind.

I never quite let go of geometry, the triangles on my graph paper smudged from my palms, from my pink eraser. Forms fade, but ghostly outlines remain.

Lynn, as it turns out, is Juliet, Anna, Emma, Natalie Wood.

Ferris Wheel as Denouement

Christopher disconnects the odometer in his father's Rambler. He drives us to the Jersey shore, the windows open on this summer day. A chiffon scarf flutters around my head.

His arm brushes mine as we lie beside each other on beach towels. Sand radiates heat. The sun bursts with sweat, steaming from the sky. Seaweed decorates the shore. Sandpipers and seagulls skitter foam to lace. We suck saltwater taffy, sugar and ocean water sweet and tart on our tongues. Tips of my wet hair cool my shoulders—hair, while damp, hanging straight as Lynn's on this one perfect New Jersey day.

That evening, the boardwalk throbs with bare feet. We drop coins in machines for candy, gum, prizes. I win a glass ruby ring. I pass it to Christopher to slip on my finger. Which one? Ten possibilities, only nine of them incorrect.

But how could he marry a Jew?

In English class, after reading *Romeo and Juliet*, we studied *The Merchant of Venice*. When Miss P. said the word "Jewish" aloud, I was aghast. For the first time in Glen Rock, I heard that word spoken outside my house. I cupped my palms on either side of my face, like blinders. If I couldn't see anyone, maybe no one could see me. I turned away from Christopher, sliding low in my chair.

Shylock. Jewish moneylenders.

My father was a banker. Worse: he was *president* of a bank.

At the end of the play, after the trial, as part of the settlement, Shylock must convert to Christianity.

If my father converted. . . . If *I* converted, I wouldn't be destined to be me.

Now we glide around the carousel, joggle in bumper cars, hurtle on the roller coaster. Soaring gondolas, dotting the circumference of the Ferris wheel, gently rock us. Rather than loop around and around, we float over the Atlantic Ocean. The miniature ships, flashing red and blue neon, bleed into night. I lean close to Christopher, his tanned skin. He holds my hand, the imprint a golden tattoo on my palm. His blond hair ruffles. I am giddy, sailing from land to sky to sea. Below the Ferris wheel, streetlights necklace the shoreline. Above us, starry ice blazes across space.

Soon the wheel slows. The breeze slows. The night slows. The motion stops. "I want to ride again," I whisper.

Does he hear me—what does he hear—in this dark absence of sound?

Christopher nods and lets go of my hand.

Swimming Like a Gefilte Fish

THE JEWS ARE COMING TO VISIT, is how you think of it, back then. As if you, yourself, are not a Jew.

Who are these Jews?

Distant relatives and old friends of your parents, your grandparents. From the Old Country. Russia. Kiev. Jews who fled.

You sit on the couch in the perfect, gold-carpeted living room—as far from icy steppes as possible—staring out the picture window. You watch Jew after Jew struggle to emerge from the interior of a black, battered car. They struggle because they are ancient, struggle because they are burdened with parcels of Jewish food (not available—thank god—in Glen Rock) and with boxes of religious totems (ditto), the contents of which—leather phylacteries, fringed tallises, yarmulkes, and siddurs—will scare you. Horrify you. Will make you feel as if you're surrounded by aliens. Struggling to emerge, because, raised in a shtetl, to them, *cars* are alien. As parcel after parcel is stacked by the curb it's as if they're unloading the entire baggage of the diaspora.

They arrive at your house smelling of musty Brooklyn or Bronx apartments where (you know because you've been forced to visit) closets smell of damp wool and lox, even though winter oranges, studded with cloves, hang on hooks. By March, the skins of the oranges have puckered and shriveled. Like the skin hanging from your great-aunt's forearms. Once you sat on the floor of her closet and plucked every single clove from an orange, hiding them in the toe of her shoe. For no reason. Or, because hiding cloves was your sole means of protest. A dislike of gefilte fish, after all, didn't warrant carrying placards or boycotting dinner.

Now, when the Jews open the door to your house with much kissing, pinching of cheeks, and *gut shabeses*, the soft murmurs of Glen Rock—sprinklers, playing cards snapping in bicycle spokes—are suddenly obliterated. The green-grass scent is overwhelmed by pickled and sour-cream herring, horseradish, borscht, tongue.

A *real* cow's tongue protrudes from a platter, the flesh goose-bumpy and pink.

The back of your own tongue shivers as if you'll never swallow again.

Matzoh, kugel, blintzes. Your mother's best china, to hold all this food, appears on the dining room table, green Wedgwood purchased in the West Indies.

You think of your Christian friends eating steaks, hamburgers, fries. Cookouts. Picnics . . . kids and parents wearing Bermuda shorts, pedal pushers, seersucker. The Jews never eat outside. The women wear slightly formal dark nylon dresses, brooches pinned to the collars. The men wear white shirts and dark ties.

As the Jews descend upon the food like schools of fish, you envision hiding in your bedroom, turning on the record player, and blasting Pat Boone.

Gefilte fish: White mysterious mounds ground up with matzoh flour, eggs, and onion and stuffed (according to the traditional recipe used by your relatives) back in fish skins. Served in a transparent jellied slippery slime.

Not one fish actually swimming in the ocean has ever been labeled "gefilte."

No taxonomic phylum, subphylum, or infraspecies exists.

How can a fish that's not a fish end up in a ball floating in jelly, stuffed in fish skin (and *whose* skin is it, anyway, if it's not even a fish?), as if it's wearing a jacket? All evidence of its fishness—its true identity—gone. (Which is probably why you've secretly identified with gefilte fish all these years in the first place.)

You eat salmon, tuna, trout, blue, sword, perch, bass: *Christian* fish.

What you don't know then, but what you surely must suspect—even as a teenager—is that you will eventually marry a man who isn't Jewish, who has never eaten gefilte fish. In fact, you will marry (and divorce) two men who aren't Jewish.

Your first husband, the director of a preservation project, in anticipation of the sale of a historic building, will one day say to you, "I won't let him Jew me down."

On this day in the future, you and he will be walking down a sidewalk together. You will stop as if you are driving in a car and suddenly slam into the iron front of one of the buildings he's trying to save. He will turn to you. Apologize.

You will be mortified. Because he dissed your religion? Or mortified because you haven't "passed," because, even though you changed your last name to his—a neat, tidy, one-syllable name—he will always know you are Jewish.

Your second husband, also a lapsed Christian, will never utter a religious slur. Instead, both he and his mother will brag about all their Jewish friends: your husband's academic mentor, for example. At Christmas, they give you books about famous Jewish people. Instead of "passing" with *his* neat, tidy, one-syllable Christian name, you will feel, instead, your very Jewishness drubbed down upon your head.

But now, back in Glen Rock, the men wrap leather bands, phylacteries, around their arms, leather bands around their heads, leather boxes attached, containing portions of the Torah. They protrude from their foreheads like tumors. Yarmulkes perch atop skulls. Fringed tallises wrap shoulders. Veined hands with gnarled fingers grasp siddurs, daily prayer books. Soon they are swaying and bending back and forth, davening in Hebrew.

You're relieved it is hot, windows closed, air conditioning whirring. None of your friends will hear them.

As the men daven, you stare at the plate-glass window. The sun, round as an orange (or a gefilte, depending), fractures the glass. White rays radiate from the center of the pane, inappropriate as a halo.

For Jews Only

TEENAGE BOYS DIVE-BOMB INTO THE POOL, spraying water. Or they sneak behind girls, grab them, and toss them in. Girls' voices shriek in mock anger, but I can tell they like being singled out, noticed.

I dab Coppertone on my nose and shoulders. Humidity frizzes my dark auburn ponytail. Here, I look like the other girls. They look like me. Is this why no one talks to me, notices me: I don't stand out?

In the distance, men in caps stroll the golf course.

Women play mahjongg, a Chinese game. Men play a Scottish game.

I slide into the water and lie on my back, barely bobbing on the surface. The mahjongg words sound like a meditation, a poem, a chant.

Women, wearing straw hats and sunglasses, sit beside the swimming pool on patio furniture speaking exotic words as they play. Tiles click.

Plum. Orchid. Chrysanthemum. Bamboo.

Dragon tiles. Season tiles. Honor tiles.

Prevailing winds. East winds. West winds.

Sun warms my face; water cools my back. I am at the Westwood Country Club in Bergen County, New Jersey. But I could be in Shanghai. I could be Chinese.

That Summer of War and Apricots

Bukra fil mishmish.
(Tomorrow, when the apricots come.)

AT THE SAME MOMENT NEIL ARMSTRONG and his Apollo 11 mission float across the Sea of Tranquility, I lie alone on the ground beneath stars and planets in an orchard of *mishmish* trees. I am in Israel, having recently quit my job on Capitol Hill, my first after graduating college. I'm not actually trying to see Apollo 11 with a naked eye. Rather, it's as if I sense the pearly skin of the moon invaded—moon dust, silent for eons, startled by thruster rockets—marred by boot prints.

Ari's boots. I press my head against the ground as if I can feel reverberations of *his* footsteps patrolling the kibbutz, his military boots circling closer to me.

I've been awake since four, just like every morning, except Saturday. From four to eleven, in the cooler air, my group picks apricots. I strap a white canvas bucket over my shoulders and carry a wood ladder from tree to tree. Before dawn, fruit is almost invisible on the dark branches. I search more by feel, my fingers distinguishing fuzz from the slickness of leaves. After filling a bucketful, I unhook the bottom. Apricots, like cataracts of sunbeams, flow into the bed of a truck. Then I return to the ladder: more apricots, more trees.

Soon I am lost to the soft *plop* of fruit dropped in my bag. Leaves rustle. Twigs snap. I prop my bucket on the top rung to lean against it, resting. I lick the skin of an apricot before sinking my teeth into pulp—leaving my own mark. My mouth wakens to small explosions of sunlit juice. I don't wipe my lips, craving this stickiness from an apricot that's *mine*, that *I* picked. I grip the ladder, dazzled. As morning rises, apricots become thousands of miniature suns lighting the air—me—my skin flush as fever. My fingertips sense shades of peach, yellow, orange, cantaloupe. The fuzz glows more golden than ancient coins—pale filaments incandescent by dawn.

Apricot: the vowels sound round as fruit.

Apricum: The sunny place. Early ripening. Precocious.

I split a *mishmish* in two and consider the pit, feeling as if I should swallow it, as if then maybe *I'll* bloom.

Israelis, after all, command even the desert to blossom.

I flew to Israel after the Six-Day War. For the first time I'm proud to be Jewish, after wishing, all my life, to be Christian. Growing up, wherever we lived, I was one of only a handful of Jewish kids. I skulked school corridors hoping to be proselytized, changed. I peroxided strands of my hair to look Christian, hoping to pass. It didn't work. I felt alien. Outcast. All my heroes were Christian. I knew no Jewish presidents, teenage heartthrobs, astronauts, or pop idols.

I cringed in English class in college reading descriptions of Wolfsheim in *The Great Gatsby*. I worried that my own nose, though small, might suddenly grow hooked as his. In *The Sun Also Rises*, Jake says of Cohn, "He had a hard, Jewish, stubborn streak."

But now, after only six short days, we are no longer defined as victims, mere survivors, or shylocks.

But do I belong here?

Am I *of* this new sun-drenched nation? Or just *in* it?

Now my fellow kibbutzniks watch the moon landing on the television in the communal dining hall. Earlier, in broken English, they invited me to join them. I shook my head no, though I long for company. But I'm boycotting everything American because of the Vietnam War.

From this morning's work in the orchards, my insteps still feel the press of ladder rungs. I stand, turn from the moon, and walk between a row of trees. My leather sandals, straps crisscrossing my calves, etch the fragile soil. I brush dirt from my arms and legs, from my brown shorts and yellow tank top. My filigreed earrings, bought in the Old City in Jerusalem, dangle like silver globes. Through the leaves, I see specks of light from the dining hall, a flicker of a black-and-white television—Neil Armstrong, perhaps at this moment, delivering his now-famous line. Light and sound dim and surge, surge and dim as the unreliable generator drones. Just past the orchard a barbed-wire fence surrounds the kibbutz, protecting us from our enemies.

A callused hand grips my forearm. A glint of an Uzi . . . Ari, the Israeli soldier who patrols the perimeter, guarding us all night. He expects me. Gently but firmly he pushes me back into the orchard, down on the moist soil between the trees. His mouth tastes of Sabra, chocolate, and nectarines. His nose is thin, his eyes green, his hair so blond he could pass as one of my Christian boyfriends.

We don't speak. I don't close my eyes. Night spills stars across the Mediterranean sky. The moon presses me to the earth—this Israeli moon, this soil, this man cradling me, our bodies crushing fallen fruit.

When dawn laces the sky I, along with the other kibbutzniks, rest for fifteen minutes. We sit on the ground beside the *mish-mish* trees drinking water from a tin cup. We are each given a hard-boiled egg and a slice of bread smeared with apricot jam. I rarely speak. I don't know Hebrew. Few here on the kibbutz speak English. Surrounded by Israelis, I am virtually silent all day. I *am* taught the word *aliyah*, however, to *make aliyah*, to return to Israel, to the homeland, to live.

"*Aliyah, aliyah?*" they ask, they ask.

I shake my head, shrug. When I don't provide a firm commitment to renounce the United States, I am more American than Jew. At eleven, we pile in the backs of trucks, returning to our bungalows. I grab a bar of soap, shampoo, a towel and head toward the corrugated-tin bathhouse, a short walk from my room. I undress in one of the stalls. I unbraid my long hair that falls halfway down my back, slip the rubber band on a peg, and shake out the strands. There is no hot-water faucet. But by noon, from sun scorching metal pipes, a tepid stream soothes my muscles. I scrub off Israeli dirt, sap, and apricot fuzz from fingertips to shoulders, returning to my more-American skin. I wait until the water chills me, as if I can hoard coolness for the rest of the day.

A scorpion hovers in the corner of the shower greeting me daily, perhaps also seeking water, a respite from heat. The Israelis, with their tough skin, don't bother to kill it. Its hooked tail, even when sodden, looks lethal, anxious, longing to sting. I admire the simplicity of *scorpion*, assured of its identity, its function.

Back in my room, I sit on a stool before a rickety wood table beneath the one window. I leave the door open, hoping for a stray breeze to wrinkle the afternoon. I place a blank green aerogramme on the table, a letter—a love letter—I'm supposed to be writing to my Presbyterian boyfriend who also works on Capitol Hill. *Dear Graham, Dear Graham, Dearest Graham* . . . I think, but don't write, on the onionskin. *Ari* . . . his red beret, his Uzi. He speaks only a few words of English, just enough for me to know that, during the Six-Day War, he parachuted from planes to kill the enemy in hand-to-hand combat . . . *tumbles from the sky like a shooting star, billows to earth in nylon clouds, his soundless stealth beneath moons desert-hard and dry, like his knife, its scentless glitter* . . . *his muscles taut, his breath ancient as sand.*

He, too, knows his identity, his function.

Ari is my first Jewish boyfriend, yet I'm relieved he and I speak sparingly to each other. Back in DC, I grew exhausted listening to Graham, to myself, to my friends. All I heard was our shrill self-righteousness, faith by slogan: *"Hey, hey, LBJ, how many kids did you kill today?"*

The Six-Day War: the indelible simplicity of capturing territory in less than a week. Now, here, I focus on Israelis planting apricot fields, while America's orange jelly is napalm, hot and endless.

How am I a Dove at home, against the war in Vietnam, while here I am a Hawk?

I put down my pen.

Beneath my bare feet the floor in my bungalow is gritty with dust and sand. Out the window, yellow-green fields flow to orchards, to the *hamsin*-hot summer, air brittle with the friction of insect wings. In the distance, a Soviet-built MiG-21 zips open the sky. It plunges toward earth—quick—dropping a bomb on an Israeli town or military encampment before blazing back toward Syria. Too far away to hear. Its silvery light ebbs to black. A plume of smoke hazes the horizon.

This, while a blank aerogramme rustles in a desert breeze.

At home, I watched the faraway Vietnam War on television in bright, primary colors, grenades seeming to explode in my living room. Here, where the war is close, only miles away, it seems distant. Here in the solitude of this small room, I feel safe.

My hair dries. I braid it, fastening the end with the rubber band. I lie on my mattress stuffed with straw and covered by a rough wool blanket. If I press a damp palm against the inside walls, my sweat almost sizzles, even the walls almost too hot to touch.

Shouts of children from the kibbutz school float through the window. A donkey brays. Sheep bleat in a distant field. I drift, my head on the hard pillow, gently rocked by slow concussions of sound. Light burns dust into air.

All day in my Capitol Hill office, typewriter keys clacked, phones shrilled, bells rang for roll calls, quorums, votes. Once I found *those* sounds exciting, meaningful. I worked for Congressman Edward Koch and was part—a small part—of the most powerful government in the world. A hippie flower child with turquoise love beads, I answered letters from Koch's constituents, drafted inserts for the *Congressional Record*, wrote "Dear Colleague" letters. I researched legislation to halt construction of the Supersonic Transport. Before I resigned my job, Koch was also working on legislation to make the tax code more equitable for single, unmarried people. *"Mr. Chairman and members of the Ways and Means Committee, I am pleased to have this opportunity today to testify before you in support of what I believe to be essential legislation correcting major inequities in our present tax system. Unfortunately, approximately 30 million, namely those who are single, are discriminated against . . . ."*

Congressman Koch introduced resolutions to halt the fighting in Vietnam.

But no words seem to change anything, seem to matter.

Dear Graham . . .

I wonder: Has he burned his draft card yet? Has he decided to go to jail or Canada?

Graham, I never told you . . .

. . . After work, I turned off my IBM Selectric in room 1134 of the Longworth House Office Building. My tasseled Pappagallo shoes tapped marble corridors. In my miniskirt, I took the elevator to the basement, rode the small trolley beneath the Capitol to the New Senate Office Building. Elevator up to the second floor to Senator B.'s office . . . thinking I could find something with him that I'd never discover with Graham. Excitement? Prestige? Power? But the power was all *his*. Me, only bruising my thighs on the senator's navy-blue leather couch.

A month ago, my first evening in Jerusalem, I phone a friend of a friend, H., a married American man I never met before. I take the number sixteen bus, Jerusalem stone pink at dusk. We meet for drinks in the bar of the King David Hotel. Too many Scotches. We sway up the elevator and along the corridor to his room. H. whispers he'll visit me at the kibbutz when he completes his business in Jerusalem. We'll get together back in the States.

The door to the balcony is open . . . open to groves of olive trees, the diesel of army trunks, the scent of history, and promises broken all across the Mediterranean.

If only H. weren't married he could have been my first Jewish American boyfriend.

The next day, waiting for the bus to the kibbutz, I wander the Old City. Serpentine alleyways of dung and opium. Drowsy men recline on Oriental carpets smoking *nargiles*, water pipes. Merchants shout indefatigably, offering their wares: embroidered Egyptian dresses, camels carved in olive wood, Hebron peaches, bottles of colored desert sand, Turkish coffee and quince, carnelian bracelets, pomegranate blossoms, jasmine, roasting lamb. I am immediately lost in a maze . . . a maze of streets, a labyrinth of scents. I list words for each item I pass in each stall as if this accumulation, itself, can weight me in this place.

It doesn't. Not yet. Not now.

Rather, I wonder: Should I turn left, right? Should I buy this or that? Live in this city or that one? Myrtle berries or almonds? This man or that man? This country or that one?

Why not all of them, everything?

Because H. and Senator B. belong to their wives. Graham belongs to the Movement—as well as to his WASPy mom and dad. Ari belongs to Israel.

Aliyah? Aliyah?

I need to learn to haggle.

We don't pick apricots the morning after the moon landing. As soon as the truck drops us at the field, we are told to climb back on. We return to the common area, shuttled to underground bunkers. The perimeter has been breached, a cut in the chain-link fence. Soldiers scout the kibbutz, searching for someone who might be searching for *us*. I wonder when it happened. It could have been last night while I lay alone in the orchard . . . or when I was with Ari, when he was supposed to be guarding us, keeping us safe.

The bunker is too cool, too damp. We sit on wood benches and are given water in tin cups. The kibbutzniks are stoic. No one cries, not even the children. Conversations I don't understand. After a half hour, someone switches on a radio. American music. *Jesus loves you more than you can know . . . Back of my neck getting dirty and gritty . . .*

Dear Graham, today . . .

Homesickness wells up from the base of my throat.

Yet if I were home, I'd long to be *here*.

For months I daydreamed of Israel while sitting in my Capitol Hill office. My fingers paused over typewriter keys, while I glanced out the window . . . imagining the El Al jet landing on the tarmac at Lod Airport in Tel Aviv. Driving to Jerusalem. Slipping a handwritten wish on a scrap of paper between rocks in the Wailing Wall: *Let me find who I am, what I seek.*

Not long ago when Congressman Koch visited Israel, his Wailing Wall wish was that one day he'd be mayor of New York City.

Why is no one satisfied with what they have . . . always seeking new borders, decisive wars, more apricots?

A few hours later we are released from the bunker. If an Arab was discovered, I am not told. We don't return to the orchard that day, however.

I wander to a pasture. A donkey, his nose pressed to a wood fence, watches me. I scratch his head, his neck. I pick sweet blades of grass, letting him nibble from my palm. I climb over the fence and lead him to a mulberry tree. I sit in the shade, leaning against the trunk. I sense faint aftershocks, deep inside the bark. Daily afternoon MiGs needle the sky. I wonder if the donkey's hooves feel the percussive shudder. But he seems peaceful, tranquil, satisfied, just munching grass.

Bedouin women in the Negev say that tea made from apricot pits increases fertility.

Samarian men consider apricot juice good for longevity.

Israelis proclaim gifts of apricots to be a sign of true friendship.

Immigrants from Russia insist that apricots are a sign of luck.

At night the skin of an apricot resembles a yellow moon even as its scent is of dawn, waking the Mediterranean Sea.

I hitchhike to the base of Mt. Tabor in order to climb to the top. I stand in a field of sunflowers, gazing at the dome, almost two thousand feet above. All I've brought is a thermos of water, an *agvaniot*, tomato sandwich, an apricot. I could hitch; a road leads to the top. I could have asked Ari to drive me. Instead, alone, I want the soles of my sandals to bear witness. I wander through stands of eucalyptus, pine, and Mt. Tabor oak trees, some six hundred years old. I pass ruins of Crusader fortifications. A snake, at least five feet long, slithers past, pouring over an escarpment into underbrush. I halt, my gaze following its wake, horrified. Most of my teenage years, I lived in the suburbs. My idea of camping is to stay in a Holiday Inn, close to a field, with the windows open. Why did I think I could make it as a pseudo-Israeli?

I am greeted by Franciscans at the top of the summit. They give me orange soda and thick *botz* in a Turkish coffee cup. I don't enter the basilica. Instead, sweaty and exhausted, I collapse on the ground beneath cypress, cedar, olive. The colors in the Jezreel Valley far below lie flat, muted, like an Oriental rug faded by centuries of sunlight. Around me stand several churches. One is supervised by Greek Orthodox monks. Another is the Church of the Transfiguration. It is on Mt. Tabor that the prophet Deborah assembled the tribes for the battle against Sisera the Canaanite. Here, too, Josephus Flavius raised fortifications before he deserted the Jews rebelling against the Romans in 66 CE.

If Mt. Tabor were an archaeological site, I would unearth bits of chipped pottery, beads, splintered vessels, tablets on which stories are written—stories of all the armies, marauders, invaders, explorers, prophets, crusaders, rapists, gods, thieves, fanatics, saints—even young American girls who think stories of the Holy Land are *their* tales to tell.

I eat the tomato sandwich and apricot. I suck on the pit until it is clean before pushing it into the ground.

I rub an olive leaf between my fingers. I shred it, inking the green scent into my skin. Sand grouse trill afternoon winds, soughing grass. Apricots and olives. Are these scents the only stories I know to tell?

After the second temple was destroyed by Babylonians, there was widespread mourning. All the trees shed their leaves, except the olive. When asked why, the olive trees responded, "You, my brothers, show your grief on the outside for all to see. My grief will be carried within for all time."

Each year the olive tree eats away at itself in sorrow until it's nothing more than a hollow strip of bark.

In Washington, *I* felt like a hollow strip of bark. I traveled here to be nourished with olives, with the honey taste of apricot on my tongue. Now I wait to feel the soul of the sand, the fiery slant of sun. The beam of the moon, cooling. The tempering metallic scent of the Israeli sky. The sting of the scorpion, the hiss of the asp. Churches. Temples. Ruins. Olive and oak. Coffee and orange soda. The pit of an apricot.

But I don't know what, of me, I have found.

Dear Graham, after a long walk . . .

That evening, when the kibbutz darkens, rather than meet Ari, I slip, unnoticed, into the kitchen just off the dining hall. Most of our meals consist of hard-boiled eggs, yogurt, rye bread. Only on Friday evenings are we served roast chicken. I am starving. I crave sugar, something sweet. I scan the cupboards, open the refrigerator. Eggs, eggs, more eggs. There is also a large jar of apricot preserves. I sit on the floor, swallowing spoonful after spoonful.

My parents left Washington DC to live in Haifa for three years shortly before the War of Independence, under the British Mandate. Then the land was still called Palestine. Though my parents weren't religious, they were Zionists, seeking a homeland. Even before the outbreak of World War II, they felt the sting of anti-Semitism, not allowed, for example, to purchase homes in neighborhoods with protective covenants. Years earlier, during the Russian pogroms, my father's father fled Kiev after being conscripted into the czar's army. He left behind his wife and my then-infant father, promising to bring them to America after he'd saved enough money.

My parents would have remained in Palestine except the British made it virtually impossible for Jews to find work. My father, an attorney, couldn't secure a job. They returned to America, though they always longed to be Israeli. *Were*, in their hearts, Israeli, and always wanted me to feel this way, too.

"Next year in Jerusalem," they always said . . .

I am given a four-day vacation from the kibbutz. Ari and I hitchhike south across the Negev toward Eilat and the Red Sea. Between rides, I pluck a red Negev poppy, weaving the stem into my long braid. We are picked up by soldiers, friends of Ari's, in a green army truck spewing diesel fumes. We sit in the back, protected from the sun by a canvas awning, its flaps tied back. Ari tries to give me a tour. In broken English, he points out desert mountains, rock pillars, cracked mud flats, craters, green ponds.

Bedouins ride camels along the old spice route in this stone and sand desert. Using my dictionary, Ari whispers the names *sun roses, swamp irises, anemones.* He seems to hiss the words *desert broomrape, Oriental viper's grass.* The soft vowels of plovers and Oriental skylarks. The harsh consonants of buzzards and vultures winging like black flames across a white sky. I'm not sure which is more beautiful, which words to savor: the language of the moon or that of Uzis? The rough stubble along Ari's jaw or the fuzz of fruit.

He presents each word to me as a gift, ribboned in gold. Will I accept this word? This language? This country? This boy?

We swim in the Red Sea, skin bronzing in reflected light from the sandstone of the Red Sea Mountains.

"*Aliyah?*" Ari asks, his voice of salt, sun, sea. "You to move here?"

In the swell of water, his callused hand holds mine tight, as if pressure alone can make me Israeli, or a Jew.

I shrug. I shake my head. Long strands of hair swirl around my shoulders never seeming to root.

My return El Al flight lands at National Airport. My tanned feet and calves, still laced in leather gladiator sandals, are freezing. I buy a Senators baseball cap in the airport and slip it on my head. From my suitcase I remove a shawl purchased in the Old City to wrap around my bare arms. I catch a DC Transit bus, unsure of my destination, not ready to return to my American apartment. An autumn breeze ripples the Potomac. The setting sun reflects off the white marble of the Capitol, all the monuments, but it is almost too blinding. I shade my eyes. I hunch in my seat as the bus lurches from stop to stop; I don't know when to pull the cord, when to get off. The driver punches the accelerator. The scent of diesel reminds me of Israeli army trucks, of air silvery with MiGs.

When Ari and I said good-bye, he pulled me from the shade of apricot trees into the white heat of the moon. Or so it felt. In one sentence of English, which perhaps he practiced for days, he said I should return here next spring. Or next summer at the latest. I shrugged. I nodded—not sure which was true. With his hands, he pantomimed wings of a plane before handing me a small paper sack. Food for the long journey home. A hard-boiled egg. A slab of bread. Two apricots.

I finished the snack on the bus before even arriving at Tel Aviv. Once in the airport, I went to the restaurant, ordered a Coke and three pieces of chocolate cake.

Then the plane arced away. I touched the two apricot pits I'd put in my pocket, wrapped in a napkin, saving them, as if I could plant them in a ceramic pot on the balcony of my apartment.

As if they'd grow.

The Invisible Synagogue

MY BOYFRIEND, GRAHAM, AND I WEAVE—weave because we're slightly drunk after a breakfast of plummy slivovitz, brandy *frit-ules*, and Turkish coffee—along the Stradun, the main commercial street of Dubrovnik, Yugoslavia. I wear an embroidered peasant blouse with jeans. My hair sways in a braid down my back. Silver filigree earrings, which I bought in Israel, pierce my ears. My leather sandals, the same ones that wandered the Old City of Jerusalem, now tramp Dubrovnik cobblestones, which must still carry the stain of centuries-old ethnic wars from before Tito . . . all the blood of Venetians, Turks, Serbs, Habsburgs, Montenegrins, Italians, Germans.

Graham also wears jeans, as well as wire-rim glasses, his hair the length of the Beatles'. We look like the clean, well-behaved, suburban-raised hippies we are. According to Graham, we're supposed to be serious, earnest. During the five years we've dated off and on, we've attended movies like Rohmer's *Claire's Knee*, Bergman's *Wild Strawberries* and *The Seventh Seal*—foreign films, serious films, films with a message. We eat at inexpensive ethnic restaurants. We read the Sunday *New York Times*. We march in anti–Vietnam War demonstrations, but peacefully, would never get arrested. Rather than be drafted or flee to Canada, Graham joined an army reserve medical unit.

Now Graham reads aloud from a tour booklet: "Inside the thick stone walls surrounding Dubrovnik are fourteen quadrangular towers and a fortress, Sveti Ivan. The most monumental is the tower, Minceta."

Graham wants to circle the full two kilometers of walls, see everything.

66

He has come here for all of this.

But not I.

I want to take Graham to the beach, hold hands, as if decisions about our relationship will be revealed in all this sun, stone, blue sky, azure water. Should we part or marry? Won't decisions clarify if, together, we sip iced *smreka*, juniper juice, . . . or if we lovingly browse shops selling lace tablecloths and silk pillows? Shouldn't we at least pretend we're shopping for our first house together? I don't want to visit historical sites. What answers for my future can be found on the grounds of ancient battles or on alters of musty churches? But I love Graham, so I follow along, behaving like the girl I think he wants: industrious, committed to causes—and Christian.

We pass a Renaissance church where, according to the tour book, the women of Dubrovnik, both peasant and patrician, carried stones for its construction. They also strengthened the mortar with milk and egg whites, causing, according to legend, the church to withstand the 1667 earthquake, which destroyed more than three-fourths of the city. *Women's Lib or slave labor?* The booklet doesn't say.

We reach Luza Square. It features Orlando's Column, a fifteenth-century statue of a knight. Here all announcements and proclamations, as well as public punishments, took place. *I should proclaim, confess all my imperfections to Graham. But then I know he'd leave me. After all, to him, my most glaring imperfection—being Jewish—is imperfection enough.*

Last night in the hotel, I was unable to sleep. I lay beside a drowsing Graham after an endless flight from National Airport, with a stopover in Paris, for this Easter vacation from our jobs on Capitol Hill. I hoped this trip might have led (dare I say it) to a honeymoon. Except Graham's parents convinced him not to marry me because I'm a Jew—even though Graham's father, himself, is half Jewish. Very few people know this, his father's secret.

Graham's parents live in a WASPY suburban neighborhood in Connecticut. They attend Presbyterian services.

Lying awake, I wondered, *Why would I love someone afraid to marry me? Would marrying into his family prove that my being Jewish doesn't matter? Doesn't matter to him, or to me?* Had I hoped Graham would love me more, see me differently, less Jewish, here in Yugoslavia than at home . . . here, far away from his parents?

Outside the open window of our hotel room, below the fortress walls, an oarlock rattled, droplets of the Adriatic trailing from the oar back to the sea. The comforting rhythm finally lulled me to sleep, wafting on a mistral breeze of lemons, almonds, stone pines.

Now Graham wanders away from me at the entrance to the Sponza Palace. He searches for the gold-plated statue of St. Blaise. I sit on a bench, the air cool, shadowed. Soon, even as I grow accustomed to the dim light, I barely see him. He's a vague form, faint as the scent of crumbling parchment and candle wax.

I know he'll take his time, so I walk back outside. I follow Peline Street past the Minceta tower to Zudioska Street. I pause, looking around. The word "Zudioska" sounds familiar. Shingles of light fade as the street descends (I soon discover) to the Jewish ghetto. In the sunless alleyway the stones grow cold, almost mossy and damp. At the bottom of the alley hangs a small sign on a door. I can't read it but, again, the word "Zudioska." It is a plain, nondescript, three-story stone building. A narrow flight of tiled stairs leads to a small office. Inside, the walls are adorned with old photos and documents: a picture of the Wailing Wall, a memorial plaque for victims of the Holocaust. A woman, who speaks almost no English, sells tickets. "Synagogue," she says, pointing. "Synagogue." I climb more steps into the sanctuary.

I'm unfamiliar with Jewish religious objects; this is one of few temples I've ever entered. I scan a pamphlet, even though it's poorly written in English. A partition, pierced by three wide arches, divides the room and the oversize bimah. A white sat-in *parokhet* covers the inlaid doors of the *aron kodesh*, which holds several Torah scrolls. The ark is decorated with woodcuts mounted on gold-painted Corinthian pillars. In Sephardic fashion, bronze Florentine lamps hang from chains like chandeliers, containing glass oil cups. My sandals scrape the wood floors, unlike the sandy floors in the synagogue in St. Thomas.

Constellations of golden stars float across a cobalt-blue ceiling.

In 1600 fifty Jews lived in Dubrovnik. Three hundred and eight Jews in 1815. In 1939, 250. Today, 30 Jews reside in Dubrovnik.

Counting me, 31. Thirty-one and one-quarter, counting Graham.

The synagogue, the second oldest in Europe, existed as early as 1352. Now, however, it's more a museum. No rabbi. No congregation. No prayers.

It's almost like the Museum of an Extinct People, proposed by Hitler in Prague, where future generations of Aryans would have paid a few coins to tour exhibits of Torahs, menorahs, ceremonial shawls, mezuzahs. Airless exhibits. Absent of people.

No one has ever seen me as anything but Jewish, I think.

Stick to your own kind, my grandmother always hissed.

In 1815 Dubrovnik Jews needed permission from Austria to marry. In 1941 Italians confiscated Jewish property. In 1942, under German instructions, the Italians interned Jews on the nearby island of Lopud. Between the fall of Italy and the German occupation, many Jews were transported by partisans to liberated territory on the mainland. The rest were sent to camps.

Is this why the exterior of Dubrovnik's synagogue is plain, unobtrusive, nearly invisible—all of its beauty hidden inside?

From Dubrovnik, Graham and I travel by boat up the Dalmatian coast to Rijeka. Here we rent a car to drive to Sarajevo and Montenegro, where we spend the night in a farmhouse. Before dinner, I sit outside and the elderly farmer, in peasant clothes and cap, approaches me. He holds out a gnarled, work-worn hand. At first I think he means to shake mine, so I extend it, smiling. But he, grinning with absent teeth, places three colored eggs in my palm: blue, green, pink. Today is Easter. I have forgotten. He speaks to me in Croatian, so I don't understand his words—yet I feel them, like a warm egg in my hand.

"*Hvala!*" I say. *Thank you!*

I hold up the eggs to admire. The dye is uneven, in places barely a transparent tint, white shell peeking through. I nod my head, still smiling. "*Hvala.*"

I long for more words but have few in his language. He motions toward the eggs, toward his mouth. Yes, I nod, imitating him. I will eat them, yes.

He smiles, satisfied.

In our room in the farmhouse, I hold one out to Graham. He refuses. *They might be spoiled. We might get sick,* he says. I sit on the straw mattress peeling blue, green, pink. I take a bite of egg. Speckles of colored shell fall to the rough floor.

On our final evening in Yugoslavia, back in Dubrovnik, I stand by the railing on the hotel balcony overlooking the Adriatic. I want to hear the oarlocks from our first night, just to know someone's out there: Croatian, Serb, or Jew. The stars in the cobalt-blue sky seem to shine through a film of night . . . as if there is only a thin membrane between me and the realm of pure light.

It will still take me several more months to see that, after all, ancient feuds and warring ethnic and religious factions do predict the future. I will see that Graham's father is right. His son and I are not meant to marry each other. Our cool, hip, 1970s accouterments only mask how different we are—mask the fact that, although earnest, Graham is not brave.

But tonight I long to tell him about the 31¼ Jews, that *I* will always be a Jew. I want to tell him I am beginning to lose my desire for his love, which is deficient by ¼, or perhaps ¾. Which means it is entirely deficient. Which means I am beginning to peel away his beautiful shell.

Concerning Cardboard Ghosts, Rosaries, and the Thingness of Things

No ideas but in things.

WILLIAM CARLOS WILLIAMS

THE MOMENT I SEE THE HALLOWEEN cardboard ghost hang-ing in the grocery store window, I unexpectedly enter its secret life. As I approach the ghost, walking home from high school, I sense the papery beat of its heart, a flutter so thin no one else hears. I pause on the sidewalk to confirm that the rhythm isn't the tap of my penny loafers on pavement—me in my autumny orange-and-brown wool outfit with matching kneesocks. I stand still, silent, now certain the sound emanates from the direction of the window, heartbeats twining with sunrays pulsing off glass.

Outside the grocery store, red and yellow leaves scatter among jugs of apple cider, pots of chrysanthemums, pyramids of pol-ished apples. I recount these details only because, in many ways, the day is seemingly ordinary. Yet because it *is* Halloween, sure-ly the earth trembles in October winds. A day moon, almost transparent, casts pale shadows. Trick-or-treaters, preparing to spook neighborhoods as pirates, skeletons, witches, cause the everyday world to shiver. And *in* this tremble, this shadow, this shiver—just as I pass the grocery store—I know how the cut-out ghost feels.

This isn't an apparition. It's not as if I'm hallucinating. I don't conclude the cutout is real. I *know* the ghost is cardboard. It won't loosen the string that secures it in the plate-glass window. It won't escape to basements or attics. At midnight, it won't conjure itself at a dead-end street at the edge of town. Nor do I fear the ghost will haunt me.

I step closer until my own vague image is superimposed upon the glass. The skin on my face pales in this palimpsest of ghost, glass, me. I feel the gossamer hem of the ghost's body. My veins sense the hoarfrost in its torso. I inhale ether on its breath. As I evanesce into this cutout, I sense the cardboard ghost's soul— transparent as the day moon and as lovely, inevitable, unambig- uous. It is reliable in its "ghostness." So in *this* way, yes, I admit the ghost *is* real: to me. In this way, *I* am the one to haunt *it*.

Then, quite simply, the moment ends. I continue walking home from school, my kneecaps above my orange kneesocks now chilled cool and white. Mandee's Dress Shoppe, People's Bank, Rock Ridge Pharmacy, all are in their correct places on the sidewalk, nothing amiss. Mothers with kids drive station wagons down Rock Road. The ghost remains hanging in the window, floating behind glass, while I seamlessly reenter this other—what some would call the "real"—world. No one witnesses my brief absence.

This event isn't entirely unexpected. For years I've known how, by mentally deliquescing, to divine the soul of inanimate things. Of my own free will, I allow objects to thrust me into their paper or glass or metal states of being, to decipher their hidden lives. So even when a ghost in a window is depicted in cardboard— immobile, lifeless—I know that molecules can be magically trans- formed. Things are alembic. I am.

In this particular way the ghost is no different from my own handkerchiefs. One square of cotton shows a drawing of Pluto, the cartoon dog. Another hankie is filigreed magenta. On an- other, my white interlocked initials, "sws," are embroidered on a white background. At least this is how the handkerchiefs ap- pear when neatly folded in my bureau drawer.

They amaze me only when, fresh from the clothesline, I lov- ingly iron them.

In first grade, to reach the ironing board, I stand on a small stool, sprinkling water—stored in an old bottle of my father's bay-rum aftershave—onto the material. As I slide the iron, Pluto wags his tail. Magenta explodes in streamers. My initials bloom like orchid petals in bay-rum mist. The rolled hems sway, ghost-like, a mirage of heat, shimmering. I lift the edge of cotton to see what breathes beneath.

As soon as I finish ironing my hankies, I wrinkle them, simply to magically iron them all over again. I pause if my mother draws near while I iron, not wanting her to know the special power I possess . . . the mystical secrets that *things* possess. This is not a world adults understand.

After we leave the States and move to the West Indies, my mother, in fact, chastises me when I linger on the verandah watching the sky through a prism of garnet rosary beads. I'm given the rosary my first day at All-Saints Anglican School. But since I'm a little Jewish girl (only temporarily attending All-Saints because the nondenominational school is full), my mother insists I put that silly thing away.

I can't.

I hold the beads toward open windows, squinting, even during school. I ignore the teacher's strict warnings to pay attention to lessons. Besides, I *am* paying attention. The sky fireworks ruby suns refracting all the ions in the universe. Since none of my schoolmates hold their rosaries toward space, I believe only mine reveals this secret: there is more than one sun in the sky. At will, galaxies of suns glitter like gems, like stars—atoms dazzling the atmosphere—redder than all the hibiscus and frangipani flowers on the island. Even though I am in the tropics, this warmth, offered by the rosary, is deeper, casting light into my soul.

The light disappears only when I put the rosary in my pocket. Rather than feel sad, I am pleased. For things are predictable, re-maining where I leave them, unmoving, waiting for me to return to them. And warmth *does* return . . . the moment I once again hold a bead toward the sky. It is this consistency—much more consistent than people—that reassures me, that offers comfort, always drawing me back.

Beauty is in allowing a thing to fulfill its potential: infusing the cardboard ghost with hoarfrost or a rosary bead with sunlight. Beauty is in hearing, in tasting, in sensing the inner life, the secret seed of a thing. The Beauty of Things is a religion; I am resolute in my belief.

We return to the States, settling in Glen Rock, where I discover that Miss C., my eighth-grade teacher, is one particular person who offers no comfort. Her handkerchief perches stiffly in the pocket of her tweed jacket. I picture *her* pressing handkerchiefs with a humorless, iron-like hand, the same humorlessness with which she reads my essays.

On the day of our final papers, for example, Miss C. requests that we each write a three-paragraph essay, with at least six sentences in each. I develop the first two paragraphs, as instructed. When I reach the third, however, I know only one sentence belongs, will fit. Confidently, I write what I'm certain is a sentence that completes the essay with clarity, with perfection. But in front of the class, after praising other students' papers, Miss C. turns to mine, claiming you *can't* have only one sentence in a paragraph. It isn't acceptable, she says.

Why not? I want to know.

But I'm too timid to ask.

Instead I learn that, compared to things, Miss C. is unknowable. I don't understand why she wants me to write an ordinary essay like other students. She is unpredictable, too. One moment she praises students; the next, she is fearsome with me. She is just like my mother, who bakes cookies, only later to call my beloved rosary "silly." Such contradictions confirm that *things* are more reliable. People like Miss C. are opaque, whereas the world of handkerchiefs, of beads, is transparent, is like ghosts, like glass.

How easily I step from one world into the other and back again as if I'm living two lives. In one, I pray to the secret life of things; in the other, I play games and attend school. How effortless to cross thresholds, invisible borders between worlds. It's perfectly natural, say, to warm my fingers on rosary beads one moment and the next to eat a peanut-butter-and-jelly sandwich in the cafeteria.

In this way the world isn't less real. It's *more*. For it's confabulated with other realities, ones that are intoxicating, primary-color bright and kinetic. Not static. Not dying. Not lifeless. Not weighted with sorrow or despair. Neither inconsistent nor dogmatic.

I'm transported, with one glance, into the reality of a seemingly monadic dime store marble, a sliver of white in transparent glass. One moment this white is frozen in its glass cocoon; the next, the tips of my fingers feel moisture from its cloudy molecules. Now free, it twists and spins, elements spewing from its core. Snow melts to oleander petals. Frost seeps ghostlike into the atmosphere, white-ing the Milky Way. Waves drizzle foam, lacy as crinolines. Beams from the moon bathe my feet. I taste the vanilla of swan feathers, of pearls. Next I gaze through quartz, enveloped in polleny sunlight. Or I see animals roam a savannah inside tigereye marbles. My tongue against glass, I lick lemon spumoni, lime agates, iridescent gumballs, wet red polish, mango crystals, a blueberry freeze, amethyst ice, the luster of mint. My marbles are planets in motion, even when they're at rest.

The more I understand the soul of things, the more I know I influence things as much as they influence me. A marble, for example, initially contains, in its purest form, one certain aspect. Then, by peering beneath the surface, it's as if my very senses violently cause a thing not necessarily to act differently, but to fulfill all its realities, be *more* of itself, down to its tiniest quark:

a marble yields the earth; a bead yields a sun; a cardboard ghost yields a heartbeat. A marble, then, isn't only a chunk of glass. A marble has scent and taste that's beyond—deeper than—a cool, glassy skin.

At the same time I, myself, appropriate the essence of each of these things. This confluence of energy flows between these familiar, intimate, unambiguous things—and me.

How, I wonder at times, can a thing, able to be conjured into a deeper self, be considered unambiguous? It's because all I need to do is blink or swallow, stretch my limbs or place an object in a pocket, for it to revert to its ordinary, simpler self. A marble is *also* still a marble. It never loses its essence, its natural, basic core.

A marble never loses its "marbleness."

Unlike these knowable things, however, it is *people* who hide behind masks. People are afraid to reveal themselves or show their various properties or dimensions. You never know what to expect, for you can't observe or contain all of any particular person. How could I have known, for example, that Miss C. would fail to see the significance of my one-sentence paragraph, of each carefully selected word?

For words, too, when written on paper alchemize into tangible objects, more reliable, more magical, more potent than people. The first word I fall in love with is "ventriloquist," twisting the letters around my tongue. In this word I understand that the ghost speaks for me just as I speak for it—that I am the light around the bead as much as I discover its own warmth within. Words are spoken with ears, noses, fingertips. By unmasking words, syllables and letters appear. Words reveal meanings of things I savor, a constant source of intrigue and afterthought. I mull a word for hours as if I hold it, too, up to the light to inhale all its facets.

But because of this, in my same English class, I am unable to learn dictionary definitions for vocabulary tests. The word "marble," for example, is defined as "a hard ball used in children's games." Nowhere does it mention iridescent gumballs, the luster of mint.

I never tell anyone about the hidden life of things. Not that I'm ashamed. Nor do I think people will laugh at me or doubt my certainty that a rosary bead transfigures into "sun." Rather, it would be as if a magician revealed the tricks of the trade. It just isn't done. But because of my silence, because I'm unable to learn vocabulary words and write six-sentence paragraphs, I am sent off to summer school. I'm urged to try harder, spend more time on my studies.

I slouch at my summer-school desk one dull day after another. With all my mistakes, all my incorrect definitions and unsatisfactory essays, the eraser on my pencil shrinks. It dwindles toward a nub. I mourn the loss of each pink particle, almost as tiny as dust. So rather than pay attention to the teacher, I focus on saving them. I gently brush the rubber bits across my paper, careful they don't gust onto the floor. My palm hovers at the edge of the desk ready to catch them, like crumbs. When only a few pink polka dots remain on the paper, I press a moist fingertip against them until they adhere. I open my plastic change purse. I brush my hand. The motes emigrate to live with nickels and dimes.

Or I hold the eraser beneath my nose. I lick it. And soon . . . soon I am barefoot on a trail in the Malaysian archipelago among towering rubber trees with glossy leaves. The air is burgundy and hot. Halved coconuts catch latex dripping from bark. But watching the incisions—liquid rubber weeping from them—it's as if my arms and legs, my own limbs, feel the cuts. Just as when I sensed the ghost's papery heartbeat, I now equally understand the quiddity of rubber. Soon, I myself no longer exist, as if I perished in a plane crash or was lost at the bottom of the sea. I am rubber.

The skin on my arms and legs remains sore for days. My fingers smell of pink acid, a hint of smoke, a trace of bark. I still feel each particle as if it, alone, holds me to the skin of the earth. Or as if each pink seed will blossom into all that's pink in the world: pigs and petunias, bubble gum and lipstick, nail polish and cats' noses, ballet slippers and dogs' tongues. Pellucid dawns. Pink tastes like sugar, satin ribbons, sapphires. Like tender wounds. All that is lush with pleasure, frail with pain. *Pink,* I say to myself, the long vowel sound lingering, inviting me into the word— the world of pink—before the quick consonant at the end snaps shut, holding me forever.

I understand that living a life of things has repercussions. I'm so consumed, not only do I fail high school essays and vocabulary tests, I also fail the sats, barely getting accepted into college. Even college classes hold little interest. I'm much more content, say, observing imbrications on a pinecone, wondering how the bracts feel overlapping in their ornamental pattern. No, I *know* how they feel, each bract hugged and loved by its neighbor.

At a funeral for a friend killed in a car crash, I begin, now in my twenties, to question whether I should relinquish my hold on things, at least a little. I sense, during the service, the warm mahogany of the casket. I am awash in red roses, white carnations, yellow lilies, the perfume and aftershave of mourners pressed together in pews. People weep. Tears runnel through makeup, staining silk dresses.

I am unable to mourn, to weep. As much as I wonder why, I am equally consumed with the idea that things don't betray you in this way, don't die.

Or do they?

I am seized by two contradictory notions: that things don't die; that they do. I am suddenly bereft when I realize I haven't seen my rosary for over a decade. During which move did I lose it? Or were the beads, at some unremembered time, inadvertently crushed? Might I have even thrown away the rosary, my affections aglow with some new object of desire? Oh, the effusiveness of color in marbles, the destiny of red and yellow on beach balls, the surrender of book covers waiting to be opened, the eagerness of Jujubes yearning to be devoured! I feel craven by my own deceit. That I am unfaithful. That I might have discarded the rosary after falling in love with an ivory button. How could I not have noticed—in *my* all-too-human way—that I, too, failed to be consistent, not always tender toward the feelings and needs of things?

Sitting in the pew in this church at this funeral, I grieve. Only now, I fully understand that, over the years, handkerchiefs shred. Ribbons unravel to lint. Ravenous moths fray feather collections. I, alone, am responsible for the loss, these deaths. Yet I never stopped to pay attention as *my* attention so willingly drifted from this sequin to that burnt sienna crayon . . . years of bijoux, bangles, bracelets. How sorrowfully I neglected my duties, even as I am solely in charge of their care.

But even if I maintain constant vigilance over my things, what will happen to them when *I* die? What will happen to my objects when I'm gone? Who will care for them, these things allowing themselves to be lovingly explored by me in all their dimensions? These things, all my things, are almost mortal themselves in the way *they* have been with me during my most intense experiences. They, in fact, have *been* my most intense experiences. I have held them, caressed them, licked them, examined them, inhaled them, heard them, savored them.

The church service ends. I find myself outside on the sidewalk, alone, here where I'm now living in Galveston, Texas. The day is sunny, hot, blue. The pallbearers slide the casket into the hearse. The door closes long before I know how to say good-bye to a human friend.

I seek therapy following the funeral, in the midst of these anxieties and contemplations. I need to understand my newly realized confusion about things—as much as I must learn to accept the everyday world of people to be as reliable, as enticing, as soulful as—well—*real* as objects, as things.

Instead, during hour-long therapy sessions with Dr. Gripon, I eye a bamboo tissue box on the coffee table. I begin, after a few sessions, to surreptitiously peel off slivers of wood. I slide them between my fingers. How delicate, this chartreuse aroma of hollow woody stems swaying in an Asian breeze.

It is *this* airy, fluty sound of bamboo I hear more than I'm able to distinguish Dr. Gripon's voice when he asks how I feel, when he tries to define what's wrong. Besides, unsure of my own voice, I'm unable to answer. How, after all, can I say I *feel* like a rosary bead, a hankie, a bamboo twig? It's as if I never learned the words of human feelings. I know how a marble feels; I can feel like a marble.

But how do I feel like *me?*

I stop therapy after three years even though I still don't know the right words to say to him. I'm unable to describe what's wrong. Nevertheless, at our last session, I want to give him a going-away present. Maybe he'll finally understand who I am if I give him my marble with the white swirl.

As I hand it to him, however, I drop it. It rolls under his desk. While I meant for this moment to be plush with meaning—presenting him the marble as if it's a new world for him to explore—instead I'm on my hands and knees poking around dust balls and bits of paper. I now consider whether I'd have felt more comfortable sitting *here*—partially obscured by his desk—inhaling powdery dust. Its grit provides texture to my own transparent-feeling skin. He chuckles as I search for the marble, asking what's going on, what have I dropped, what am I doing?

I finally retrieve the marble, but I'm too mortified to show it to him, let alone give him this present. Despite his name, I realize I'm unable to "grip on." To him. To what he considers real. He'll never understand the marble. Things. Me.

I return home, placing the marble on a bed of gauze in an antique ORIENTAL TOOTH PASTE jar, which I found at an excavation site in Galveston. It's as if the marble, feverish in its swoon after inhaling the fumes of Dr. Gripon's office, is contaminated. It rests, quarantined, quietly recovering from its brush with reality.

It will take years—and the threat of divorce—before *I* am the one to understand: understand the words and the world of people. Eventually, after ten more therapists likewise fail to correctly diagnose my condition, I finally find one, Randy Groskind (after I move to Georgia), who does. I present a conch shell to him, one from St. Thomas. He nods when I explain that in its whoosh of breath, I hear words circling the whorls of my own ears. He doesn't laugh. Nor does he smile. He is perfectly quiet— as still and quiet as a thing—not rudely disturbing the presence of things.

Randy is always Randy. Like his last name, his kindness is large. Unlike other people, he never loses his essential quality, the reliable properties of "Randy Groskind."

In his silence, in his consistency, I finally find a way to say that when I was a girl my father hurt me. He, my own father, was *particularly* opaque, unpredictable, unknowable. One moment he was a loving daddy who built me a dollhouse out of construction paper; the next moment he wasn't a daddy at all.

I tell Randy about dropping the marble in Dr. Gripon's office. I explain what I have now come to understand about that moment. That, for the first time, it's as if I saw the marble for what it was—lying alone, helpless, hiding in shadows beneath the desk, as if ashamed, as if it had lost its magic. The white swirl seemed shriveled. The incorporeal essence of the marble dead.

Or maybe I, as a little girl, was the one who lost my own personal magic, only discovering the magic of childhood in things. *I* was the one who would have been feverish without them. I would have been dull, dark, contaminated, soulless in the heavy folds of loss without my beloved things.

It is then that I say, "But I was really a little girl. Not a marble. Not a thing."

I don't believe there's only one reason why I became this way in the first place. Yes, maybe it was the particular betrayal of parents and teachers. Maybe I suffered chronic metaphysical crises or semantic fugues. Maybe, lacking real religion, I found comfort in totems, artifacts, and talismans. Or maybe the fault is solely mine—a daydreamer, a slothful, lazy person who loves to commune with marbles and beads. I allowed myself to be porous, to become things, to be transported wherever they lead.

Years later, the marble remains in the ORIENTAL TOOTH PASTE jar ("CLEANSING, BEAUTIFYING, PRESERVING THE TEETH AND GUMS ~~ PREPARED BY JEWSBURY & BROWN"), with its gray and white marbleized surface. The rim of the jar is chipped from when my cat once knocked it off my desk. Now I accept such flaws and inconsistencies in things, in people. In me.

Yet on days when the earth seems paused on its axis, or when the day moon fails to rise, I remove the marble from its nest. I savor its cool wonder in the palm of my hand.

Prepositioning John Travolta

Major things are wind, evil, a good fighting horse, prepositions, inexhaustible love, the way people choose their king.

ANNE CARSON

PERHAPS IT'S BECAUSE YOU RECENTLY MOVED to Texas and
can't figure out if you live *in* Galveston or *on* Galveston Island
that you begin to confuse prepositions. In any event, the first
serious outbreak of this prepositional virus blooms at (during?)
the time you find yourself, rumpled and damp, before (against?,
beside?) the barrette counter in the "notions" aisle in the un-
air-conditioned Woolworth's. You believe that if you purchase
a white silk camellia—a clasp attached to its short stem—and
use it to pin up the left side of your hair, away from your face,
that you will resemble Stephanie, John Travolta's love interest,
in *Saturday Night Fever*.

No, you will actually *be* Stephanie in *Saturday Night Fever*.

But—what with phrasal prepositions compounding your
problem—will you be her *in addition to* yourself? *In spite of* your
own obvious self? *Apart from* yourself? Or *with the exception of*
your rumpled and damp self?

Maybe an unhappy marriage, maybe the fact that you gave
up a good job on Capitol Hill to move here for (with) your husband, maybe Galveston's humidity that clings to (upon) your
skin like a moist membrane, or maybe simple longing contrib-
ute to the prepositional crisis that causes you to stare into (toward) the tarnished, wavy mirror, fasten the fake camellia, and
hope for the best.

You tilt your neck to catch a different view of yourself from (in) another mirror, one aisle over in "makeup." This double, wavy image casts you, you're convinced, in a more romantic light. A soft-focus-publicity-photo kind of light. Which helps.

Because the thing is, you aren't particularly upset to find yourself floundering in this psychotic-cum-prepositional break. *In* (inside, within) this break, or *during* this break, you can actually believe that this warped wood floor in Woolworth's is mere prelude to the neon dance floor of 2001 Odyssey, the disco in Bay Ridge, Brooklyn. Surely you already smell polyester-y cologne, taste Seven and Sevens, inhale salt-grit air rising around the Verrazano Bridge, all more pungent and real than this dusty Woolworth's.

In other words (or toward other words, or concerning other words, with respect to other words), *in* this prepositional confusion, you actually feel a modicum of comfort *by reason of* or *with respect to* the fact that reality, even in the best of times, is slippery and unpredictable. Not unlike prepositions.

At the same time, however, here in notions, because of this prepositional impasse, you're not, ironically, able to consider the notion that it's as if you, yourself, are trapped between (inside, within, against) two tarnished, wavy mirrors. Prepositionally speaking, you do not see that your love of (for) John Travolta occurs *in spite of* your trapped life. Or is it *on account of* or *due to* it? Do you love him *in place of* any other life whatsoever? Love him *in lieu of* a life of your own?

In short, in this prepositional chaos you don't see the Big Picture. Or even know if there is a Big Picture, let alone its origins or what it means.

A few years later, now divorced from (without) your Galveston husband, and with (beside) your Houston husband but still entrenched in (or with, during, among) your prepositional crisis (but definitely not *between* prepositional crises, thus crossing one preposition off the list), you stand before (but thankfully not between) racks of shoes in Marshall's searching for a pair of cow-boy boots. You just saw *Urban Cowboy* and want, more than any-thing, to resemble Debra Winger, or the character Sissy, whom John Travolta's character, Bud, marries, loses, loves again.

You don't have enough money to purchase Tony Lamas. You pull on a pair of red-fringed, faux-suede boots, instead . . . Tex-an enough to dance the two-step with John Travolta at Gilley's.

John Travolta films *Urban Cowboy* in Houston. You almost see him in person, but don't. You haven't quite recovered from the near miss.

As you sit in your therapist's office (or *on* the couch *in* his office) for your weekly appointment, you discover how close you came to seeing him. Before you're able to speak, however, you can't help but silently ruminate about whether one sits *on* a porch or *in* a porch . . . and do you sit *in* or *on* a wicker chair *on* that porch *beside* (inside of) the railing? As you try to sort out these prepositional conundrums, you begin (dare you admit it?) to succumb to the weariness of this confusion. You even won-der if whoever invented prepositions in the first place ultimately ended up in (around, near, inside) the eighth or ninth circle of hell. And decide probably the latter.

Dr. Gripon, due to your delay in speaking, finally says, "Guess what?"

Still in your Stephanie phase, you wear the white camellia (now shredding) with a polyester outfit and platform shoes.

"My wife and I saw John Travolta last night having dinner . . ."

"The *real* him?" you ask, incredulous.

Dr. Gripon has never been informed about your personal prep-ositional maelstrom or the cause and effect between it and your crush on John Travolta. In fact, by now, you yourself aren't one hundred percent sure which came first, the chicken or the egg, or in this case, the prepositions or John Travolta, though you suspect the former.

Nevertheless, what with this unsolved mystery—coupled with the dilemma as to which preposition would best express your love for (with, of) John Travolta—you have only mentioned him in passing to Dr. Gripon.

"He's in town filming that movie."

Urban Cowboy.

"My wife got his autograph."

So now John Travolta has fallen madly in love with your thera-pist's wife, you actually think. Because, after all, if he has seen her *in place of you,* isn't it just as likely that he has fallen *in* love with her . . . now, for the first time, worrying that people, just like prepositions, are interchangeable.

Interchangeable because, though you don't like to admit it, even John Travolta is interchangeable.

You once equally had a crush on Paul Newman. Whom you *did* meet in person.

This was when you worked on (in) Capitol Hill and helped out at a Democratic fund-raiser. At one point during the evening, you found yourself standing beside (around, near, within speaking distance of—or to) Paul Newman, who asked you for a cigarette. Unfortunately, you don't smoke. Which is what you told him.

Which caused your first missed opportunity.

Because you should have told Paul Newman to just stay put while you found a cigarette. And you should have moved both heaven and earth—above, across, behind, below, underneath, off, inside—and every other possible prepositional direction—*on account of* your search to find one. Because then he might have fallen in (into) love with you. Except you didn't. So he didn't.

But even if you had (you try to reason), by the time you actually found your way out of the smoky prepositional maze, Paul Newman would probably have found a cigarette from some other girl hovering before, behind, around him. And he would have fallen in love with her. Because if prepositions and movie stars are interchangeable, aren't, likewise, lonely girls?

Before your mind further descends into a prepositional melt-down, you say to Dr. Gripon, "But you didn't call me from the restaurant!"

Thus resulting in the aforementioned missed opportunity to drive there to meet John Travolta.

Now, what with a growing number of missed opportunities—and, by association, loss, alienation, an existential crisis—all entering the (prepositional) equation simultaneously, you wonder whether your prepositional breakdown is the root cause of *all* your problems, from the get-go.

Maybe your prepositions were never neatly aligned inside (throughout, within) your mind in the first place.

How *can* they be when even your religious beliefs are *out* of alignment by reason of (with respect to) your Jewish father's damaging love—to say nothing of the seduction of popular culture and its ever-changing fads. Why wouldn't you want to dance with (beside, along with) Catholic Italian John Travolta, aka Tony Manero and/or good ol' Texas boy Bud, whether it's disco or the Texas two-step? After all, if Jewish Debra Winger can masquerade in (with) what surely must be Christian cowgirl boots (real Jews, after all, never wear cowboy boots), why can't you?

So how can you possibly expect prepositions to clarify life when your whole identity from day one decidedly stood apart from (beside, without) whoever might be the "real" you?

For the very first time since beginning therapy you weep. Though you aren't really sure if it's because of John Travolta, Paul Newman, your Galveston (ex)husband, your fast-fading Houston husband, or the state of your soul—as confused as prepositions.

Compounding the problem is that you are now so endlessly mired in (with reference to) your prepositional nightmare, you can't even explain it to Dr. Gripon. You likewise generally avoid discussing your childhood—and its religious implications—to him altogether, due to (on account of) your inability to select the one correct preposition to highlight the divide between (among!)

genuine love, movie-star love, spiritual love, pop-culture love, and/or your father's so-called love.

To make matters worse, while still sitting on the couch in (within) Dr. Gripon's office, you realize that *his very name itself* is adrift in the equivalent of a prepositional hazardous waste site. You worry you are losing your grip on him. For how can you grip *on to* him in order to save your sanity, with his name morphing (and why not?) into Dr. Gripoff.

In any event, there is simply no way to discuss life and its various losses, confusions, and missed opportunities within the context of—and given the nuances of—so many prepositions and phrasal prepositions—even if you cross one (such as "between") off the list—as you tried to do. Though you suspect, given the right circumstances, it could just as easily return, as in "you are *between* two no-win prepositional propositions. Unless you are *among* more than two lose-lose prepositional proposals."

Years later, as it so happens, your doctor prescribes an antibiotic for an infection, and the antibiotic severely disrupts your intestinal tract.

While you wait to either recover or die (now, without any husband), you watch old movies on television and see a young, glistening Paul Newman in *The Long, Hot Summer*. One Saturday evening, channel surfing, you also catch *Saturday Night Fever* . . . now sure that your life is flashing before (beyond, near) your eyes. How young and healthy John Travolta likewise looks in (with) that white suit boogying on (across) that neon-flashing dance floor. (It should be noted that although you have, by now, lost the camellia, the red-suede boots still occupy space on the floor of your closet—or perhaps simply in the closet—but at any rate not *on* your feet, which is where they should be if you are to die nobly.)

You now wonder, in your frail condition, if you want(-ed) to be Stephanie and be *in* (within, inside) *Saturday Night Fever* because then you wouldn't be *outside* it, susceptible, as you are, to disease, grammatically challenged childhoods, failed marriages, death . . . well, susceptible, after all, to *life*. Because you would forever be inside (within) the screen itself.

To be dead is to be *in* (below, beneath, underneath, within) the ground. Or to be *up* in crematorium smoke. Or, if you believe in the hereafter—heaven, hell, limbo, purgatory, or whatever—which you don't (or do you?), you'd still be above, beyond, off, outside the earth.

Which would be all right if you are an astronaut. And now that you think of it, you always wanted to be an astronaut.

But as you grow older, well, as you *age* and opportunities lessen, while, at the same time, prepositions metastasize out of control, you realize you'll never be an astronaut—a stretch even in your twenties unless you played one on screen—which you would have liked to be—or to do. Just float in space . . . watching the marble of the earth sink farther and farther away, observing the earth (life, death, etc.) with perspective, while, at the same time, also gain perspective on prepositions and, finally, yourself.

Imagining all this—as if you *are* either inside a movie or outside gravity—you realize: it doesn't really matter if you mess up a few prepositions in your life; the problems, after all, of 56 little prepositions don't amount to a hill of beans in (with regard to) this crazy world—because we all die anyway, boots on or off.

Which leads you to (toward) the realization that you deliberately trapped yourself inside (among, below, behind, or underneath) prepositions in the first place because you *want* to be trapped as if between (yes, for once, you're sure this is the right word) those wavy, almost-funhouse Woolworth's mirrors in lieu of (in spite of, in addition to, or even in place of) reality, of life.

All of which is to say: you might have figured out the Big Picture earlier if you'd confided in Dr. Gripon. But what with prepositions running amok, you lived in (inside) John Travolta's world, a beautiful friendship, except for (with the exception of) the fact that it wasn't yours to live.

Have you missed me? Not to worry. I'm still here (though who the "I" is remains anyone's guess), chronicling every misstep of our long-suffering gefilte. Israel, though pretty, was a bust in the identity department. Even my own sorry attempt at playing the role of Supplicant, which I previously neglected to mention, resulted in a zero as round as I am.

Nevertheless, imagine this little gefilte rolling along with the best of them down the dusty path of the Via Dolorosa. Did you not see me dodging the blistered feet of priests, rabbis, clergy-men, and American tourists radiant on the Way of Grief, the Way of Sorrows, the Painful Way. Oh, I roll past Stations of the Cross, one after another, even though my own station remains one big Matzoh of Confusion. By the end of my trek down the Dolor-ous Way, I have a headache this big—as if I myself wear a crown of thorns hooked to my head—not that gefiltes have heads. But what with Romans, Catholics, Christians, gefiltes, and Jews, who can possibly find the Path to Salvation let alone manage not to get lost in that maze of alleys in the Old City. In short, from all the tumbling and wrong turns I end up gritty and flattened, a gefilte latke, along the same Path that Jesus himself might or might not have walked. This possible (mis)direction just another of my own crosses to bear.

Nor did I find my identity *in, with,* or even *in spite of* John Tra-volta . . . bearing in mind the enormity of the miracle (think, here, water into wine; loaves and fishes; being cast as female lead, etc.) that would have to occur for a gefilte to discover her Jewishness (or, let's be honest, any realistic self) with a Hollywood Scientologist. If this isn't looking for miracles in all the wrong places, what is, I ask you? Can you say I've been barking up the wrong tree? Except for the fact that a gefilte is hardly a dogfish—let alone one that barks—and we've got enough identities going on here as it is.

By now the role of one long-lost gefilte has grown so depressing that I have a vision of a breakdown in my future. Are there rehab centers for gefilte fish? Twelve-step programs? *My name is Gefilte and I am not a fish. My name is Gefilte and I am not a Jew. Or am I?*

Now, just to be clear, chronologically speaking, I still live in Galveston and haven't, in "real" time (whatever that is), moved to Georgia as yet or started therapy with Randy. Miles to go . . . journeys, as you well know, rarely proceeding in one straight line or direction. In short, this gefilte swims one league forward, two leagues back.

And speaking of backward, when you think of it, as much as I wanted to marry Christopher and live as a Christian suburban housewife in our own brick ranch in Glen Rock, let's analyze this notion for a moment. Can you really imagine *this* gefilte fish wearing an apron or driving a station wagon full of my wiggling spawn?

I thought not.

S.W.S.

Galveston Island Breakdown

The Neon Penises of Galveston, Texas

FALL IN LOVE WITH A MAN who drives a blue Chevy convertible. You and he—along with his wife and a group of friends—are dancing at the Kon Tiki, a gay bar just off The Strand, across the street from the apartment you share with your husband. You're here because the Kon Tiki has the best disco music, the best dance floor: clear Lucite underlit with neon penises. They flash on. They flash off. Red, green, blue penises strobe to the beat. "Stayin' Alive." Tonight, caught in the melodrama of the moment, you think, *The penises strobe in time to the aching beat.* Or, better yet, *The aching penises strobe in time to the beat.* This amuses you. Of course, you've been drinking Seven and Sevens all night long, you, in your jivy platform sandals, cutoff jeans, polyester tank top. You're also celebrating April fourteenth, your birthday, your husband out of town on business.

Don't consider that marriage—blue Chevy convertible's or yours—an impediment to falling in love. Especially here on the Gulf Coast past midnight, just drunk enough to believe he dances like John Travolta in *Saturday Night Fever*, a movie you've seen upwards of twelve times. Thirteen times. Since in your present condition nothing is an impediment, slither against blue-convertible man during a slow number. Whisper "let's fuck" into his ear.

When these two short words—*let's fuck*—slam together, blue-convertible man ditches his wife for you.

93

You and he drive thirty-two miles to the west end of Galveston Island—with a bottle of Seagram's to go. The convertible top is down. Music from KILE blares on the radio. You cross the San Luis Pass bridge, cruising the curve of the Gulf Coast, distant towns lit like radioactive dust. He stops in Matagorda, the Paradise Motel, its neon rendition of paradise consisting of a palm, a seagull, a sun. You have read *Paradise Lost* (or at least the Cliffs Notes). He's maybe read *Jonathan Livingston Seagull*. Or *Love Story*. Or at least seen the movie. But why *can't* paradise be neon palms, seagulls, suns? Why can't paradise be the strobe of neon penises? Why can't it be a motel room with humid sheets?

In fact, why can't paradise, why can't love, be like Sylvester Stallone's line from *Rocky* since, right before you fall asleep, blue-convertible man whispers, "I've got gaps. You've got gaps. Together, we fill each other's gaps."

Don't dwell on exactly what each other's gaps are. Tonight, your synapses crackling from the fire of alcohol, you're sure your gaps are manageable. It's only later you realize your gaps are gaping.

When the weekend is over and he returns to his wife, counsel yourself: *This love of your life lasted less time than you spent alone in the movie theater watching John Travolta dance.*

Dancing the Quadriplegic Two-Step

By May, alone, answer an ad in the *Galveston Daily News* for a furnished apartment. Drive your un-air-conditioned green Volkswagen bug to a Victorian house on Market Street. Paint peels from loosely hinged shutters and galleries. One window pane is repaired with corrugated cardboard. The three-foot brick pier on which the house stands is cracked—many houses having been elevated above sandy swamps after the 1900 hurricane. Ring the doorbell. A disembodied voice, booming over an intercom, intones, "Door's unlocked."

Enter a parlor where a quadriplegic man lies hoisted onto a hospital bed with pulleys, buttons, buzzers situated so he can raise and lower his bed with a flicker of movement. His massive bald head rears from an obese body covered with a sheet, soggy with sweat. In his static stare, not even his lids blink. His protruding eyes x-ray your heart.

You are too sober to speak. Your first impulse is to stick a fork in your eye before you even see the apartment. Nevertheless, take the second-floor apartment, sight unseen. The rent is cheap. You're broke, desperate.

Carry your one canvas suitcase up the outside steps. Before you open the door, you know the apartment's archaeology of scents: stained undershirts, empty ice-cube trays, faulty electrical wiring, chipped lead paint. Sit on the couch, the plastic upholstery reminding you of the seats in the blue convertible. Across from you is a bright square of wallpaper where a picture must have hung for years. From age, sun, neglect, the remaining wallpaper is the color of water-stained magnolia petals. A solitary cobweb trails from the ceiling. In the bathroom, rust corrodes the toilet, the sink. The mirror's silver backing is tarnished. Avoid looking at yourself when you open the medicine chest. Dry mercurochrome smears one of the shelves.

A toaster, leaking crumbs, is plugged into a scorched socket in the kitchen. Open the refrigerator to discover an empty, washed mayonnaise jar, even the rim wiped clean. Remove, from your suitcase, a small slab of roast beef wrapped in aluminum foil. You brought it from the apartment where you lived with your husband, ten blocks away. Place the beef in the fridge beside the empty jar.

Open windows. Across the street is a rooming house. A man's arm leans on the sill in a second-story window. In the lowering sun, you barely see his shadowed face. But you know a frayed rope belts his stained jeans. He eats deviled ham out of a can for dinner. He thinks it still costs three cents to mail a letter. Dry skin cracks his heels. You want to wave but know that's not a good idea.

That evening walk to the seawall. Another day slips into the gulf, below water. No longer believing in romantic sunsets, enter the first club you pass, the Jean Lafitte; believe in the permanent neon night of bars instead. Slide onto a stool. Order bourbon and fries. One by one, dip them in ketchup. Glen Campbell sings "Galveston," an obvious jukebox favorite. On the dance floor, not nearly as interesting as the Kon Tiki's, sailors sway the Texas two-step, girls wearing western shirts with plastic, pearlized buttons. Ceiling fans churn cigarette smoke. Inhale it. Deeply. Glance at the pay phone by the front door. Think about calling blue convertible. Or your husband. Think about returning to the apartment you shared with him. But across from that apartment is the red door of the Kon Tiki. It would only be a matter of time before, lonely again, you watch neon penises flashing off and, better yet, on.

Besides, while you suspect what's wrong, you don't know how to explain it—to your husband or to yourself. You don't quite know how to say that you once had a good job on Capitol Hill. But you left it, as well as your friends and your apartment, to move here to be with him . . . where he has a job directing a project to restore The Strand and the Victorian residential neighborhoods. Whereas you have no job at all. Nor do you know how to say you are angry he works long hours and weekends. At times, he doesn't seem to remember he's married. You might as well be a table or chair. He never says "I love you." Nor can you explain your confusion as to why he never bought you an engagement ring or a wedding band. He ignored you during your wedding reception, dancing with virtually everyone else but you. He never apologized. But remember that love means never having to say you're sorry.

Now what to do? Return to DC? Work on your marriage? File for divorce? Buds of indecision bloom—all you're able to grow.

A drunken sailor approaches your bar stool. His face and clothes are wrinkled from salty air, alcohol, age. Halfheartedly, he attempts to pick you up, but you're both too far gone to give it anything but a feeble try. Still, perhaps in his sadness as to what might have been—another night, another year—he generously produces a twenty-dollar bill from his wallet, shoving it into your hand. Think about refusing.

Back outside, walk along the seawall lined with palms, wind-whipped fronds permanently molded in a northerly direction. Motorcycles roar along the strip. Teenagers blare music in Trans Ams, headlights and taillights dim portholes through night. Down on the beach jellyfish, washed ashore, lie strewn across sand like discarded wedding veils. Oil rigs, out in the gulf, flicker more brightly than stars, melting in the humid sky. Think about throwing yourself into the harbor. Instead, watch waves surge and collapse until you're exhausted by their constant, useless movements.

That night, lie atop the chenille bedspread in the valley of the mattress, still in tank top and cutoff jeans, the edges frayed. Worry the sheets haven't been washed since the Eisenhower administration. From downstairs, pulleys and levers whir as the quadriplegic lowers himself to sleep, while his breath bubbles from watery lungs. Imagine his soft, slug-like body. No. Don't. Fumes from your own mattress rise around you. Be afraid to yawn or close your eyes. Be afraid, if you move, tethers will shred. You'll slide deeper into inertia. Think about the man who lives in the rooming house across the street. Feel the breaths of all three of you becoming gossamer—or fog.

Through the double-hung windows, humidity swells the night with longing. Display the sailor's twenty-dollar bill on the dresser, a memento of your first night alone in Galveston.

Stalking for Love in All the Wrong Places

One dusk a week later, strolling the east-end neighborhood, see the blue convertible. The car isn't parked outside his own house. This is not the street where he lives. Feel a tremor behind your knees. Stumble on a magnolia root that cracks the sidewalk. Glance at surrounding windows and doors. Guess which one. Think about ringing the doorbell, calling his name. Instead, sit on a seesaw in a playground at the end of the street, watching for him. You want to say something, though you're not sure what. Maybe you and he can try again. Maybe he can still save you, though you don't know from what. Your need is indefatigable as waves.

He still hasn't appeared by eight o'clock. Lights have gone on in windows. Off. On and off in all the Italianate, Carpenter Gothic, Victorian houses being restored—part of your husband's project—the yards dense with pin oaks and crape myrtles. Retrace your steps to the blue convertible. Glance through the windshield to the upholstery where you once sat driving to Matagorda, pretending he was John Travolta, though a short, blond, nearsighted John Travolta. Recall that the inside of the car smells of plaster casts and distilled alcohol from the hospital where he works. But now the scent would seem foreign. You don't understand the dislocation of time—how you sat in this car thinking you'd be part of it forever—whereas now his car and he are a distant vibration of memory.

Follow your instincts. You know what he is doing and what you will watch him do. Drag a porch chair down a narrow path between two Greek Revival houses. Stand on it. Lean forward, palms against the frame of a dimly lit window. Sheer curtains cast a faint pall on bodies. He is naked. So is she, where they lie together on a rumpled bed. Roy Orbison sings "Blue Bayou" . . . and you inhale the slow decay of cypress roots, the stagnant tremble of muddy sludge. Your own pulse deepens, to blue. His fingers trace her skin. Feel it on your own, small eruptions that ache. Your breath mists the window. Palm fronds rustle like words spoken a long time ago.

Place your own fingertips on the pane. Your prints are smudged evidence of all that's tangible of you—as if there's no "you" behind your skin. Even your skin feels like a filigree of foam . . . you, yourself, transparent water draining down panes of glass.

Watch the apartment you shared with your husband in one of the restored iron-front buildings at the corner of Tremont and The Strand. Here, the third-story arched windows are dark. Picture the marble tabletop you and your husband bought in Portugal. Miss the sunflower plates, the silver candleholders from Mexico, your pretty dresses hanging in the closet—even though you don't want to claim any belongings. Rather, you want your old life to be a museum, as if a ghost of you still lives there.

Glance across the street. A spotlight illuminates the red door of the Kon Tiki. The soles of your feet feel the bass disco beat, neon penises throbbing.

At Thorne's, a new restaurant a few blocks away, stand on the sidewalk gazing through floor-to-ceiling windows. Candlelight flickers on forest-green walls, white tablecloths, the mahogany bar. The ornate mirror behind the bar reflects bottles of liquor. Your husband, holding a Black Russian, sits with couples who used to be your friends, before you caused a scandal by running off in a blue convertible. Now they no longer speak to you.

Reflected in the window, see yourself superimposed on the room. But imagine the way you looked when *you* dined here. You wore long skirts, silk flowers in your hair. You sipped Sambuca with a coffee bean garnishing the bottom of the crystal glass. All evening your husband talked about the restoration project. He loves these buildings . . . and, sure, you love them, too. But you want him to love you more.

Leave before anyone sees you lurking.

Back in your apartment open the refrigerator. See the roast beef in shiny aluminum armor. Peel open the package. Smell the meat's greenness.

On the Lam without a Thing to Wear

By September, almost broke, consider what illegal act to commit in order to be locked up either in jail or an asylum. Don't be fussy, don't care which. Free room and board. Except you're not sure how to pull it off. Recall that for the past year an arsonist has set fire to a few buildings on The Strand. Some were razed. Others can still be restored. Maybe you should buy matches.

Instead, drive to the air-conditioned Rosenberg Library for relief from the heat. Glance through *Crime and Punishment* and *Notes from Underground*, books you read years ago. You've always admired the dramatic gestures of Russian novelists, authors who know how to pull out all the stops. Both war *and* peace. Crime *and* punishment. On a grand scale. The beating of chests. The pulling of hair. The whole shebang. On the first page of the library copy of *Crime and Punishment* is a faded smear of blood. Someone else with the same idea as you? Someone who takes her Dostoyevsky literally? But consider yourself on the seedy Gulf Coast, wailing country-western. Wilting beaches instead of frozen steppes. Shiner beer instead of Stolichnaya. You're not sure you have the fortitude, the depth of character of Raskolnikov or the underground man.

Beside you on the library table is today's *Houston Chronicle.* Flip through it. See the ad for a temporary employment agency in Houston. They claim they'll find you jobs by the day, the week, the month. On a whim, drop coins into the library's pay phone. Set up an appointment. Write down directions to San Jacinto Street. Wonder whether a temp job is better than suicide or arson.

At the Olga Employment Agency, pass the typing test. With flying colors. Although you've had responsible jobs, this feels like a stunning achievement. You are told to report to Schroeder Oil Company the next day. They anticipate the assignment will last a week.

You are on the lam without a thing to wear, however. For the interview you dressed in your best floral bell-bottoms, but you need a few additional outfits.

Drive around the Loop to the Galleria. Park your rusty, dented Volkswagen beside Cadillacs and Lincoln Continentals. Since you've lived almost in isolation the past few months, now, inside the mall, feel overwhelmed. But persevere. Check price tags on dresses. Technically, you could charge clothes. Technically, you're still married. Nevertheless, technically, the credit card belongs to your husband so, up until now, you've used it sparingly.

Decide—although you more or less knew it all along—to shoplift.

Perhaps this is due to *Crime and Punishment*. Perhaps this is your sorry attempt at a grand gesture. Perhaps if caught and arrested, sent to jail, you won't have to return to your apartment. Your life.

In the dressing room slip on a red-and-pink polyester dress, flimsy enough to fit beneath your clothes. The clinging material is the kind worn in *Saturday Night Fever*. That won't wrinkle. Ever. That you can rinse in your bathtub. That will air dry, even on the damp Gulf Coast, immediately.

Glance in the mirror. Wonder if you're sexy. Pretty? On your honeymoon night, in a suite in the Plaza Hotel, your husband fell asleep without so much as kissing you goodnight. Right now, this one fact—that you married someone who doesn't love you— scares you. Slide onto the floor in the dressing room. Hug your knees to your chest. The song "People" plays on the Muzak. This version—thin, pathetic, yet trying so very hard to please—causes despair to cascade through your heart.

Stop! Don't feel sorry for yourself. Continue with your plan.

Pull on your own clothes over the polyester. It bunches across the thighs. Smooth it out. Better. If caught, don't make excuses. Admit guilt. Accept responsibility. Demand a prison sentence. But only if caught, of course.

Back in your car, feel drunk with success. Not altogether unlike how you felt when you ran away with blue-convertible man.

Shoplifting: A Cautionary Tale

When your Volkswagen drops a rod on I-45 outside Texas City on the way home, consider crime *and* punishment. You are now hunkered on the shoulder. Semis and Texas-sized Caddies whiz by, your car shimmying in the gusts. The wind, however, is more like an equatorial nightmare than a fresh breeze off the gulf. Especially wearing two layers of clothes. The polyester feels like a hair shirt against your skin (which of course you deserve). The stuffing, leaking out of the split in the upholstery, pokes your left thigh. Smoke billows in the distance, tarnishing the sky, oil refineries processing crude. Take a deep breath. Think about sitting in your car until your skin grays with soot. Think about penance.

A police cruiser pulls onto the shoulder behind you. Glance in the rearview mirror to make sure no price tags stick out from under your arms or the back of your neck. Notice that, having driven with the windows open, your ponytail looks like a bristle brush.

"Trouble?" he asks.

Explain.

When he offers to call the nearest service station, accept.

Think about confessing. After all, he is cute, with blue eyes and black hair. *He*, in fact, looks more like John Travolta than the blue-convertible man. If he forgives you, you will be saved. *He*, in fact, will save you. Don't heroes love to save sinners? Consider what it's like to be married to a cop. Wisely decide not to ask.

Two hours later your car is in the shop. Lacking options, call your husband for a ride home. By now, you've sweated through both layers of clothes so that, if you look closely, the red-and-pink polyester is visible beneath the bell-bottom outfit. If your husband notices, he says nothing. At this point, however, you no longer care.

His Ford Mustang is air conditioned. Cold slices you like a blade of ice. Sweat freezes your skin. Develop a headache behind your right eye. Press a palm against your throbbing lid.

He stops the car outside the quadriplegic's house, the engine idling.

"Oh, we sold the Tremont Building," your husband says. "With façade easements."

The Tremont Building is part of his restoration development project. Façade easements protect, architecturally, the exterior of the buildings, requiring owners to give the fronts facelifts. "Super."

He explains how the developer plans shops on the ground floor, apartments upstairs.

You sit beside him in the car feeling cold and frail, but he doesn't ask how you've been, if you've been eating, if you're lonely. Never mind.

By dusk, as sweat evaporates, your skin feels gritty, sandy. The polyester outfit, which you are now regretting on every level, hangs in the bathroom, drying. Lie on your bed in your underclothes, a washcloth on your forehead, your body settling into the familiar hollow in the mattress. Your palms are up, forming shallow, empty cups. Feel like a Victorian girl with ague. The vapors.

Notes from High above Ground

In December, begin your thirty-fourth temp job in Houston, each in a different downtown high-rise. Every morning cross the causeway over Galveston Bay to the mainland, returning every afternoon, back and forth, north and south on I-45, now in your Volkswagen with a rebuilt engine. Which cost $750 to fix. Which your husband loaned you. Which you are now repaying from weekly paychecks, depleting the four to five dollars an hour you earn.

At each job sit at a desk that is yours for the day or the week. Liken it to renting a motel room for an hour. Aspire to nothing else. Instead, on an IBM Selectric, type reports for oil companies. You are a good typist. You proofread. No one complains. Typing is clear-cut, keeps you focused on punctuation, on minutiae. Little time or energy to consider a failed marriage, neon penises at the Kon Tiki, shoplifting, spying on blue-convertible man . . . or the distant, unseeable future.

Pass entire days barely speaking. You aren't allowed to make personal phone calls. There is no one to call. During lunch sit at your desk reading. Or, through lowered lashes, watch coworkers, women efficiently dressed in pantyhose and business suits— women with real jobs, families, homes. Photographs of children adorn their desks. Their closets do not contain shoplifted clothes. They do not live across the street from rooming houses.

These women seem unknowable. Different. *Adult*. You fear you are not. You *know* you are not, you, with your Monday-Wednesday-Friday peanut-butter-and-jelly sandwiches. On Tuesdays and Thursdays you bring strawberry yogurt and an apple for lunch. Pack a dented spoon from your furnished apartment in your brown-paper sack. To save money, drink a glass of tap water. Use a paper towel from the bathroom for a napkin.

Feel as if you are sliding far away from normal behavior. Hope, at least, you are more interesting than your coworkers—like a starving artist. Or begin to feel almost *Russian*, that *you* are living underground. Take a revolutionary stand against capitalism, civilization.

Perhaps you are having an existential crisis.

Also suspect, however, you are simply unoriginal, lost, confused.

Don't think about the permanence of a temporary life.

You are asked, at one oil company, only to answer the telephone, no typing. Buy Rilke's *The Notebooks of Malte Laurids Brigge* and read it, day after day, nine to five. Remove a piece of stationery from the desk drawer and print out the following line from the book: "There are people who wear the same face for years; naturally it wears out, it gets dirty, it splits at the folds, it stretches, like gloves one has worn on a journey." Finish the book while sitting at your neat desk under fluorescent lights on the fifteenth floor. Wonder whether human faces, like buildings, can have façade easements.

Attend a Christmas buffet lunch at one of the offices. Fill a paper plate with ham, sweet potatoes, a gingerbread man. Employees gather in small groups, talking and eating. Return alone to your desk, carefully setting down your plate. With your plastic knife, cut a wedge of ham. Put it in your mouth. Focus on food: cutting, chewing, swallowing. Wipe your mouth with a napkin decorated with Santa. Feel invisible.

Out the window, a forest of high-rises stretches to the Loop. The pocked roof of the Astrodome, resembling the moon, darkens in the gray afternoon. Grackles swarm in the distance, though you can't hear their raucous cries. Sounds in the office fade as well. Feel as if you occupy a monastic cell—all the windows in the buildings, all the office workers, all these sequestered faces suspended behind glass—hovering high above the earth.

The Shrouds of the Kon Tiki

Late one night awake to the clang of fire engines. Leap from bed and look out the window. Flames, from the direction of The Strand, stain the black sky. The arsonist is burning another building. Slip on flip-flops, cutoffs, hurry outside. Your lungs are heavy with humidity, your mouth smoky. Run as if you can save the building, worrying it might be your old apartment.

It is the Kon Tiki.

Pause in the alley across the street. If a building must burn, at least this one is no longer adorned with its original iron-front façade, isn't worth much architecturally. Over the years the structure's been decimated, reduced to stucco slabs.

But where are the patrons? Upstairs from the dance club are steam baths for the gay clientele. Probably the baths operate all night. Probably men are still up there, though hopefully, at this hour, not many remain.

Flames spire from the roof. Red paint peels off the front door. Behind windows, fire shimmers and roils. Your husband, in robe and pajamas, whom you just noticed, grabs a fireman. He points to the surrounding buildings. Probably he worries the fire will spread, will leap the alley to buildings waiting to be restored. The fireman nods before rushing off. Your husband backs away but continues to watch.

Slide down, your back against your old apartment building. The brick-lined alley is warm beneath your legs. The air pings as windows crack before shattering. Imagine water pipes bursting, nails bending. The notes on all the vinyl records warp. The Lucite dance floor blisters before it melts—red, green, blue neon puddling to black, to a char, to soot, to dust. The air smells dark, a whoosh of exhaled ether.

As if in a mirage, they emerge from cataracts of spraying water, walking single file. An orderly line of men wrapped in white sheets follow a fireman from a side door. They look like a procession of shrouds. Dazed, they pass an ambulance, trickling down the alley one by one, their forms watery, as if leaving the Kon Tiki not having found what they sought. They reach the end of the block. You can no longer see heads or outlines of bodies. Wispy sheets seem to drift on air currents, though the men's soles leave moist footprints on hot asphalt, as they stumble toward what will be the worst decade of their lives. Perhaps their last.

Across the street, your husband's shoulders tremble as if he is crying. Even though this building isn't on the list to be restored, still, it's in The Strand district, which he loves. *This* is his love.

Walk over to him. Hug him. Your voice would never be heard above the fiery night, but you hope he understands you are sorry. About the fire. About the blue convertible. About everything.

Imagine relationships ending like drops of water sizzling in flame.

Worn-Through Faces

One Saturday morning toward the end of March, see the entire man who lives in the rooming house across the street, not just his forearm in the window. He's opened the door and stepped outside. How do you know it's him? You just do. Imagine he's a sailor, unemployed for a while, fallen on hard times. Now you're sure he's found a new job on a freighter bound for Venezuela. He pauses on the front stoop, a cardboard valise in one hand, a cigarette in the other, as if he's stepping off a 1940s movie set. Crewcut hair. The leather of his western boots is cracked, but polished. He's younger than you imagined. But perhaps an old, previous, down-and-out face has worn off, as Rilke suggests, to reveal another face, one that's pale, yes, from his long captivity, yet now setting sail into the future. As he walks down the sidewalk watch his footsteps as if you could follow them, each step a point on a map. Direction. A destination.

The thing of it is, the moment is banal. Watching this man is the opposite of the melodrama of running away in a blue convertible. Today it is just solitary footsteps moving in one direction . . . and a new face. Today it is only the air that's spring yellow, oleanders falling all over themselves to bloom.

The man disappears at the end of the block. Rather than feel abandoned, imagine the tether that's lightly bound you and him together, now pulling you forward, too.

A few weeks later, almost a year after you ran away from home with the blue-convertible man, you are financially solvent. Pay off the rebuilt Volkswagen engine. Purchase new clothes. Pack them in the canvas suitcase and throw it in the backseat of your car. One of your temporary jobs has become permanent. You plan to move. You want to feel the throb of Houston, a city that grew in proportion to Galveston's demise. Although Galveston was once the largest port on the gulf, after the Houston Ship Channel was constructed, the island slumbered, leaving blocks of Victoriana to decay.

Until your husband was hired to restore it.

Or is he really only preserving it? Preserving decay, you now think. Consider that the old buildings should remain in ruins, the palmettos and crape myrtles jungled and rampant, cypress shingles stained with saltwater, wrought-iron fences rusted. The scent of verdigris.

Consider only your own preservation.

One last time, drive the causeway linking Galveston to the mainland. Speed, as if you are levitating, leaving the low-lying barrier island far behind. Windows open. Wind caressing the tender skin of your new face.

GENTLE READER,

But gefiltes are tough to caress. So don't get your hopes up, I'm sorry to say. Houston doesn't pan out any better than Galveston. Not learning from past mistakes, I remarry.

After serving time in Texas, I, along with my second husband, embark upon a two-year stint in Missouri. The highlight? He teaches at a college belonging to the Southern Baptist Convention. I actually believe that I belong, as well. In fact, we live in an apartment across the street from the Second Baptist church. (Recent Second Baptist Church Facebook posts: "We are loving 'Jesus Knows the Blues' class on Wednesday evenings." "How has God used Scripture to shape you in the past? How is God using Scripture to shape you now?") Back then, I would have friended their Facebook page, posting comments using the handle "gefilte-1."

After all, it takes a shtetl.

But my husband then secures a job at another college. Once again I wash up on a foreign shore, this time in Rome, Georgia. But since inland Rome doesn't have a shore, this gefilte journeys across dry land, legless . . . and, let me tell you, that is not a pretty sight.

By the time I reach Rome, anchored to my husband, I'm dirty and sweaty and have lost a layer of scales from all that rolling up and down highways from one very nasty, bitter state to another.

S.W.S.

The Fireproof Librarian

Can't start a fire without a spark . . .
BRUCE SPRINGSTEEN

TO: All Employees
FROM: Abigail Kane, Director
SUBJECT: Regarding the Possibility of Asbestos in the Building

Some concern has been expressed that not enough information regarding the investigation into the possibility of asbestos in the library building has been disseminated to the staff.
This memo/notice contains all the information I have in my
possession at this time.

I APPROACH THE RED-BRICK SARA HIGHTOWER Regional
Library on Broad Street in Rome, Georgia, where I work, hoping
to see a skull-and-crossbones sign nailed to the door. A modern
addition mutates from the rear of this original Carnegie library,
friable asbestos molting from the ceiling. Since last December,
library employees have awaited results of the "Asbestos Survey
and Testing Report," an official document to confirm exact levels
and locations. Yesterday, March third, concerned about the delay,
I myself called Dennis Scott, Floyd County health inspector, to determine the report's status. He said he planned to collect samples
today. When I expressed concern about the three-month delay, he
refused comment. No steps to fix the problem will be implement-
ed until this report is completed. No public warning signs will be
posted until the suspicion of asbestos is scientifically confirmed.

Belle, my supervisor, head of the Fine Art Department, waits at the downstairs checkout counter, watching the door, watching for me. Wide as she is tall, Belle, today, resembles a puffy pink square of bubblegum. She has two emotional settings: perky and trouble. As I approach her, the lids of her eyes flatten, so I'm thinking *trouble*. Busted. Dennis Scott blew the whistle on me—whereas I'm planning to blow it on *him*. Shrilly.

"I heard a little rumor," Belle says. "I'm hoping you'll tell me it's not true."

Given my lowly, part-time status, I deliberately bypassed her authority by calling about the report. Caught, I confess. "But did he show up today for the samples?" I nod toward the ceiling, then walk behind the checkout counter.

"You went over *my* head, over *Abigail's* head. That kind of be-havior is . . ." She clamps her mouth shut, unable to finish her sentence. Her bleached-blonde hair, polyurethaned into a hel-met, seems to tremble.

"You don't think we should at least warn the public?" I say.

"This isn't an asbestos factory." She slaps her palm on the counter. Probably it's just dust, but a few white particles spew into the air on impact. "I'm going now," she adds. "You think you can stay out of trouble the rest of the evening? Get something done here?" I work the five-to-nine-p.m. shift.

I prop open the downstairs door for fresh air, though it's just as likely a breeze will disturb the ailing asbestos. I breathe as shallowly as possible. The ceiling resembles drifts of fake snow or clumps of Ivory soap flakes, a niveous compound supposed to adhere to the structure. When the air-conditioning fan cy-cles on, however, ghostly clouds spew on books, desks, light fix-tures, floors. Deep gouges pock the ceiling where books on the top shelves brush against it. Previously, unaware of the asbes-tos, we all simply blew the stuff off book jackets or dusted them with rags—the equivalent, perhaps, of cleaning up nuclear melt-downs with mops.

I perch on the stool behind the downstairs circulation desk, awaiting patrons. The upstairs floor of the library—fiction, reference, children's books—is always busier. Tonight, my department is quiet. I'm relieved. I hate to check out books. They're only returned a few weeks later to be shelved all over again. A never-ending cycle. My official title is "Fine Art evening supervisor." Yet I'm hardly a librarian and know nothing about art. This department, however, is also a quasi-paradise for "how-to" junkies, with books on how to sail, how to train your dog, how to raise chickens, how to shoot a rifle, how to identify wildflowers, fix your plumbing and electricity, gamble, recover from cancer, nervous breakdowns, depression. All that's missing, which is what I really want, are books on how to muckrake and scandalmong.

The library's scent of sun-hot brick, musty paper, and chipped linoleum (probably likewise manufactured with asbestos) settles over the evening. From amid the stacks, I slide out the Chilton's *Kawasaki 900z1 New Repair and Tune-up Guide*. I've been studying it the past week—flaunting authority yet again—since we aren't allowed to read while on duty. On the cover looms a black-leathered man wearing a red helmet, sitting astride a Kawasaki with a red-metal fuel tank. I don't own a motorcycle. I've never owned one. But . . .

In the movie version, I grab the handlebars, heaving the Kawasaki off the stands. I press the choke with my thumb and switch the ignition. I jam my leather-booted feet on the pegs. I gun the engine, the bike's growl reverberating through my body. The silver mufflers, shaped like horns, streak above asphalt, the drive chain spinning sparks across pavement. A camera pans my race down Broad Street. Motorists wheel toward the curb. Pedestrians don't dare step from sidewalks. *I* own the street—*me*, peering through eye holes in red satin that masks my face. A cape—a *red* cape—streams behind me. Tires hiss to a stop in front of the library. I swirl through the building, the cape magically casting

asbestos into black holes in the sky. The citizens of Rome cheer. Pistons firing, chains spinning, I disappear into the night.
"Who *was* that masked girl?" everyone asks.

A few minutes before closing time, a woman plops a box stuffed with romance novels on the counter. She wears an Atlanta Braves t-shirt, the red-and-blue logo bleeding into the white fabric. I sigh, me in my own smudged t-shirt, probably sprinkled with asbestos particles. I'm tempted to tell her to go upstairs to the fiction department, but both stations are required to check out books. Besides, I figure I've caused enough trouble today. So I slam the rubber stamp with the due date onto the cards, inserting them into the pockets. Covers portray women with indigo hair, crimson blossoms pinned behind their ears. The male model Fabio (or facsimile) wears a pirate shirt. He's poised to rip bodices.

Finally the woman staggers out the door with her cardboard box of romance. I tally up the few pennies from overdue books. I turn off the downstairs lights in the Georgia Room (which houses the archives), the music room, and the windowless periodicals room. I dog-ear the Kawasaki repair manual on page twenty-seven, 629.2877 in the Dewey Decimal System. Which, by the way, is the only thing about library work I love: the exactness of each book owning a private number. It belongs *here*, in this one and only location, nowhere else in the universe. The back cover of the book appears scorched, perhaps accidentally ignited by an acetylene torch soldering valve refacers or sprocket teeth. I hide it in the stacks behind the *Handbook of Wild Flower Cultivation* (635.967) so no one will check it out. I lock the downstairs door behind me. Finally, I take a deep breath.

I switch on the engine to my sixteen-year-old green Volkswagen bug and drive down Broad Street toward home. I wonder if Belle will report me to Abigail, the library director. Probably. But I'm not sure I care. For what I did *not* say to Belle is that I hate this job. I did not say this job is a default plan for my life, nothing else to do in Rome, where I moved with my husband for *his* job. I did not say this is a second-rate library in a fading rural town, hardly Atlanta, more than an hour away. I did not say *you*, Belle, will never aspire to anything grander than overseeing a bunch of books laced with asbestos. I also restrained myself from saying that *if* I felt at home or even *slightly* welcomed in the library, I might not have called the health inspector in the first place. I did not say that I feel like a Yankee. A foreigner. An alien.

Or maybe none of this about Belle and Rome is true. Maybe it's just me—bitter, confused—who is the real problem, who has brought this all on myself.

No, surely *that* can't be true.

To reach the decrepit log cabin in which I live, you turn left off Martha Berry Boulevard onto the Berry College campus, where my husband teaches English literature. I pass the gatehouse, a low-tech security checkpoint, and drive down a narrow three-mile road plowed through a nature preserve, to faculty housing. Tonight, my foot barely on the gas pedal, the gear in second, I feel as if I'm pouring through a dark funnel. I follow thin tunnels of my own dim headlights, leading nowhere I really want to go. I pass the turnoff to the dirt road leading up Lavender Mountain. On top is the House o' Dreams, a cottage once belonging to Martha Berry, the college founder. Beside it stands a fire tower, high enough to see Alabama and Tennessee. High enough to watch for trouble-making Yankees approaching.

I maneuver a hairpin turn, pull into a small clearing, and park beside the screened porch. A light burns in my husband's study. He's probably reading Wittgenstein's *On Certainty* or Foucault's *The Archaeology of Knowledge and the Discourse of Language*, research for a book he's writing: *Literary Realism and the Ekphrastic Tradition*. He tells me that it focuses on the novel's representation of an ekphrastic art form as a reflexive device of mimetic self-definition, exploring how a shift in realist paradigms has taken place in this century from an empirical, correspondence theory of signification to a foundational model emphasizing discourse and a coherence theory of meaning.

It's virtually impossible to imagine such an incomprehensible book, with its own Dewey Decimal number, sitting on the shelves of Sara Hightower Regional Library. Certainly I myself do not, on any level of my being, understand what it's about.

I've been married to this second husband—and all his obtuse sentences—for only a few years. I met him at the University of Houston, where he taught an adult education class I took. Initially, I was impressed by his eclectic knowledge, his collection of classical records, only belatedly realizing we have little in common. I, after all, love disco—undeconstructively, I might add.

Now, I quietly close the car door, so he won't know I'm home yet. I sit on the front stoop. The humid night dampens the scent of pinestraw and of Floyd County's paper mills, slightly acrid with chemicals grinding bark to pulp. I almost hear the whoosh of bats, the twitch of white-tailed deer, the rustle of wild turkeys. Through breaks in the trees, the moon rounds the sky—a thin Necco wafer, an old-fashioned candy belonging to the past. Even though I've lived in Georgia only a few years, perhaps it is the regretful past of the South I sense. Do I myself feel the chafed hopes of elderly widows—dusty African violets in their windowsills—attired in floral dresses for Southern Baptist church services? Afterward, they gather at Shoney's for breakfast . . . widows sprinkled with carnation talcum, dusting themselves with dreams of long-ago summers. I feel this, as if I am an abandoned widow lady, too.

I masquerade with the alias of "Smith," my husband's name. "Smith" is camouflage. If I use my real name, my Jewish name, I'll blend even less well into this Bible Belt landscape. Over the years, I lived in DC, the West Indies, New Jersey, Boston, Israel, Galveston, Houston, Missouri. I am an island girl, a Jersey girl, a Sabra, a Texan, a Midwesterner, changing masks, identities, wanting to blend with the locals. I've shed my father's last name as well as the name "Flint," that of my first husband, before now evolving to "Smith." Yet I don't *feel* like a "Smith." Ironically, despite (or *because* of) all the names, the disguises, I now worry I've never blended anywhere, never felt at home, never felt like a "me" who belonged.

Belle would probably call me "*Trouble*smith," because I'm good at creating it.

The name is Smith. Trouble Smith.

Growing up in St. Thomas, I secretly spent hours at the public library in the Lange Building on Dronningens Gade, the main street of Charlotte Amalie. My father told me that I—just a girl— didn't need to learn history, English, French, science. So I told no one I went to the library. No one knew of my contentment, at one with books, sitting at a wood table on the second floor. Termites tunneled most of the books as if they, too, devoured words. The result resembled miniature portholes. I could see straight through a book from cover to cover, as if I peered through a portal onto the world itself.

I loved all elements of books indiscriminately: the covers, the paper, paragraphs, sentences, punctuation marks, ink. I equally loved the way words lined themselves up in sentences. I could not have said that I understood the concept of "ideas" back then, but it was, nevertheless, the first time I sensed a relationship between an idea and a concrete word. So I also loved the way words could all be shaken up, used in any order you liked, thus establishing an entirely *different* set of ideas. It was magic. Black, inky magic. It was the first time I ever felt powerful, learning things girls weren't supposed to, as if I knew voodoo, too. For a few hours, I was no longer the daughter of my father, that bank president who uprooted my stateside life by bringing me to an isolated, insular island.

The next morning I call my mother in New Jersey to tell her about the asbestos. I stand by the kitchen window watching deer graze on weedy grass at the edge of the forest. During the night, pollen from loblollies settled over my vw, green mingling with red dusty clay, like a pointillist painting.

"What should I do if they just sit on the report?" I ask. "Or never even write it?" I slide a piece of bread into the toaster.

She's a lover of causes. In the 1940s, before I was born, my mother sat in the backs of buses with black passengers when she lived in Washington DC. Earlier, my Russian grandfather, to avoid his draft into the czar's army, emigrated to the United States, where he joined the Socialist Party. So the idea of "protest" is entwined in my DNA, my personal gene pool.

"Call the newspaper," my mother says. "TV."

"You think it's really dangerous, you know, if you aren't actually working with it in a factory?"

"Children go there," she says. "Anyway, research it. In the library."

We laugh. The toast pops. I spread peanut butter on it. "Guess I could call the EPA."

Or, I could be that red-masked Wonder Girl swooping into town on a Kawasaki. . . .

"Sure." My mother's voice warms to the fight. "And write your congressman and senators."

In case of emergency call . . . Smith. Trouble Smith.

I park in front of the public library a few minutes before five. Broad Street, 130 feet wide, hovers like a mirage in the damp afternoon, automobiles floating down asphalt. The buildings have faded to bleached brick and stucco: Koman's in the old Kress building; the Forrest barbershop with its ancient red-and-white pole; the Cherokee Lodge in the Masonic Hall; Lynn's Uniforms; the Partridge Restaurant, established in 1933, its neon sign mute, unblinking; Esserman's department store shrinking out of business. Only a few remaining metal canopies jut onto the sidewalk, offering a suggestion of shade. The marquee of the old DeSoto Theatre—which first opened on October 29, 1929, the day the stock market crashed—is blank. All the once-fulgent buildings, back when cotton barges flowed along Rome's Oostanaula, Etowah, and Coosa Rivers, now droop and sag. The three rivers themselves are stained magenta, amber, puce—dye runoff from carpet factories—the water sludgy with chemicals from paper mills. The street resembles a deserted stage decades after the play ends. Façades of buildings are mere trompe l'oeils. Knock on a plywood door. No one answers.

Belle, I'm relieved, is gone for the day. But she taped a note for me on the counter, face up, for all to see. "It has always been my policy to 'love it or leave it,'" Belle writes, in part. "To stir a cauldron often results in unpleasant vapors. One must be willing to accept the consequences." She adds, "We expect you to continue to work as assigned."

I stomp into the music room, cranking up the feeble record player. Maybe the racket will drive away the patrons. I play soundtracks from Grease, Saturday Night Fever, Urban Cowboy, and Xanadu. The vinyl records are dusty and scratched, the needle blunt. I march down aisles, straightening books.

Earlier today I spoke with Dr. Jim Hubbard, an asbestos expert at Georgia Tech in Atlanta. He said that EPA guidelines state that if a ceiling compound or mixture contains more than 1 percent asbestos in public schools, concern is shown. He promised to send me a bunch of brochures outlining the dangers.

I also did some research at the Berry College library. From a study conducted by the Environmental Sciences Laboratory of Mount Sinai School of Medicine in New York, I learned that mesothelioma (asbestos-related lung cancer) killed the actor Steve McQueen, whose naval ship contained asbestos. "Only a few asbestos-related diseases occur prior to twenty years from the first time of exposure. However, the duration of exposure need not be long, only a few days for mesothelioma," Dr. Irving J. Selikoff writes in the May 1984 issue of the *EPA Journal*.

Now, seated behind the checkout counter, I skim dictionaries and encyclopedias for additional information about asbestos. *Asbestos*, "quicklime," from Greek. The letter *a*, "not"; the word *sbestos*, "extinguishable." Once, wicks for eternal flames of vestal virgins were made from asbestos. It also insulated suits of armor. According to legend, Charlemagne tossed asbestos tablecloths into fires to convince barbarian guests he possessed supernatural powers. Egyptians embalmed pharaohs with it. Bodies of kings were cremated in shrouds of it, cocoons to preserve their ashes, preventing their remains from mingling with the wood of funeral pyres—religious miracles if ever I saw them, which I haven't.

I'm so engrossed in asbestos I'm surprised, when I glance at my watch, that only a half hour remains before closing time. I meant to straighten more shelves. I've vaguely been aware of patrons roaming the aisles, but I failed to ask if I could assist them. But since I'm not, in fact, a superhero, I don't particularly envision myself as placed on this planet to serve them, anyway. I am the person who gives librarians a bad name.

No. That's not entirely true.

Some of my fellow librarians, the *real* librarians, prefer hoarding books to checking them out—would prefer the library be a museum, a jail. Belle, for example, is content only when rows of books sit orderly and pristine, each locked in its own Dewey Decimal slot. Books tilted sideways, or shelves with huge gaps, make her apoplectic.

And who can blame her? You finish shelving one cart of books only to discover someone else returning every book they've checked out since the Gutenberg Bible was printed. Once I replace a book I, too, expect it to remain there. Indefinitely. Until the end of time. To reshelve the same book two or three times is an imposition. In fact, I'm a firm practitioner of William

Faulkner's riposte upon quitting his job in a post office: *I won't be at the beck and call of every son of a bitch who has two cents to spend on a stamp.* Or an overdue book.

Yet I worry I *am* beholden. Not so much to the patrons or to this job but to this *life.* How did I end up working in this library in a town I never knew existed until my husband got a job here—setting the bar so low for myself, I trip over it.

I feel trapped in my own Dewey Decimal slot, unable to budge. I've been divorced once. Twice would compound the failure. Besides, I feel as if I'm running out of masks, disguises, identities. Would another town, a different last name be any better?

Before I leave the library that evening, I re-read Belle's memo. I consider unpleasant vapors in the library. I consider stirring cauldrons. I consider consequences.

A few days later, I sneak a stack of EPA brochures into the library. How to pass them out? Maybe I could just "happen" to leave them in the break room. But when I go there at 7:30, the usual time for my break, Mr. W. stands pouring a cup of coffee. I pretend to busy myself straightening napkins and paper plates. Mr. W.'s green suspenders are stained, his collar frayed. I've heard rumors he was angry when Abigail was named director, feeling he'd been passed over. "I guess no word yet from the county about the report?" I innocently ask.

He sniffs. I want to warn him to breathe shallowly. Then, without lowering his voice, as if no need to keep this a secret, he says, "Miss Abigail's known about the asbestos for *two years.*"

"You're kidding!"

"Suspected it since they found it in the library over to Cave Spring."

As if losing his taste for coffee, he sets the mug on the counter and stalks out. I pour the coffee down the drain, then sit on one of the chairs, the upholstery worn and ripped. I shake the brochures out of the envelope. On the covers, with a red ballpoint pen, I write, "Welcome to the Asbestos Factory!" I slip one into each employee mail slot.

That evening, after I return home, I set up my Smith-Corona portable typewriter on the kitchen table. I scroll a piece of paper into the roller and type out a letter to Senator Mattingly. I type a duplicate letter to Senator Nunn "to bring to your attention the fact that your constituents are at risk." Next I type a petition to be signed by myself and other employees to send to the Board of Trustees of Sara Hightower Regional Library. I state our concerns about working in an asbestos-riddled building.

The following morning I again call Dennis Scott, the county health inspector. "I'm sorry to bother you," I say. "But I wonder if you have the report yet?"

"It's locked up and I won't show it to you," he says. "But you have nothing to worry about."

"Then why can't I see it?"

"It's in Commissioner Smith's office."

He slams down the phone.

I look up the number for Ronald Smith, one of the county commissioners. Since we share the same last name, maybe he'll think we have something in common. However, by the time I dial, Dennis Scott has warned him. As soon as I identify myself, before I even ask about the results, he says, "I'll release the report when I'm good and ready. I'm through talking to you. Do you know what I mean?"

He, too, slams down the phone.

Abigail waits for me at the circulation desk holding one of my EPA brochures. "How dare you." The pulse in her temple throbs.

Later that evening, I convince seven other part-time employees to sign the petition for the Board of Trustees. None of the full-time employees, not even Mr. W., sign.

I drive to the *Rome News-Tribune* building the following morning. I ask the receptionist if I can speak to a reporter. I tell Kim Leighton about the asbestos. I explain about what I am now calling a "cover-up."

He introduces me to the newspaper's publisher. I repeat my story. They plan to check other sources and print an article.

During this conversation, I learn that a few years ago Floyd County voters rejected a bond referendum to build a new library. I surmise that the library and county officials don't want to spend money removing asbestos from an outdated building. They want the money for a new one, instead.

After the interview, I stand alone in the newspaper's parking lot. A flag wilts against the silvery pole radiating spirals of heat.

Something is wrong.

I want to turn around, go back inside, find the reporter again. Wait! Stop the presses! That's not the *whole* story, I long to say.

What I did *not* tell the reporter is that I am the emotional equivalent of General Sherman's march to the sea. I actually want to burn Rome to the fucking ground because I'm angry at unbalanced librarians, bungling county officials, small-town prejudice, polluters, Foucault, an unknown arsonist in Galveston who torched several buildings that my first husband was restoring (where's asbestos when you need it?) . . . and angry at that husband for loving those buildings more than he loved me. I'm equally angry at my current, overly intellectual husband, as well as angry at each and every page in his book—even angry at termites—because, likewise, where are *they* when you need them—need them to devour every single word he writes? Or devour every book in *this* library. I'm angry at voters, President Reagan, the Chamber of Commerce, Rotarians, anti-Semites, standardized tests, deconstructionists, Republicans, literates, illiterates, faulty engine rods in Volkswagens, Sylvester Stallone, the "Just Say No" campaign against drugs, the movie *E.T.*, people researching genealogy, furniture-moving companies, slow drivers, organized religion, pecan pie, people who fail to see the beauty of kudzu, and restaurants that serve presweetened iced tea.

I also did not tell the reporter that existentially speaking—and in my heart of hearts—I don't really give a damn about asbestos *or* the library. And yet I decide—standing in the parking lot—to show all these sons of bitches that asbestos *is* dangerous—even if I have to snort it.

I call Don Hatcher, the Rome bureau chief of *11-Alive News*, WXIA-TV in Atlanta. "There's a cover up in the library," I say.

He asks if he can interview me at 6:30.

He films me checking books in and out. I stand behind the circulation desk and tell him the story. "This isn't a safe building for patrons," I say. "Especially children. But no one in authority wants to post warnings or let the public know."

None of the "real" librarians who work upstairs happen to come downstairs while Don is filming.

In the movie version, the *New York Times*, the *Washington Post*, ABC, NBC, and CBS dispatch reporters and film crews to the library. I stand on the top step of the entrance, microphones crowded before my face. *What did Abigail know and when did she know it*, I insist.

The following afternoon, I find an "Employee Warning Record" tacked to my mail slot at the library: "This employee has taken it upon herself to circumvent management in her zealous pursuit of her cause. She has taken it upon herself to contact the investigating agencies, thus bypassing authority. When warned in person by the director, she was flippant to the point of insubordination. If she continues to cause trouble, or does not stop the agitation and get on with her work, or refuses to do the work, she will be dismissed."

I make copies of the "Employee Warning Record" for Kim Leighton and Don Hatcher.

STAFF MEETING MONDAY, 4:00 p.m.

BOARD MEETING REPORT: Health insurance says that you have to work 30 hrs. per week to be eligible. If working less than 30 hrs. will continue to be covered but possibility that may be challenged. THIS DOES NOT APPLY TO ANYONE AT CIRC. DESK.

NATIONAL LIBRARY WEEK: *Savannah Smiles* to be shown 4/20, 10 a.m.

I hear a rumor that Hollywood plans to film *The Dead Poet's Society* on the Berry College campus, reportedly starring Harrison Ford. I stalk the main campus looking for movie stars: *lights, cameras, action!* I abandon jeans and a t-shirt for a flowery skirt, a crisp blouse. Lip gloss. Eyeliner. I visit my husband in the English Department, a pretense for wandering around looking for Harrison Ford. My husband's in class. On his desk is Paul de Man's article "The Epistemology of Metaphor." But no Harrison sighting, metaphoric or otherwise. I continue to scout corridors before heading outside, past the science building, the gym. I stroll through fields with windrows of hay, past stands of magnolia, pine. *In the movie version of the movie,* I glimpse Harrison Ford just beyond that next tree wearing his *Raiders of the Lost Ark* hat. I sit, shaded beneath an oak, crimson blossoms pinned behind my ear. He kneels beside me, glowing, the camera lens in soft focus. . . .

The next morning, still hoping to be discovered, I stake out the Henry Ford complex on campus, built in English Gothic style, with money from Henry Ford himself. Today, however, the grounds appear different. The grass is *painted.* I've missed something important. I rush over to the English Department. The secretary tells me that the movie people experimented to see if they could make the grass appear . . . *grassier*. But no Harrison Ford. "They're looking for extras, though," she says. "Probably *Yankees*. Like you. It's supposedly set in New England." She tells me to go to Hermann Hall and fill out a form. "You'll need a photograph of yourself," she adds.

I slam back in my car and race home. I yank out photograph albums. I find one that's not too bad. If they're looking for Yankees, surely I'm qualified. I'll tell the casting director I went to college in Boston.

I wait for the phone to ring.

Instead, a film crew from Italy arrives on campus to film a "spaghetti" version of *Gone with the Wind*. Italian look-alikes of Clark Gable and Vivian Leigh, dressed in Confederate finery, pose on the steps of the Hoge Building, the oldest structure on campus, more or less (less) resembling Tara. Student extras stroll in hoop skirts and gray uniforms. I'm too demoralized to try out as an extra. But I skulk around, trying to avoid bayonets.

I wonder how they'll re-create the burning of Atlanta. Set fire to Broad Street? Only the Sara Hightower Regional Library will remain.

Later, as it turns out, *The Dead Poet's Society* is filmed elsewhere and stars Robin Williams.

I sit at the library counter flipping through research books. The use of asbestos dates back thousands of years. Strabo, a Greek geographer of the first century, discovered one of the first asbestos quarries on the island of Evvoia. The name "chrysotile," the most common form of asbestos, is derived from the Greek words *chrysos*, "gold," and *tilos*, "fiber." Gold fibers. Early on, it was used to make pottery as well as insulation to fill chinks in log cabins in what is now Finland.

Ancient Romans wove asbestos fibers into towels, nets, and head coverings for women. Roman restaurants used tablecloths and napkins made of asbestos. They could be thrown into fire to remove food stains and crumbs. Afterward, the cloth was whiter than before. So the Romans named asbestos *amiantus*, "unpolluted."

Pliny the Elder, doctor and historian, observed that asbestos was a magical material providing protection against spells. Yet he also noted that those exposed to high concentrations were prone to lung sickness. He recommended that quarry slaves use respirators made of transparent bladder skin to protect them from asbestos dust.

During medieval times religious crosses, resembling wood, were constructed from asbestos. Merchants claimed they were made from the cross on which Jesus was crucified. They proved their claims by setting them on fire.

Ancient Persians imported asbestos from India to wrap their dead. They believed asbestos to be hair from a small mythical animal that lived by fire and died by water.

I sense a presence. I glance up. A young girl stands before the counter, thin as a noon shadow, her gray eyes watching me. She raises an almost-invisible eyebrow, and I sense she has a question. I glance around, but no adult seems to accompany her. Her nose slopes to a small button. She places all ten fingers on the counter, the nails stubby, rimmed with dirt. Her dusty-blonde hair is chopped off below her ears. Her checked shirt strains across her shoulders, her dungarees rolled at the ankles. On her feet are plastic flip-flops, one of the straps split. She smells of grass and apples. I want to say her gray eyes resemble smoke or that gold streaks her hair. This isn't true. Yet, as I watch her, the rest of the room fades to wallpaper.

"Hi," I whisper. I stand up, leaning toward her. "Can I help you?"

She nods, a slight tightening of her neck as she swallows. *In the movie version*, she will tell me her parents abandoned her. No, she will tell me her mother died in a car crash and her father of cancer. She will tell me she has no brothers or sisters, that she never knew her grandparents. She will tell me she is orphaned, has no one. She will ask me to save her.

"I have a goat," she says. "How do you raise him?"

Goats, goats, goats. My mind races. Goats roamed St. Thomas; goats grazed fields on the kibbutz where I searched for my unplanted Jewish roots. But I never so much as touched any of those goats.

"Oh," I say, suddenly realizing she wants a book about them. "Here, let me help you."

I lead her to the card catalogue and flip to "G," to "goats." One book. *My Pet Goat.*

I rush to the shelves. It's not there. I hurry back to the counter, searching through the checkout cards. It's been checked out or else permanently "disappeared" for over three months. I show her the card, carefully explaining the procedure: that if she gives me her name and phone number, I'll call her the minute it's returned. I don't say it's probably gone forever.

She nods. I print her name and number on the form, tagging the card. "I'll call you the second it's returned," I reiterate.

Then she is gone. For a long moment I watch the spot where she last stood as if her shadow remains.

I look at her name, the number. I retrieve the phone book to learn her address. No listing. No one with her last name with that number. Suppose the book on goats is returned when I'm not here? Suppose Belle is on duty when she picks it up? I remove the tag from the card, fold the form, and put it in my pocket. Every day I'll check to see if the book's returned.

A week passes. The book remains missing. One evening, I dial the number to tell the girl how sorry I am. The phone rings and rings. No one, not even an answering machine, answers. I never see her again. I don't understand my sense of bereavement.

On April 10 the Floyd County Commissioner's office finally releases its report. Laboratory tests confirm the presence of dangerous levels of asbestos fiber particles in five areas of the library.

In the April 11 edition of the *Rome News-Tribune*, County Commissioner Ronald Smith is quoted as saying, "We're concerned. We're going to take whatever steps are necessary to make sure there's no risk to anyone." He goes on to explain that they plan dust- and ventilation-control measures. They will post warning signs. They will wet-mop the floors.

Kim Leighton from the newspaper calls for my reaction to the report. "'While I'd like to continue to work there, the asbestos is a very serious health problem that should have been acted upon sooner. Then I wouldn't have had to get involved,' said Sue Smith," he writes.

Prisoners from the Floyd County jail arrive at the library to mop floors. They wear no face masks, no gloves or rubber booties. They laugh and joke, happy to be out of jail for a few hours. Every day it's as if the ceiling itself metastasizes, producing more and more poisonous particles.

I prepare a letter to hand-deliver to Abigail Kane. "I cannot afford to breathe asbestos even one more hour. My resignation is effective immediately." I xerox copies of the letter for the *Rome News-Tribune*, the Georgia Library Association, the American Library Association, and the Board of Trustees of Sara Hightower Regional Library.

The next day Don Hatcher of wxia follows me up the steps of the library, camera whirring. I open the door to the business office. As luck would have it, Abigail sits at her desk as if expecting me. I march over and hand her the letter. "I resign," I say.

The April 15 edition of the *Rome News-Tribune* reports my decision. "'That's a sick building,' Mrs. Sue Smith said."

I petition to present a statement at the April 23 meeting of the county commissioners.

I spend days writing and revising my four-page speech, as if I plan to address Congress.

The courtroom where the commissioners meet, in the county courthouse, smells of floor wax. The five commissioners sit on a dais. I stand before them wearing a plain oxford shirt and gray skirt. A large, curious audience sits behind me. "Every hour counts," I begin.

"In one particular case," I say, after a few introductory statements, "a person died of mesothelioma simply because she lived in the same house as an asbestos worker. In another case, in London, several people died who lived within a half mile from an asbestos plant. . . ."

Commissioner Smith, a Marine Corps veteran, tries to cut me off. He moves to adjourn the meeting. The other commissioners, however, won't "so move." I continue my speech, but before I finish, he again interrupts. "She's through so far as I'm concerned," he says, leaving the room.

The audience applauds when I finish.

For a week or so after the meeting, I receive crank phone calls from an unidentified man. "Silverman, you better leave town."

How does he know my birth name? Why does he use it?

The crank calls don't scare me too much, or not as much as if he would have said, "Smith, you better leave town." What scares me more is that he knows my *real* name, my Jewish name, even after all my efforts to dodge that name, dodge the bullet, as it were, after all my efforts of disguise. Collective hatred is more dangerous than personal vendettas. For long moments after I hang up the phone, all I hear are those three syllables reverberating: *Silverman, Silverman, Silverman.*

I stand in a cinder-block bunker at the 7 Hills Firing Range. I wear yellow-lens protective goggles and earplugs. I plant my feet.

I grip a Colt .22 Diamondhead in my left hand, my right hand steadying my wrist. Before me, several yards down a lane resembling a bowling alley, hangs a target of a male figure.

I know nothing about guns. I've never held one before, nor do I plan to purchase one.

But the thing is, I'm a good shot, I discover. Even if I miss the "important" parts of the paper anatomy, I rarely miss the figure itself. After I finish one round of bullets, I press a lever that activates a chain mechanism. The target whirls back to me. I clip on a new target.

I love the cool metal trigger against my index finger, the heft of the barrel in my palm. I love the scent of gunpowder, the residue lingering on my fingers. I bring the silhouettes home with me to admire. At least one shot pierces the paper heart.

In the 60 Minutes *version,* Mike Wallace asks about the cover-up. He asks if I fear for my life.

In the tragic play, I'm a mummified Egyptian pharaoh, my body wrapped in gold-fiber asbestos, skin forever preserved against conflagration.

In the movie version, Clint Eastwood enters Sara Hightower Regional Library. "I tried being reasonable. I didn't much like it," he sneers.

In the sequel, Meryl Streep as Sue Smith glances in the rearview mirror. Menacing headlights follow her, closing in.

All summer, my husband researches and writes his book. He's immersed in Riffaterre's *Fictional Truth,* Remi Clignet's *The Structure of Artistic Revolutions,* or Kant's *The Critique of Judgment.* Since I am now unemployed, he asks if I'll help type his manuscript. I agree. "The generic and world-testing characteristics of the realistic novels I describe bear a similarity to Bakhtin's description of the menippean satire and its carnivalization of discourse. . . . An intertextual theory of realism precludes the possibility of extratextual denotative reference because the linguistic sign refers (or, following Derrida, *defers*) not to an external reference but to a connotative series of other signs. . . ."

By the end of summer, I hate words. Every single one of them. Whereas once I loved them, studying sentences for hours in that library in the West Indies. But now, I wonder, maybe words—all words and ideas—simply get in the way of things. Real things. Things like goats. Things like girls with hair the color of wet sand in August. Things like regret. Or pure old-fashioned, unadulterated angst.

I climb the rutted road to the top of Lavender Mountain to escape my husband's book for a few hours. I'm sticky and damp. I cross brittle grass past fruit trees and berry patches designed with the same plan as Castle Nemi in Italy, where Martha Berry's sister lived. I cup my palms to the sides of my eyes and peer through a window of the rarely used House o' Dreams. In 1926 students and faculty constructed this cottage for Martha as her hideaway. They even built the furniture and wove the fabric for curtains and slipcovers. Today the air feels vacant, as if I'm the only one who's been here in a long time. The top of this mountain is the House o' Dreams, but it's also the end of the road.

Where to go now?

Why do I even remain married? Buried in his philosophical books, deconstructing words and sentences for a living, my husband never notices the absence of a *real* me.

Which must be what I've wanted.

After all, because of his inattention, I'm never exposed for the poseur, the fraud that I am: a hollow woman. One not yet constructed enough to be deconstructed.

In my secret life, unable to find an identity that lasts, I change roles like fads. I seek one style to fit this year, another for next year. But I end up as neither one thing nor another.

Nothing: on my way to nowhere.

At some point must I find my own fireproof—or fiery?—garments. But how? Where? When?

In another hour, the sky will deepen to the tint of the sea. Silhouettes of birds, the color of rain, wing toward evening, only the tips of their feathers studded with diamonds of light. I think of those mythical creatures living by fire, dying by water . . . floating across a shimmering edge of a soon-forgotten dream.

No, you *can't* start a fire without a spark. Sometimes you can't start one anyway. Sometimes you just smolder, waiting for your chance to burst into flame.

Fahrvergnügen

A ROAD TRIP THROUGH A MARRIAGE

Fahrvergnügen: Driving enjoyment.
VOLKSWAGEN ADVERTISEMENT

Synchronicity

ONE CHRISTMAS VACATION MY HUSBAND insists we drive (instead of fly) from Georgia to Houston to attend his mother's second wedding. Which means we're to drive in his 1972 dual-carburetor Volkswagen camper despite the fact, as I frequently point out, that the carburetors aren't, ever, in sync. Despite the fact that the hubcaps periodically frisbee off the wheels at any speed over forty miles per hour, that the heating system works only in muggy weather, that the windshield wipers wipe depending on mood and climate, although infrequently in actual rain. To say nothing of the fact that, only last week, the camper sprung a gas-line leak. It dripped a combustible trail from our house to the mechanic—me, waving good-bye to my husband from the front stoop—expecting to see a fireball at any moment, unsure, at this point in our marriage, whether this would be an altogether upsetting event.

My husband loves the pumpkin-colored camper to distraction. He invests hundreds of dollars on the carburetors, their synchronicity lasting only as long as it takes to pull out of the mechanic's garage. He spends hours tinkering and cleaning. He snaps Polaroids, displaying them on his desk. Once he asked me to crank the engine while he investigated under the chassis to determine the cause of its latest ailment. When I turned the key I forgot to put the transmission in neutral. The camper lurched forward. I almost plowed over him before I slammed on the brakes, stalling the engine. He survived with nothing worse than pale red tire marks on his stomach. Although I apologized, profusely, he never again asked me to help.

The Intricacies of Foreign Car Repair
in Lanett, Alabama

I'd prefer to fly to Houston, but I don't want to attend his mother's wedding in any event. As maid of honor, I've been coerced into wearing a pink dress as frothy and frilly as cake icing. But the preparations are finalized. My husband washes and waxes the camper. He cleans the orange upholstery, the matching stool with metal legs, the storage chest. He vacuums the carpeting and shines the windows. He pops the top to dust for cobwebs. Two days before Christmas we pack up the camper, setting out for our initial stop in Pensacola to collect my husband's aged aunt before continuing on to Houston.

We pull out of the Berry College campus, where we still live in that log cabin, onto Martha Berry Highway, follow US 27 south to US 29 before reaching I-85. We have driven 124.85 miles, a total of two hours and twenty-two minutes (but who's counting?), when the camper drops an engine rod outside Lanett, Alabama.

We've barely made it over the border from Georgia. Really, we're on the cusp of the border, hardly in one state or the other. We're stranded on the side of the road, loaded down with Christmas and wedding presents, suitcases, frilly dress, duffle bag, Styrofoam cooler.

While my husband walks to a service station, I (fuming) theoretically guard the camper, as if anyone would want to—or even could—steal it. He returns, hours later, with a tow truck and driver. We stand on the shoulder, vehicles whizzing past. My husband discusses cars, engines, options, while the driver hooks the bumper to the towing mechanism. I, meanwhile, consider pushing my husband into the path of an oncoming semi.

The driver tows the camper to the only place in Lanett where he thinks, maybe, if we're lucky, a mechanic might work on a foreign car. A sign taped to the door says it won't reopen until after Christmas. We unload the presents and suitcases, piling everything into the tow truck. We're driven to a Super 8 on the edge of town.

"How long will you be staying with us?" the receptionist asks.

"One night," my husband says. "Maybe two."

I glance at the ceiling. *Indefinitely*, I think.

The room is cold, airless. Still in my jacket, I lie beneath the blanket and bedspread. My husband turns on the combination air conditioner/heater window unit. The fan rattles like out-of-sync carburetors.

Years ago I find my own 1969 green Volkswagen beetle, used, at a dealer in Washington DC. I work on Capitol Hill at the time, am tired of relying on DC Transit, so finally save enough money to purchase it, my first car. The salesman, young and blond, accompanies me on a test run. Since I've never driven a stick shift before, we stay on flat streets. I have considerable trouble shifting from neutral to first on a hill, or even a small incline, if stopped at a red light. I can't simultaneously synchronize the brake, clutch, and accelerator. Therefore, the car drifts backward, which means trouble when another car pulls up too close behind. Really, I have trouble shifting, period. But I love the *putt-putt* engine. I love the sound of the *Blaupunkt* tuned to my favorite rock-and-roll station. I fill up the tank for three dollars. I slide it into a space less than half the size of one of the ubiquitous limousines with diplomatic plates. I get a House of Representatives staff parking sticker for the underground lot beneath the Longworth Building. Sure, the two little heating levers on either side of the gearshift are more for show than actual heat. Still, it's all mine. And I'm in love with the sheer *bugginess* of it. Yet my love affair is problematic almost from the start.

One evening a week or so after I purchase it, I receive a crank phone call. The sound of a man's heavy breathing floats through the phone line into my ear. I slam down the receiver. A few days later, the man whispers obscenities. Worse, he knows my first name, which isn't listed in the phone book. His voice sounds familiar. After a few weeks, I recognize it: the man who sold me the car.

Then, mornings when I leave my apartment for work, I suspiciously eye the car as if *it* is making the phone calls. I unlock the door, almost afraid the man lurks inside.

Keeping It on Mute

My husband finally reaches the owner of the car-repair shop by phone. But the mechanic says he won't have time to examine the camper until after the first of the year, more than ten days from now. My husband explains about his mother's wedding, the Super 8 motel. The owner himself is on his way out of town. Ten days. Take it or leave it.

My husband calls Greyhound Bus Lines. He can't get through. Two days before Christmas, everyone's calling.

I'm awake most of the night watching soundless images on the television screen.

The next day, about noon, my husband finally reaches a person at Greyhound. No bus station in Lanett. We have to go to Opelika, a half hour away. I don't ask my husband how long it'd take to walk carrying presents, frilly dress, etc. Assuming we even get to Opelika, it's an eighteen-hour bus trip to Houston, with two transfers. Plus, there's still Aunt Beulah waiting for us in Pensacola. Opelika to Pensacola is ten hours, one transfer. Pensacola to Houston is another eleven hours with one transfer.

By car or camper, which we no longer have, it would be only an eleven-hour drive, total.

I don't mention it to my husband but, given the options, I'd prefer to stay in the Super 8 in Lanett, Alabama, for the rest of my life.

As the Crow Flies

"Let's see if we can rent a car," I say.

We both glance out the motel window. Across the street is a field of winter grass. No Avis or Hertz. I look up car rentals in the phone book. After calling an 800 number, I learn that the closest car rental is at the airport in Columbus, Georgia. Forty-six miles away, about an hour on US 27 north, Martha Berry Highway. In other words, retrace our footsteps. Or tire tracks.

It takes another night and most of a day before we locate a taxi willing to drive us to Columbus. For a small fortune. On the way out of town we pass the garage, the orange camper hunkered in the lot.

German Engineering

A few years earlier, when we live in Missouri, where my husband teaches at that Southern Baptist college, he arranges for a Holocaust survivor to speak to a class of students. The temperature hovers near zero on the appointed day. Should he pick up the Holocaust survivor in the camper or the bug? The heating and defrost system work about as well in each, but he figures he might as well drive the camper since it's roomier. On the return forty-five-minute trip, the Holocaust survivor begins to shiver. My husband apologizes for the lack of heat. The survivor asks if there's a box in the car. A box? My husband pulls over to the side of the road and, in fact, finds a corrugated box in the back. The survivor props his feet on top of it. He says he learned in a concentration camp that you're less likely to get frostbite if there's space between your feet and the ground.

Volksmarch

Our first October in Rome, we plan a day trip in the camper to Helen, Georgia. We follow us 53 to Dalton, meandering through the Chattahoochee National Forest to Dahlonega, before cruising north on us 75 into a 1970s re-creation of a Bavarian mountain village. Oktoberfest is in full swing. We drive amid traffic and crowds along cobblestone streets until we find a parking spot close to the Chattahoochee River. We wander boutiques and specialty shops selling beer steins, candles, and cuckoo clocks. During the rest of the year, Helen boasts winefests, Alpenfests, all-American Fourth of July fireworks, as well as Bavarian Nights of Summer.

Sun drills the north Georgia air. I wear a short-sleeve t-shirt and sandals, which balance precariously on the uneven cobblestones. After an hour of tramping through hoards of sullen children and beer-crazed parents, I'm ready to go home. But first we decide to eat. Restaurants sell schnitzel, sauerbraten, and sausages. Others offer country ham, grits, biscuits and gravy. Street vendors hawk funnel cakes and homemade fudge. I buy a Caesar salad, my husband a brat dripping grease. We carry the boxes of food back to the camper, open the sliding door, and sit on the cushioned seats in the back, our food on the table. I prop my feet on the camper stool, watching the Chattahoochee flowing south to Atlanta.

After eating, we buckle ourselves into our seats. My husband turns the key in the ignition. It starts right up. I'm surprised, having convinced myself the camper would develop some new ailment in order to stay in this German village, no matter how faux.

We Have a Problem

We rent a gold Plymouth at the Columbus, Georgia, airport and drive south to the Pensacola trailer park and Aunt Beulah. Originally, we planned to spend the night, but now we're running late.

We can't miss the wedding, so we pack Beulah and her suitcases into the backseat before heading west to Houston . . . Houston, which floods during rainstorms since it's built at about sea level with too much asphalt and concrete.

During the time I live there, after leaving Galveston, the starter on my Volkswagen, placed *beneath* the engine (an engineering breakthrough that no mechanic can explain), floods out. Three times. All three times I have to replace the starter box.

One flood is so severe that, glancing out the window of my small house, I watch my Volkswagen float down the street.

I run through near-hurricane conditions to rescue it.

I Spy

My husband, Aunt Beulah, and I partially follow the route a boy-friend and I once took, years ago, in his tan Volkswagen camper. Then we drove cross-country from Washington DC to California before traveling the Pacific Coast Highway north to Portland. Where the Volkswagen stripped its gears. Where we lost second, third, and fourth. Where we were stranded for several days waiting for a mechanic to fix it.

Later, following the northern route back to Washington DC, somewhere east of South Dakota, after visiting Mount Rushmore, I got food poisoning from eating at a Stuckey's. I vomited for more than three hundred miles in the rear seat of the camper.

Now, for eight hours, from Pensacola through muggy Alabama, stifling Mississippi, humid Louisiana, and into east Texas, Aunt Beulah points at swamps out the window and says, "I bet there's a lot of cottonmouths in there."

Superbug to the Rescue

Once, when I fly back to Georgia from visiting friends, my husband plans to pick me up at Atlanta's Hartsfield Airport. The plane lands a little after eight o'clock at night, but no husband at the gate. No husband at baggage claim. I try calling from a pay phone. No answer. We recently purchased a Ford Escort station wagon to replace the camper (foreshadowing here), the first new car for either of us, so it can't be car problems. It is, however, storming, so I imagine a collision or accident on a slick I-75.

I sit in baggage claim until two o'clock in the morning, virtually alone in the airport. The custodians sweep the floor around me.

My husband finally rushes in. He'd made it halfway to Atlanta, over an hour away, when the Ford developed (we later find out) vapor lock. He left it on the side of the road, walked to a gas station, had it towed, called friends who picked him up and brought him back home to get another car. We owned three.

He decided to try the yellow Opel next, figuring it'd be more reliable than my Volkswagen. The secondhand Opel was a dubious present from my parents. It had to undergo a complicated and elaborate ritual—almost an exorcism—in order to start the engine in such a way that it wouldn't stall out: pump the gas five times, wait a full sixty seconds, pump the gas ten times, wait exactly three minutes, turn the key with your foot off the gas, allow the engine to idle precisely four and a half minutes, slowly, *slowly* ease the automatic stick from neutral to drive. Put your foot on the accelerator.

My husband must have either missed or rushed through one of the steps. Or, since it lacked a working gas gauge, perhaps it ran out of gas. In any event, a mile from home it stalled out on the side of the road.

He walked home and got the Volkswagen bug. Which made it to Hartsfield Airport without a hitch.

Taking It and Leaving It

After the wedding and Christmas, we leave the aunt in Houston and drive the Plymouth back to Lanett. It feels as if we're returning to the scene of a crime. The mechanic, at whose place the camper has taken up residence since the breakdown, says it'll cost at least a thousand dollars to fix. Probably more. My husband is tempted but says he'll think about it. He asks the mechanic if he'll consider purchasing the camper as is, for parts? Or, of course, the mechanic could fix it and sell it, recoup his investment. I'm mum about the dual carburetors. Hubcaps. Windshield wipers, etc.

We return to Rome in the Plymouth, while everyone considers options. We pick up my Volkswagen, and I follow my husband back to the Columbus airport to return the rental car. Then we cruise over to Lanett again. The mechanic says he'll give us $200. We say we'll take it. No hesitation.

We clean out the rest of our stuff from the camper. Even though, officially, the stool belongs with the camper, my husband takes it, a souvenir. He majestically places it in the backseat of the bug.

Of My Own Accord

I secure my first teaching job, earning enough to buy a new car: a Honda. I sell my Volkswagen.

The man who purchases it is overjoyed beyond all reason. After all, the plastic seats are cracked with straw-like stuffing leaking out. At some point, the *Blaupunkt* was stolen. The left-side molding is a shinier shade of green paint than the rest of the car, a result of a repair job following a minor accident during one of the Houston floods. The right-side molding, from another mishap, remains bashed in, never repaired. The windshield has a small, spiderweb crack. The heater has never worked.

But its original hubcaps shine like only slightly dented moons.

After my parents die, we inherit their Toyota Corolla. We sell the Opel to a woman who wants it solely because her fondest memory of adolescence is driving in her father's Opel. I write out detailed instructions on how to start the engine. We sell the Ford Escort station wagon as well since, shortly after we purchased it, a drunk driver rear-ended us. Despite five or six trips to the Ford dealership, the rear window still leaks. Whenever it rains, water drips in around the rubber gaskets, soaking the carpet. The ongoing vapor lock is also problematic.

At the same time that we inherit the Toyota and sell the other cars, we buy our first house. It's a split-level ranch with a two-stall garage and automatic door opener in the suburbs of Rome. The spotless, well-ordered house, along with the Honda and Toyota, are all clean, reliable, watertight, dependable. So we soon grow bored without the drama and distraction of a monthly breakdown or crisis. How else to explain why, for my husband's birthday (using money that was a gift from my parents), I buy him a car he covets. It's a white 1963 Ford Galaxie convertible with Rangoon-red leather seats and a 352-cubic-inch engine. *His* fondest memory of childhood is working on his family's Galaxie with his father.

This Galaxie, which he happened to notice in a used-car lot, is *not* in mint condition, which, of course, is the appeal. He wants to restore it. He, sometimes accompanied by me, scours salvage yards for replacement parts: grills, bumpers, a toggle switch to activate the hydraulic pump that raises and lowers the convertible top. Followed by a new hydraulic pump itself. Then, of course, the car requires a new white canvas top to go with the toggle switch and pump. Soon one stall of our garage resembles a salvage yard strewn with bumpers, metal molding, lug nuts, levers, spark plugs, cables, knobs. My husband purchases a subscription to *Hemmings Motor News* to search for additional parts. After about a year, he's replaced over 60 percent of the engine and body. He proudly enters it in classic-car shows, even wins trophies, which he displays on the mantel. By the time we move to Michigan from Georgia, it's his prized possession. Afraid something might happen to it during the move, he hires a carrier that specializes in classic cars. They ferry the Galaxie in an enclosed van so it won't be exposed to the elements—or rude, oncoming cars.

My husband and I are in Michigan only about a year before we divorce. We own three cars to divide between us. We decide I'll keep the Honda, he the Toyota. I also request the Galaxie. I don't know why. After all, I bought it for him as a present. He's restored it. I wouldn't be able to repair it when parts need replacing. Besides, it's *his* car.

Maybe I only want to spite him, since I know how much he treasures it. He spends time lovingly restoring it, more time than he ever spent with *me* (my italics).

I finally concede it to him, in the end.

After he moves out, I remain in the Victorian house we purchased together. One day, a year or so after he leaves, I discover the pumpkin-colored camper stool in the basement. It glows like warm autumn sunlight amid the dark disorder of boxes, cobwebs, broken furniture, discarded books, old computers, and long-forgotten knickknacks. I wonder if he *meant* to leave this questionable memento. I sit on the stool. The metal legs wobble on the brick floor as if on uneven cobblestones, in a tourist town you drive hours to reach, just to experience history whose worst moments have been so carefully expunged.

Almond Butter in the Ruints

METEOROLOGISTS PREDICT A BLIZZARD FOR March 12. Everyone in Rome, Georgia, scurries to Kroger and Piggly Wiggly to stockpile bottled water, flashlight batteries, food staples— everyone, that is, except me. I ignore all warnings. I pooh-pooh the approaching storm. The entire state, after all, virtually shuts down if so much as two snowflakes drift from the sky. Surely this is another false alarm. Initially, when I moved here from Missouri, I took winter storm warnings seriously. Now I go about my business, anticipating, at most, one-eighth of an inch of snow. Besides, my husband, my cat Quizzle, and I recently moved into our sturdy brick ranch house after living in that log cabin on campus for years. Now we're snug and secure in our new home.

Starting around midnight, we lie awake in bed. Thunder cracks. Lightning flashes. The ground shakes with the thud of loblolly pines crashing in our yard. The trees, high as telephone poles, are unable to withstand severe winds because of their shallow root system.

"We should go to the basement," my husband says. He worries a tree will crash onto our roof.

"But in the basement both the roof *and* the first floor could fall on us," I say, comfortable beneath the quilt.

Quizzle, usually a calm and fearless cat, hunkers between us in bed.

The next morning we stare out the glass sliders in the kitchen. About seven loblollies, huge root bulbs exposed, crisscross the snowy yard. Luckily, all crashed to the ground away from the house, though they severed power and phone lines.

We're without heat and electricity. No working flashlights. No phone. No logs to burn in the fireplace. The South, lacking snow-removal equipment, can't plow streets, now several feet deep in snow. We don't even own a snow shovel. Plus, we're probably the only people in the state out of food.

We sit at the kitchen table bundled in jackets and caps eating almond butter on crackers for breakfast. Lunch. Dinner. When we run out of crackers, we dip a teaspoon into the jar and lick. I don't remember whether I bought the almond butter or whether it was a present, but it has languished on various shelves for years, continuously moved from house to house, refrigerator to refrigerator. Not that I'm much of a cook—a fact that contributes to our present lack of food—but I've never used, let alone seen, a recipe that actually calls for almond butter. Yet since it's relatively expensive, and packaged in such a cute jar, I've never thrown it away.

Our only means of communication is a shortwave radio belonging to my husband. Miraculously, it has a set of working batteries.

Hour after hour, Romans who still have phone service call the radio station. They share their storm emergencies, anecdotes, and general feelings. Can anyone provide an elderly woman with a ride to Floyd County Hospital? Can anyone stop the snow and clear the streets for a young woman supposed to get married today? Can anyone airlift in a prescription of Prozac? Can anyone obtain kerosene for a heater for someone's grandmother?

Most calls concern food stockpiled in refrigerators and freezers. Now, lacking electricity, it's being ruined . . . or, as it sounds to my Northern-Yankee ears, "ruint." Chickens, roasts, deer and rabbit meat, ice cream, sweet potato pies. All ruint.

"How can food go bad when their houses are cold as a freezer?" I ask.

My husband glares at me since I convinced him the storm wouldn't be, well, a storm. He'd suggested we purchase supplies like firewood or kerosene or, at least, groceries.

"But five hundred years!" We'd just heard on the radio that this type of freak storm occurs only once every half millennium. "Plus, it's March," I add. "What are the odds?"

In between reports of ruint food, we learn that in this storm near-hurricane-force winds gusted over fifty-five miles per hour. It slammed most of the East Coast as far south as Cuba. A disorganized area of low pressure that formed in the Gulf of Mexico merged with an arctic high-pressure system in the midwestern Great Plains. Both swarmed into the midlatitudes because of an unusually steep southward jet stream. In Georgia temperatures plummeted from sixty-five degrees to the teens in a matter of hours. Thundersnow, it's called on the radio. A cyclonic blizzard. A Nor'easter.

I just bought twenty-five dollars of stew meat to get us through the storm. Now it's ruint.

"See," I say. "If we'd stockpiled groceries, it'd all be ruint."

"Bread? Bottled water?" my husband says.

"We've got water." I clomp over to the sink in my boots and turn on the faucet.

I run the hot water till it's steaming. I fill up a mug and drink it. Then I refill it, holding the steam close to my face. Who knows how long the water in the heater will stay hot? Quizzle jumps on my lap when I sit down again. I press the mug against her fur before tucking her under my jacket. She purrs.

Anyone with pickups and chainsaws, Georgia Power's looking for folks to help cart logs from downed power lines.

My husband spends the day grading student papers. I also have a batch of freshman essays to grade, but I'm too cold to remove my gloves, too cold to grip a pencil. After being unemployed for several years (when I quit my job at the public library), I returned to school for an advanced degree. I now teach as an adjunct at the community college.

I remain in the chair, Quizzle on my lap, seemingly incapable of movement. I just stare out the sliders at the snow and fallen

loblollies. I wish, at least, we had television. I hate to miss episodes of my favorite show, *Mystery Science Theater 3000.*
All NASCAR *races in Atlanta are postponed until . . .*
All classes cancelled . . .
I should be pleased by this news. And I am, but only partially. Most of my students, in this rural Georgia county, are women, and most are the first members of their families to continue their education past high school. I admire and miss them. At times they good-naturedly poke fun at what they call my "Yankee accent." I start saying "y'all" to humor them, to fit in.

A few months ago one of the students asked why I liked teaching English. "I guess I like words," I said, having finally recovered from typing my husband's indecipherable book on ekphrasis.

Marcee, a quiet student but a good writer, came up to me after class. "I like words, too," she said, her voice low. "But I never heard anyone ever say that before."

A month later she switched her major from dental hygiene to English.

Previously, I taught at another college here in Rome, one belonging to the Southern Baptist Convention. I attended church services on Wednesday evenings. I held hands with colleagues as we prayed over meals. Before Christmas break, I sat in the chapel scented with candle wax and deep-red poinsettias. The choir sang Christmas carols and hymns, warming the windows overlooking a gray winter sky. *Loving God, help us remember the birth of Jesus, that we may share in the song of the angels.* A Christmas tree, decorated with gold-colored crosses, silvery stars, and white lights, shone at the college entrance.

But the job was temporary. Maybe if I still taught there I'd have believed in the fury of this storm, a storm of biblical proportions, instead of ignoring the warnings.

Saturday night, before dark, I search the kitchen drawers for matches. I find an old matchbook from Thorne's restaurant in

Galveston, hunter green with white lettering. The cover is bent, the sticks crumpled, but I manage to light a few candles. Flickering flames reflect in the glass doors leading to the deck. I once read that, back before electricity, mirrors were frequently hung in houses in order to multiply light.

My husband carries Quizzle down the hall to the bedroom. I remain by the kitchen sliders, long past midnight. In the glass, my face grays, ghostly, surrounded by licks of fire. As my eyes adjust to darkness, slivers of moonlight whiten the snow . . . snow blanketing all of Georgia, the whole East Coast.

The last time I felt this cold was last August, a Friday evening in the bar at the Holiday Inn. The room was over air conditioned and frigid. Condensation formed on windows overlooking the parking lot, blurring the night. My husband and I were with a group of friends from his college. We all drank Long Island iced tea: vodka, tequila, rum, gin, triple sec, sour mix, a splash of cola. A variation: white crème de menthe, a splash of real iced tea.

An Elvis impersonator.

I danced with a man to "Suspicious Minds." This man, who was not my husband, wore a black shirt and white tie, faux tough guy.

I barely noticed my husband or what he was or wasn't doing.

The air conditioning chilled my skin, to say nothing of the layers slowly numbing beneath the surface.

The bar was also packed with out-of-towners sentenced to a Holiday Inn on business.

Why did I think that the scent of chilled air, the scent of skin sweating alcohol, was romantic? That an Elvis impersonator, whose career apex would be chain motels on the outskirts of oblivion, was romantic?

Or was I the one on the outskirts of oblivion?

Who was I impersonating that night? Who am I now?

I glanced up. My husband sat at a round bar table, beside the window, gripping his drink. He wasn't smiling. He didn't seem to hear the music. His face was expressionless, his reflection in the glass, vague. He seemed to be staring at me . . . or, no, staring past me, or through me. How could he see me when I was barely able to see myself? I wanted to go to him. I wanted to apologize, apologize for dancing with someone else all night, apologize for not warning him, before we married, that I'd be a bad wife. A hollow wife. For not warning him that, in my previous marriage, I'd run off with a man whose biggest attraction was that he drove a blue convertible.

But I didn't.

When Elvis's simulacrum crooned "Always on My Mind," I nuzzled my face against the neck of the black-shirt-and-white-tie man. I closed my eyes so I no longer saw my husband or so, magically, he—no one—could see me. But in my transparency, surely no one saw me anyway.

Now, outside, the night is still, quiet. No cars, snowplows, or people. The houses surrounding mine are equally dark.

Only disembodied voices on the radio calling for help, recognition, comfort.

The radio itself is like the mother ship, the heartbeat of Rome, a solitary light burning in the universe.

And I realize why people prepare for storms, even as no one can ever be fully prepared: the camaraderie of gathering in the supermarket to stockpile groceries; the camaraderie when plans fail, so neighbor helps neighbor.

But I stockpiled nothing, nothing to ease me through the storm.

All night, the radio spools out voices. I don't turn it off.

My pork chops are ruint.

It's an act of God.

Drifts of snow press against the sliding door.

If only my telephone worked, I could call into the radio station with my own emergency: *My marriage is buried under cataracts of snow. I am encased in ice. I am ruint.*

I remain in the kitchen, hungry and cold, gripping the jar of almond butter on the Sabbath—a totem, a talisman, an artifact—among my Southern Baptist neighbors. Centuries hence, I will be discovered by archaeologists in this same position, beneath slabs of ice in the ruints of Rome.

I Was a Prisoner on the Satellite of Love

(FEATURING CROW T. ROBOT, STAR,
MYSTERY SCIENCE THEATER 3000)

CAST OF CHARACTERS (in order of appearance):
SUE: a wife, a human
M.: Sue's husband, a human
CROW T. ROBOT: a robot living on the Satellite of Love
   (SOL), the stage set for the television show *Mystery
   Science Theater 3000*
RICH: a realtor, a human
JOEL: a human living on the SOL
TOM SERVO: a robot living on the SOL
RANDY: a human therapist in Atlanta

I SLUMP BESIDE MY HUSBAND, M., barely speaking to him.
We're on the Northwest Airlines flight from Hartsfield International Airport in Atlanta to Grand Rapids with a layover in
Detroit. In the Hartsfield gift shop I was comforted by familiar
Braves baseball caps, Dawgs t-shirts, the drawl of slow, fluid syllables. Now, after landing in Michigan, I'm confused by foreign
midwestern logos, sights, and sounds: Red Wings hockey sweat-
shirts, "M Go Blue" pennants, flat accents, heavy on my ears. I
want to be home in Georgia. But my husband has a new job offer, so we're flying here to look for a house prior to our move.

We wait for the realtor outside the terminal of the Gerald R.
Ford International Airport. It's Memorial Day weekend, and I'm
wearing a sleeveless floral blouse and hot-pink sandals. Freez-

ing, I might add, in sleeveless blouse and sandals. While it was over eighty degrees in Georgia, it feels less than fifty here, practically still winter. Indeed, everyone at the airport wears dreary tans, grays, blacks. All the footwear seems to be sturdy boots. Everyone looks as if they hike. I am the only one in floral, the only one in sandals, in pink. Is tan actually a color? All my boots have stylish heels. Besides, I hate ice hockey. I don't know what "M Go Blue" means. [*"Get your shoes on,"* Crow T. Robot quips from his front-row seat on this movie of my life. *"We're at the monster."*]

Rich, our realtor, glides to the curb in a black Jaguar. He leaps from the car, enthusiastically welcoming us to west Michigan. I barely shake his hand before collapsing in the backseat, forcing M. to sit in front. Let *him* schmooze with Rich, listen to the glowing Chamber of Commerce sales pitch. Let *him* hear about this "perfect" house, that "perfect" neighborhood. [*"Hour after hour of heart-pounding small talk,"* Crow says, in a mock-stentorian voice.]

Just two years ago, after renting that log cabin, we bought our first house, only recently completing the redecoration. *That's* the house in which I want to live. But now, because of this job offer, we must sell it. I must give up my adjunct teaching job. I must leave my therapist and my group. [*"Goodbye,"* Crow calls. *"Thanks for the Valium!"*] Worse, I fear I might also have to leave Crow—Crow, the robot, whom I think I love more than my husband. At least it *feels* as if I'm leaving Crow behind. Surely, though, I reassure myself, cable television stations in Michigan—just as in Georgia—*must* air the Comedy Central series *Mystery Science Theater 3000* (MST3K), in which Crow is one of the stars. But all in all it feels as if I'm leaving my life behind—or as if I'm being abandoned. [*"Does anyone have a copy of* Final Exit?" Crow asks, innocently.]

We've planned to buy a house in one of the lakeshore communities about forty minutes west of Grand Rapids. During the drive to the coast, I notice trees still leafless and bare [*"Enjoy our bleak landscape,"* I hear Crow say.], whereas in Georgia, spring rains are funneling toward summer. I want to ask the realtor to turn on the car heater, but I'm too exhausted to speak. The thought of finding a house during one long weekend seems impossible. Besides, Georgia is the longest I've lived anywhere. While initially, upon moving there, when I worked at the public library, I had a troubled relationship with the State of Georgia, now it finally feels like home.

To be totally honest, however, I don't really want to live in Georgia either. Rather, I'd much prefer to live with Crow T. Robot (the letter "T" is short for "The") on the Satellite of Love, a satellite floating, obviously, in outer space—or at least floating on the television show MST3K. Don't get me wrong: even though it's true I've only recently been released from a twenty-eight-day rehab program, recovering from my family of origin and other disasters, I'm not really crazy. Sure, okay, I have a couple of issues, just a bit of a skewed vision of the world. [*"This is my world and welcome to it," Crow crows.*] Nevertheless, even though *of course* I pretty much know the difference between make-believe and reality, still, Crow *seems* so real. I *want* him to be real. He and Joel, the human on the show and Crow's creator, are the ones with whom I want to live, the ones whom I want for my family.

Now, just worrying about this move, I begin to imagine Crow as living only inside *my* particular television set in Georgia—even though, technically, I know this isn't true. But suppose I can't find him in Michigan? Comedy Central is, after all, a fledgling network, not yet carried nationwide. Even now, leaving Georgia for a few days, I'll miss him. [*"The Bataan Death March was less painful than this," Crow commiserates.*] I gave detailed instructions to a friend in my therapy group to videotape all the weekend shows, but suppose his VCR breaks? Suppose the timer doesn't work? Suppose he forgets an episode by mistake? [*"Do not adjust your set!" Crow commands. "We can make it stupid."*]

STAGE DIRECTIONS: Rich T. Realtor drives along the shore of Lake Michigan, the main selling point of the area. But this stage set of

Sue's life should not be designed as a summery beach. The day is gray, cool, gusty. No trees or dense foliage, only a few sprigs of dune grass. No boats on the water. No one sunning on beach towels. No boardwalk or carnival rides. Miles of deserted sand. [*"Once a garden spot, now a playground of death," Crow intones.*]

After a fade-out, the camera focuses on the Jaguar stopping beside the first house on Rich's list, a mustard-yellow, wood-frame Victorian with purple trim. It is surrounded by evergreen trees, not loblollies like the ones in Georgia, I notice, sighing. I straggle behind Rich and M. toward the front door, while Rich gleefully details the pros of the house. To him, of course, there are no cons, even though the carpet is electric green. Pepto Bismol–pink paint drenches walls clogged with sad clown paintings. [*"When knickknacks ruled the world," Crow groans.*] The kitchen is decorated in a heart-and-duck motif. [*Sue, sotto voce: "Country-psychedelic Victorian on crack."*]

My head is spinning as if I've just staggered off a Tilt-a-Whirl. I sit on the green velveteen couch in the living room, thinking I might feel better if I put my head below my knees. Surely this technique cures both dizzy spells *and* nausea. [*"I'm up here, honey, with the DTs," Crow yells. "Could you get the yellow lizard out of the bathroom?"*]

"I happen to know they had a professional interior decorator," Rich says.

The remote for the television set is propped beside the screen. I can't resist. I channel surf: ABC, CBS, NBC, CNN, TBS. *Comedy Central, Comedy Central, where are you? Do you read me? Where is my favorite robot?* Right then I decide to refuse to buy a house without Comedy Central, without Crow.

SOLILOQUY, SUE, WITH YEARNING: Crow, I can't live without you. Sure, even with your gold-lacquer finish, you're probably not the most handsome robot. Your head is crafted from a lacrosse-stick pocket with a bowling-pin snout attached. Your ping-pong-ball eyes have plus signs for corneas. You have rod-like arms and a thin neck. Your chest looks like two Frisbees glued together, while your lower torso is (more or less) an indented paint can. Nevertheless, dearest Crow, you stole my heart with your irony, your sarcasm, your lack of illusion, your intolerance of deceit . . . you, Crow, who are just the opposite of my deceitful father. [*"Bad movie?" Crow says of Sue's life. "You're soaking in it."*]

Sue continues [*"As the God of Exposition rears its ugly head," Crow laments.*], Crow doesn't live alone on the Satellite of Love. His robot brother is Tom Servo, whose head is a transparent gumball globe with a small tin mouth. His Slinky arms are attached to a red-barreled chest that sits atop a hover skirt.

The robots aren't orphans, however. Far from it. The head of this household is Joel, the human, who, both on MST3K *and* in reality, is a low-key, sweet-faced, blue-eyed, blond Minnesotan. [*"In real life, your landlord is a butane addict who sneaks into your apartment and looks through your underwear drawer," Crow warns.*]

Why do they live on the satellite? How did they get there? Joel, the janitor at the Gizmonic Institute in Minneapolis (or maybe it's St. Paul), irritates the two mad scientists in charge. To vent their annoyance they shoot Joel into outer space to live on the Satellite of Love. There they force him to watch bad movies (mostly science fiction) from the 1950s and early '60s, thus punishing him further. But their ulterior motive, in their twisted minds, is to discover a movie to inflict on the world that is *so* bad, they'll be able to conquer the universe.

The mad scientists come close. They screen the worst movies ever filmed, the worst of the worst, emphatically bad: *Attack of the Giant Leeches, Fire Maidens of Outer Space, Santa Claus Conquers the Martians, The Pod People, The Killer Shrews, Attack of the Eye Creatures, Manos: The Hands of Fate, Eegah!, The Crawling Hand,* and *Monster A-Go-Go.* So Joel, lonely and depressed [*"The first step to recovery is recognizing you have a problem," Crow reminds*

Joel.], missing his roots, his family and friends (this isn't Minnesota anymore), and being something of a scientist himself, constructs the robots for friends. (In reality, Joel, as part of the creative team Best Brains, pieced together his 'bots using gizmos found in a Salvation Army basement.) Now, not only does he have company as he floats in space, he has companions with whom he can suffer the daily dose of bad flicks. [*"I've got a headache this big, and it's got this movie written all over it," Crow moans.*]

So now imagine me, Sue, in my ranch house in Georgia, the television set turned to Comedy Central. I sit on my couch watching bad movies at the same time as I observe the silhouettes of Crow, Tom Servo, and Joel *also* watching the movies, sitting in a mock theater. Lights dim. The opening credits for *Earth vs. the Spider* [*"I'm putting my money on the spider," Crow guesses.*] or *The Castle of Fu Manchu* begin to roll.

Joel and the 'bots don't just watch the movies. They riff, groan, make snide comments, combining literary allusions with references to both high and low culture. [*"I love the smell of lizard in the morning," Crow says over the climactic scene of* Attack of the Giant Gila Monster. *"It smells like . . . chicken!"*]

STAGE DIRECTIONS: A close-up of Sue, still in the Victorian house, with the TV remote in her hand.

Rich T. Realtor: "What're you doing?"

Sue: "Seeing if they get Comedy Central."

Rich T. Realtor: "But this house is only *six blocks* from the lake."

Rich informs M. and Sue that the goal of all homeowners in west Michigan is to move from one house to another, closer and closer to the lake, eventually buying a grand house overlooking Lake Michigan. "It's climbing the ladder," he says, authoritatively. "Our younger couples might begin in a starter home," Rich adds, "before moving to a restored house in the older downtown area." Beaming, he gestures at the green-and-pink Victorian nightmare. [*"There's a fine line between surrealism and costume-*

shop closeout," Crow says, so loudly Sue thinks the realtor must hear.]
"Then, from here, you can move into a house even closer to the
lake," Rich says. "And soon, before you know it . . ." [*"Jupiter:
America's heartland!" Crow exclaims.*]

AN ASIDE: This is the place in the script where additional exposition must be inserted. It must be clear *why* Sue loves MST3K.
The *what's the motivation?* question must be addressed. Therefore, it should be clarified that, to Sue, the bad movies on MST3K
are emblematic of dysfunctional families everywhere, such as
hers. These families, after all, maintain the pretense that they're
perfect, that they're *not* dysfunctional. Likewise, in these movies the actors pretend, for example, that a jolly Santa Claus *can*
conquer the Martians. Or, in *Attack of the Eye Creatures*, the actors deliberately overlook the sneakers peeking from beneath
the eye creatures' costumes. No one notes the inconsistency of
a character wearing Ray Ban sunglasses in a film supposedly
set in the thirteenth century. In *Teen-Agers from Outer Space* the
actors are, as Crow notes, "really *old* teenagers," while their uniforms are decorated with what looks suspiciously like duct tape.
The creature in *It Conquered the World* looks like a "giant Vlas-
ic pickle with horns," according to Crow. But the actors play it
straight, as truth. No one winks. No one (except Joel and the
'bots, of course) inserts even a touch of irony into the films. No
actors groan or smirk at inconsistencies. No one shatters these
façades . . . in the way Sue's parents' friends believed her family was perfect, believed the façade . . . in the way Sue's parents,
themselves, knew the truth but lied: Sue's father claimed to love
her; he pretended to be the perfect father by providing his family with nice homes and expensive cars. Everyone played their
roles with straight faces.
    In short, there was no Crow to point out that Sue's father was a
child molester. Had there been, Crow would have noted, as he does
about *City Limits*, "There's no place like home for the Holocaust."

FLASHBACK, INTERIOR. Actors costumed in circa mid-1960s clothes and hairstyles.

Sue's father, the new bank president, is officiating at the opening of the Saddle Brook Bank and Trust Company. Cameras flash. Champagne flows. Flower arrangements are situated on tellers' windows. [*"A long line at the petty larceny window," Crow observes. "I'd like to deposit some guilt, mistrust, and denial."*] A family photograph is taken where Sue's father stands between her and his wife, Sue's mother. With his left arm he encircles Sue's waist.

[*Voice-over (vo), Sue: "Look how happy we are!"*]

[*vo, Crow T. Robot: "Define happy."*]

Everyone at the party fails to see his tight grip, insisting that Sue smile, insisting this family portrait appear perfect. [*"Well, you're rich and white," Crow interjects. "I don't see a problem with it."*] If Crow were a silhouette in the corner of the photograph he would ask Sue's father, "Are we evil yet?"

Meanwhile, at the party, sounds of laughter. Champagne corks pop. Vaguely heard snatches of conversation: "What a wonderful mother," says an unnamed pod extra.

[*Crow: "I don't have a mother. I have an alligator."*]

"And a wonderful father and husband, too," says another pod.

[*Crow: "Yes, Satan speaks to me through this song."*]

Drunken laughter.

[*Crow: "Vodka sandwiches for dinner!"*]

Quick glimpses of men pressing too close to women.

[*Crow: "Oh, no, there're Kennedys on the planet."*]

"What a lovely family."

[*Crow: "These are not simple utilitarian lies that satisfy you and me on a daily basis."*]

Of course I need Joel, too. He's a nurturing figure, the good dad, who reads sections of the big book from Alcoholics Anonymous to the 'bots to ensure his little family stays spiritual and sober. Or, during breaks from the movies, he'll tuck the 'bots into bed at night and read *The Velveteen Rabbit*. [*"When slumber parties go bad," Crow whispers.*] Other times, he'll teach them human character traits or tell them about life on Earth. "Back in the sixties," Joel tells the 'bots, "it wasn't uncommon for your mom to serve you a great big charbroiled steak while she smoked, drank a Tab, and made your dad another Manhattan for the road. And that was just breakfast."

FLASHBACK, THE RECENT PAST: M. and I sit at the dinner table in our home in Georgia. M. has the television turned to TBS, watching an Atlanta Braves baseball game while we eat. I flip through the mail, finding a bill from Randy, my therapist.

"I don't have enough money in my checking account," I say.

[*vo, Crow T. Robot: "Yeah, boo-hoo, we all have problems."*]

M., still watching television, says, "That's because you only teach as an adjunct."

He knows that's the only opening available.

"Maybe you need to get a second job to help pay your bills. Work at Target. Anything," M. says. "Or else stay home and have a baby, so we can be a *real* family."

[*Crow: "Leering in from the back is chief editor of* White Male Perspective, *Wilhelm Studman, visibly upset with the intrusion of a mere girl into a man's world."*]

STAGE DIRECTIONS: The camera focus blurs before jump-cutting to present action where Rich, without winking, without irony, tells M. and Sue that the green-and-pink decor is sophisticated and classy. [*"Either these drapes go, or we do," Crow threatens.*]

I continue to channel surf until, finally, on channel 22, I find an episode of *Politically Incorrect*. This must be Comedy Central, since *Politically Incorrect* frequently airs after the morning episode of MST3K. This means the cable station in this neighborhood carries Comedy Central! This means maybe this house isn't so bad after all! [*"Sanctuary!" Crow cackles.*]

Rich ushers us out of the house. Consulting his list, he says, "The next place is in Ferrysburg, farther from the lake, but it's a beaut in the popular subdivision of River View."

"But wouldn't that be climbing *down* the ladder?" I ask, innocently.

Rich forces a smile. "Just wait 'til you see it. It was built in the fifties, back when we were all worried about nuclear fallout and what have you, and you can't get a sturdier house."

[*"I'm the Angel of Death,"* Crow hisses.]

Rich pulls up to a brick house with a bay window. "It's a spacious three bedroom, two bath. Open floor plan. Sliders off the dining area," he demonstrates how they work, "that open to a beautifully landscaped backyard. Finished lower level." Rich opens the door to the basement, which is pitch black. He tries the switch, but the bulb is burned out. [*"Hey, it's Boo Radley's house!"* Crow says, darkly.]

M. and I walk around the house, devoid of furniture. Nevertheless, determined, I search for a television set. None is visible.

"Do you think I could call the owners and see if they get Comedy Central?" I ask.

"We don't like clients contacting the owners directly," Rich says.

[*"Allow me to knee you right in the groin,"* Crow offers.]

STAGE DIRECTIONS: Quick cuts to show Rich, Sue, and M. driving from one house to the next. The houses are clean, pristine, antiseptic. [*"The parade of shame and wasted lives,"* Crow pontificates.] During the tour, Rich also shows them various sites. Churches adorn a disproportionate number of streets, though there are no synagogues or mosques. All the shop windows sparkle in Grand Haven's five-block downtown. Early spring flowers in window boxes are perfectly petaled. [*"Let's take you back to the days when* DDT *was safe,"* Crow says, nostalgically.] Sidewalks are virtually deserted, almost as if citizens are afraid to dirty them by actually walking.

Rich T. Realtor: "No gridlocks here. No traffic jams."
[*"One thing about the apocalypse," Crow opines. "Plenty of parking."*]

Rich T. Realtor: "No teenagers getting in trouble with drugs. No violence."

[*"How many times have you gone rooting through your junk drawer muttering to yourself, 'Where have I put my gun?'" Crow wonders.*]

Rich T. Realtor: "We've got the Musical Fountain. Largest in the world. Coast Guard Festival every August. This is a beautiful resort-type area, yachting all summer, swimming, sand dunes, wildlife. People come *here* from all over the world to vacation."

[*"Here at Phillips Petroleum we've found ways to replace the environment. Take, for example, these plastic self-cleaning ducks," Crow instructs.*]

Rich T. Realtor: "And here's the pièce de résistance." He pronounces the French with a flat, midwestern accent. "Thought I'd save the best for last." He parks in the driveway of a custom-built home.

[*"And now it's our cross to bear," Crow says, crossly.*]

Rich T. Realtor: "This classic, in the village of Spring Lake, has an open staircase with natural oak treads and painted risers winding around the great room with a fireplace and cathedral ceilings." He points out features to M. and me. "Private office and computer center on the main floor. Spacious master bedroom with a large private bath . . ." [*"And it can all be yours if 'The Price is Right'!" Crow announces.*]

"How much would this set me back?" M. asks. He glares at me to remind me yet again that I don't earn enough money.

I look around but can't find a television.

STAGE DIRECTIONS: The sun lowers in the west over Lake Michigan to denote a break in action, time passing.

INTERIOR SHOT: Rich, M., and Sue sit in Rich's office. Rich is behind his desk, Sue and M. on wingback chairs across from him. General conversation ensues, reviewing options, deciding whether to make an offer or look at additional houses tomorrow.

"I'm still leaning toward the ugly Victorian," I say, "that we *know* gets Comedy Central."

Rich, in an upbeat tone, tries to please everyone. [*"Dying is easy," Crow points out. "Comedy is hard."*] He acknowledges that, while it might need a paint job, and while it's not *on* Lake Michigan, it *is* close to downtown, which, according to Rich, is still a step up the ladder—albeit not the top rung. He confesses (scraping of background violins) that he and his wife began their marriage in a two-bedroom ranch in a subdivision, before moving to a four-bedroom ranch, before restoring a Victorian, where they installed a Jacuzzi in the bathroom. [*"Hey, you're getting into a real weird area here," Crow grimaces.*]

"Now, me and my family," Rich gestures to a photograph (violins moan to a crescendo), "live right on the lake and own three boats." [*"Five more minutes with him, and I'll open fire on a crowd," Crow snarls.*] "You'll love this whole area." He sighs deeply, with satisfaction. "There's no nicer place in the whole of these United States."

"I want to put down a deposit on the last one," M. says, caught up in the moment. "In Spring Lake."

"You can't go wrong!" Rich says.

"But I don't know if it gets Comedy Central."

M. and Rich glare at me.

"Okay, okay, why don't we call the cable company and ask," M. says.

Rich digs out his phone book and dials the number. He hands the receiver to me, without a word, some of his enthusiasm fading. After going through a complicated automated voice system [*"If you'd like to speak to the monster," Crow instructs, "press one."*], a real person (though I'd prefer talking to a silicon chip) answers. I ask the cable company operator if they carry Comedy Central in Spring Lake.

Cable company operator: "Not at this time."

Sue: "Might you at some time in the future?"

Cable company operator: "It's possible."

[*vo, Crow: "When apathy ruled the world."*]

Sue: "Do you know when that might be?"

Cable company operator: "Not at this time."

Sue: "But when? What time?"

[*vo, Crow: "Something out there is beyond the limits of our knowledge."*]

Cable company operator: "We don't have that information in our computer."

I slam down the phone.

"Christ, that stupid show," M. says. "You won't even remember it in a few months."

[*"We're getting you a lobotomy,"* Crow threatens.]

Rich, anxious for a sale, leafs through his realtor listings for additional houses. He holds up a photograph of another Victorian in Grand Haven, about three blocks from the psychedelic one. "This just went on the market yesterday," he says. "I don't have a price yet, but we could take a look-see. I think all of Grand Haven gets Comedy Central."

STAGE DIRECTIONS: Rich drives M. and Sue to Howard Avenue, to a house over one hundred years old. All the windows rattle. The refrigerator is located behind a door leading to the basement. The kitchen cabinets are scratched. Electrical wires protrude from walls in odd places. The basement is streamered with cobwebs, while a furnace shaped like the octopus in *Bride of the Monster* hunkers in a corner. [*"All we need now is a plague of locusts,"* Crow snorts.] Rich promises to find out the list price.

Exhausted, M. and I check into our room at the Holiday Inn where we're spending the weekend. I collapse on the bed, staring at the ceiling. M. changes into swimming trunks before heading to the hotel pool.

Even I know that, regardless of the price, the house in Spring Lake is the safer deal—better resale, more reliable. You never know what you're getting into with an old house, what with outdated wiring and plumbing.

But what about Crow? [*"We're all going to die alone and afraid,"* Crow says, realistically.]

I retrieve my AT&T phone card from my wallet, deciding to call my therapist in Georgia. I've never called him at home before, have never had such a dire emergency. *Can I really make a hundred-thousand-dollar decision based on a fictitious robot? What's the meaning of life, anyway?* I wonder, dialing the phone. [*"I wanted to play hopscotch with the impenetrable mystery of existence,"* says Crow, *"but he stepped in a wormhole and had to go in early."*]

Clutching the receiver, I explain the MST3K issue to Randy, telling him about the two houses under consideration. "The nicer house doesn't get Comedy Central, and the one that needs a lot of work *does* get it," I say. "I mean, I *know* Crow's just a robot. But . . ."

[*"We'll always have Encino,"* Crow reminds me.]

"But what does he *mean* to you?" Randy asks.

"Family," I say, without hesitation. "But a *good* one."

"Given how unsafe your father was, of course you'd want to live—"

"On the Satellite of *Love*," I interrupt. Pausing, I glance at the blank television screen in the hotel room, almost as if I can see Crow. "Sure, Joel and the 'bots joke around all the time, but they really *love* each other."

[*"I can hear my heart breaking,"* Crow sighs.]

"I don't see anything wrong in buying the house with Comedy Central," Randy says.

"But my husband's so angry. He thinks it's ridiculous to make a decision based on . . ."

[Crow, butting in: *"Honey, why can't you just once let me take over the world?"*]

"Still, you're moving all the way to Michigan just for him," Randy says.

The next morning Rich phones to tell us that the house on Howard Avenue is twenty thousand dollars less than the one in Spring Lake. M. and I discuss the two houses while eating breakfast in the hotel dining room.

"That settles it," I say. "It makes financial sense to buy the Victorian."

"But we'll spend that much fixing it up. And the Spring Lake house is a better investment."

I glance down at my plate, at the untouched food, shaking my head.

"Fine, then," M. says. "But you're going to have to earn more money to fix it up."

[*"It's after the apocalypse, dickweed," Crow notes. "No one's hiring."*]

SUE AS THE GODDESS OF EXPOSITION: We return home to Georgia from the weekend in Michigan. I'm resigned to the fact that we are definitely moving. In preparation, I videotape every episode of MST3K. I need to possess every movie, even though we buy the house on Howard Avenue with Comedy Central. [*"Sad, really," Crow says, sadly.*] At some point, after all, the show might be canceled. It might go off the air. A freak storm might knock out the cable. Besides, you can never tell when you might need a Crow fix—night or day. I must be prepared with a stockpile of MST3K tapes for all emergencies, all contingencies. [*"In case there's no Supreme Being," Crow confirms.*]

By moving day I have about fifty tapes of MST3K, with two or three movies per tape, for a grand total of 132 episodes. I, of course, am pleased to possess probably the largest private collection of bad movies in the history of the universe. While I allow the movers to take the artwork, my best shoes, the set of china in their van, I, myself, carefully place all the MST3K tapes in a special suitcase that will accompany me in my car. I refuse to let Crow out of my sight. I can't bear to be separated from him for a minute.

STAGE DIRECTIONS: The pages of a calendar flip through a year. The trees outside the windows change from green to red to bare branches to green once again.

ADDITIONAL STAGE DIRECTIONS: A wide-angle shot of the Victorian house on Howard Avenue in Grand Haven. INTERIOR: Some rooms are empty or sparsely furnished. The camera moves in for a close-up of Sue sitting alone on the couch in the living room. It's clear she's totally alone, that M. is gone [*"Don't worry,"* Crow reassures. *"We had him put down."*], that they've divorced. [*"We can't have a plot twist this late in the movie!"* Crow grouses.] The only light in the house comes from the television. She watches the end of *It Conquered the World*, tears streaming down her face.

SKIT OF JOEL AND THE 'BOTS IMMEDIATELY FOLLOWING THE END OF *IT CONQUERED THE WORLD*, STARRING ROBERT GRAVES: Joel, Crow, and Tom Servo have left the theater and are now in the living room of the Satellite of Love. Crow wears a plaid bathrobe, Tom Servo a red one. Joel, holding a dinner plate, feeds them. He slides a spoonful of food into Crow's open mouth before turning to Tom Servo. A nurturing mood is conveyed. Background music from *It Conquered the World* plays, while the camera remains on Joel and the 'bots.

They, themselves, are now watching a television set while listening, for a second time, to the voice-over of Robert Graves as the final credits roll: "He learned almost too late that Man is a feeling creature. And because of it, the greatest in the universe." Music soars. "There can't be any gift of perfection outside themselves. And when men seek such perfection they find only death, fire, loss, disillusionment. Men have always sought an end to toil and misery. It can't be given. It has to be achieved. There is hope, but it has to come from inside."

"Talk about it," Joel says. "You'll feel better."

[*"We're all going to die," Crow points out.*]

I want to be in my bathrobe. I want to sit beside Crow. I want Joel to offer *me* a spoonful of food. I see no irony that this moment between a human and two robots—with a sentimental voice-over from a B movie—is the most loving moment I've witnessed on television. This is the true American family. Not the Cleavers on *Leave It to Beaver,* not the Nelsons on *Ozzie and Harriet,* not the Andersons on *Father Knows Best.* [*"Shallow stereotypes of midfifties sociopaths," Crow dictates.*] And certainly this family on the SOL is more real, more loving than families like mine, where parents hurt their children while pretending to be perfect. More real than my marriage, where we thought a new job, a new home, a new state would make us whole.

EPILOGUE: [*"The gathering gloom," Crow predicts.*] I carry my dinner plate into the living room. I insert one of the prerecorded MST3K movies into the VCR and sit on the couch. *"In the not too distant future . . ."* the theme song begins as I place a forkful of food in my mouth. I don't want to eat alone, so this is my nightly ritual. I want to believe I'll eat dinner for the rest of my life with Joel and the 'bots on the SOL. [*"Something unspeakably horrible!" Crow warns.*] When I can't fall asleep and am awake at three in the morning, I watch one of the tapes. Instant comfort. Instant family. *This* family is always here—just inside the TV—fighting the evil of bad movies that tries to destroy civilization. [*"Oh, the humanity," Crow cries.*]

One evening I tape a new movie, *Mitchell.* It becomes increasingly clear that this is Joel's last episode. I later learn that "creative differences" force Joel to leave the show, even though MST3K was his idea. But now, during each skit between breaks in the film, an escape route is planned for Joel's return to Minnesota.

Toward the end of the movie, Crow has a meltdown over Joel's departure. I rush from the room. I continue to tape the episode to watch at a later date, but I can't bear to witness it now. [*"Oh, Lord, let it be quick," Crow pleads.*]

What'll I do without MST3K as I know it, without Joel? Does this mean Crow and the show might soon go off the air as well? I've been lulled into thinking we'll all grow old together. So what'll I do? [*"Please remain seated until the movie grinds to a complete halt," Crow advises.*]

Sure, I could return to Georgia, return to Atlanta Braves logos, southern drawls, loblolly pines. Or, maybe there *is* robot life in outer space! [*"Yeah, and there could be dogs and light-rail and tofu. What's your point?" Crow asks, characteristically.*] But if I were a character in *It Conquered the World*, I would say, unironically, "It doesn't matter where you live—outer space, Georgia, Michigan. 'Man *is* a feeling creature.' So home, after all, is where the heart is. *Isn't it?*" [*"Is the pope Catholic?" Crow queries.*]

Months later I finally watch the end of *Mitchell*. I have to. I must. If I don't face the reality of Joel's departure, as well as feel the loss suffered by the 'bots, won't *I* be living with my own denial—that all is fine when it's not? [*"You can't handle the truth," Crow challenges.*] Wanting to grow old with Joel and the 'bots won't make it happen.

"Hey, what about us?" Crow calls out, as he and Tom Servo watch Joel floating away from the SOL in a launch pod. "What're we supposed to do without you? Who's going to teach us about what it is to be human and stuff?"

"Listen, you guys," Joel says, his voice growing faint. "At this point, you guys know as much about it as I do." The 'bots watch the pod fading from view. "Be strong," Joel adds. "Be true. I love you!"

I love you, too, I think.

I turn off the television. I stare at the blank screen. No, I stare at the image, the afterimage, of my husband driving away from me. [*You can't walk out on me, I'm Charles Foster Kane,"* Crow asserts.] After all, as much as I have to watch the truth of the final episode with Joel, I must also watch the final episode starring M. . . .

I'm relaxing on the couch after dinner when my husband comes to sit beside me. With no preliminaries, this husband of eighteen years announces he wants a divorce. He's seen an attorney, found an apartment, is moving out. Tomorrow—on the Fourth of July.

He met Cheryl from Akron in an Internet chat room. *She understands me*, he says. [*"I know how much you love your turtle, but there are other things in the world just as important," Crow says, categorically.*]

I lie awake all night imagining him in his downstairs study, night after night, face lit by the glow from his computer screen.

The following morning, before he moves out, as previously planned, we arrive in Allendale, about twenty minutes from home. We're in his 1963 Ford Galaxie convertible to participate in the Fourth of July parade. A friend, running for re-election to the Michigan House of Representatives, asked if he could sit on the rear boot of the car, wave to the crowd, toss candy. [*"Oh, and who died and made you president of the capsule?" Crow challenges.*]

My husband slowly cruises the main drag, amid high school marching bands, Ronald McDonald clowns, Masons in fezzes, homecoming queens, and cheerleaders. [*"It's so painful being a crappy special effect," Crow grumbles.*] I sit beside him. The state rep smiles to the sparse crowd strung along the sidewalk. A warm breeze gusts small American flags held on sticks. [*"Rampant jingoism," Crow smirks.*]

After the parade, back at the house, my husband throws a suitcase of clothes in the backseat. He says he'll return for his other things later.

I wonder if Cheryl from Akron is visiting him in his new apartment for the holiday weekend. I don't ask.

I stand in the driveway watching him leave. My first thought is that I must drive to Home Depot to buy a fire extinguisher. I am now solely responsible for this wood-frame Victorian house with questionable wiring. [*"You close the hatch, I'm bitter," Crow says, a grin on his metal beak.*]

But I *can* survive alone, even with questionable wiring, can't I? [*I want to decide who gets to live and who dies," Crow proclaims.*]

But now, staring at the blank television screen, I realize that I miss him, miss *them*. Joel floating off into the galaxy . . . M. floating away in *his* Galaxie. I miss something. Maybe I miss the idea of Home, a home I've never found, or found only long enough for it to qualify as one of those temp jobs. [*"Maybe you should have brought this up in group," Crow says, helpfully.*]

I must also watch the truth about myself: I was a bad wife. I was an invisible wife. Too many selves, or none.

Joel seeks his new identity back on planet Earth. Crow will seek his with a new human on the SOL. M. seeks his with Cheryl from Akron . . . or with someone, anyone, who will be a better wife than I. [*"There's more action in the wallpaper," Crow points out.*]

And what about me? Isn't *this* what Joel and Crow have really taught me: how best to survive—and triumph over—the losses, the bitterness of it all?

Joel speaks to me as well as to the 'bots when he says he's taught us all he can about being human. Human *and* spiritual, *without* hypocrisy. [*"Heavy!" Crow exaggerates.*] But more than this, I now finally realize that Crow no longer lives inside a television. As sappy as it sounds, he lives here with me, inside my heart, me, behind the wheel of my own galaxy, celestial and bright. [*"In real life, of course, your roommate is a stinky high school dropout who fills your life with head lice, crusty laundry, and furry cans of SpaghettiOs," Crow snorts.*]

Good-bye Joel. Good-bye M.

[*"Goodnight, sweet crustacean," Crow bows, "wherever you are."*]

See the Difference

Clostridium difficile (klo STRID-ee-um dif-uh-SEEL)
is a bacterium that causes diarrhea and
more serious intestinal conditions such as colitis.

CENTERS FOR DISEASE CONTROL (CDC)

AFTER THE DEATH OF MY THERAPIST in May, followed by that of my cat in August, I wait. Not that I'm overly superstitious— but *don't* bad things happen in threes? So when amorphous, ghostly pains whisper through my lower abdomen, I fear I'm entering my own deadly portal. I schedule an appointment with my doctor for October 19, her practice only ten minutes from my house in Grand Haven. Dr. Sharon Fields pokes my stomach. She shakes her head: no grapefruit-sized tumor. She performs a Pap smear since I'm due for one anyway. "*Here's* the problem," she says, diagnosing a vaginal infection on the spot, without awaiting lab results. She prescribes an antibiotic, clindamycin, 300 mg capsules to be taken twice daily for a week. I leave her office, vaguely satisfied I'll survive this relatively mild diagnosis, that *I* won't be the third in a fateful series. I stop at the pharmacy to fill the prescription at 10:30 in the morning.

I swallow the first turquoise pill, the color of a chlorinated, antiseptic pool of water. I'm convinced a pill wearing such a delectable, albeit chemically colored, jacket will cure me. I don't read the warning label. I rarely do, since pharmaceutical companies tend to list every conceivable side effect from hangnail to death. How can you tell? I simply trust my physician. I don't notice, therefore, that clindamycin "should be used only for serious in-

171

fections because infrequently there are severe, rarely fatal, intestinal problems (pseudomembranous colitis) that can occur." And then I get sick.

Ten days after starting the antibiotic regimen, on October 29, I awake to a warm west Michigan morning. I also awake to mild intestinal distress. But since the evening before my partner, Marc, and I celebrated his birthday by dining out, perhaps I have a touch of food poisoning. Or maybe a spice disagreed with me. Since I don't feel too poorly, Marc and I go for a walk, enjoying one of the final days of sunshine before the veil of a midwestern winter descends. We stroll the quiet streets of Grand Haven before heading to the library. But here, amid the stacks, I weaken. I rest on a chair while Marc carries our books to the checkout desk. As I walk home, the muscles in my legs soften. They feel unmanageable, wayward, drunk. My black clogs, which usually clomp on pavement, now listlessly drag. I'm too tired to lift my feet. Exhaustion flares behind my eyes. I want to be in bed. Asleep.

Community Hospital, October 30

Clostridium difficile . . . infections [can result in] Colitis,
more serious intestinal conditions, sepsis, and rarely death.

CDC

"What're your symptoms?" Dr. Larson asks, after I'm admitted to the emergency room.

I consider mentioning Randy, my therapist, who died of heart failure in his early fifties, and Quizzle, my cat, dead at eighteen of lung cancer. I consider mentioning fate—that I'm ill simply because bad luck occurs in groups of three—whether the catastrophes are plane crashes or mysterious illnesses.

In fact, I wasn't the least surprised to find myself bundled into the car at 6:00 a.m. Marc drove us the five blocks to the emergency room along deserted Sunday streets. Last evening, collapsed in bed, wearing a sweatshirt and kneesocks to protect my diminishing body, I made trip after trip to the bathroom. I counted nineteen strides from bed to toilet. One way. I was afraid to sleep, convinced I'd die if I let down my guard. At any rate, I *couldn't* sleep, egesting what seemed at least a month's worth of food. At times I drifted in an opaque haze, gazing at—if not actively watching—the Turner Classic Movie cable channel all night, beginning with *South Pacific*. After that, I time-traveled through a midnight film noir stupor, movies reeling one into the next, indistinguishable.

Between movies, I self-diagnosed various ailments with which I might be afflicted. The litany began when I (belatedly) read the warning label on the phial of clindamycin: "pseudomembranous colitis." The list expanded when I Googled "diarrhea" on my laptop, an instant link to a World Wide Web of infection, disease, plague, and disorders.

"I took this antibiotic," I now say to Dr. Larson. I hand him the clindamycin warning label.

He nods. "I've seen this before." He explains that a pseudomembranous colitis infection is caused by *C. diff.* bacteria, short for *Clostridium difficile.* "It's nasty stuff," he adds. "We'll run some tests. Start an IV. You're probably dehydrated."

I lie on the hospital bed in the emergency room, watching transparent yellow fluid drip into my vein. Still early, it's relatively quiet. Small bleeps in the distance, perhaps a machine breathing life into a body. . . . Randy suffered a heart attack in his office, but I don't know if he died immediately or if an ambulance rushed him to the hospital. With Quizzle, I asked the vet to come to my house to put her to sleep. She was already thin with cancer. I thought she'd be more comfortable fading away on her kitty condo beside her favorite window. Now I want to doze, but the emergency room's searchlight-voltage fluorescent lights preclude rest. Also, I must roll the IV pole back and forth across the corridor to the bathroom. My body has a will of its own. It desires to be lighter, more deficient.

"The test is negative for *C. diff.*," Dr. Larson says about an hour later. "But that doesn't mean a whole lot. This is one of those tests that frequently shows a false negative."

He prescribes fourteen antibiotic metronidazole pills, 500 mg each, plus dicyclomine for cramping. "Stay on the BRAT diet—bananas, rice, applesauce, toast—for a week. Come back if you have additional symptoms."

Community Hospital, November 2

C. difficile symptoms include: Watery diarrhea (at least three bowel movements per day for two or more days), fever, loss of appetite, nausea, abdominal pain/tenderness.

CDC

"What're your symptoms?" Dr. Harkness, another ER doctor, asks, peering at me.

I explain that for the past three days I have nibbled only bananas, rice, applesauce, and toast. Small sips of Gatorade. But my body feels threatened even by bland food, impolitely rejecting it. "I'm exhausted," I add.

"We'll hook up an IV and run more lab tests," he says, glancing at my chart.

"What if it's *not* a *C. diff.* infection?" I ask.

"That'll be good."

"But what're the other options?" I ask.

"Maybe Crohn's disease," he says.

"But isn't that bad? Worse?" He disappears before the question is fully asked, much less answered. From the little I know, Crohn's disease is chronic, possibly life threatening, whereas a *C. diff.* infection can be cured . . . I think. But now I'm distracted by a man in the next bed, a curtain separating us. He moans every fifteen seconds as if on schedule. A nurse is telling him he probably has diverticulitis.

"What's that?" he asks her.

"Usually a bit of nut or seed gets trapped in the intestine," she answers. "We need to run a CAT scan."

I try to remember the last time I ate a nut or a seed. Yes! I *did* eat canned nuts about a week or so ago. I want to make sure I don't have diverticulitis. I want the doctor to order a CAT scan for me—a full-body x-ray. But then I remember the x-ray of Quizzle's lungs, pinpoints of white, multiplying spots. The vet carefully reviewed all her symptoms. At the time, I told the vet that I wished she were my doctor. She spent more time with Quizzle than any doctor ever spent with me and was gentle, patient, smart.

"The tests are negative for *C. diff.*," Dr. Harkness says. He adds that I should continue taking that *second* antibiotic to counteract the effects of the *first* antibiotic, clindamycin, just in case. That's all he can do. "There's no way to know for sure without a colonoscopy," he says.

"Then why can't I have one?" I ask.

"The gastroenterologist wouldn't order one yet. You have to wait and see if the metronidazole takes effect."

"You can't order it?" I ask.

"There's a procedure to be followed."

Community Hospital, November 3

People in good health usually don't get *C. difficile* disease. People who have other illnesses or conditions requiring prolonged use of antibiotics and the elderly are at greater risk of acquiring this disease. The bacteria are found in the feces. People can become infected if they touch items or surfaces that are contaminated with feces and then touch their mouths or mucous membranes. Healthcare workers can spread the bacteria to other patients or contaminate surfaces through hand contact.

CDC

I awake with blurred vision. I stare at a line of text on my computer. Each letter possesses a shadow. I try another pair of reading glasses. The shadowed letters remain. *I am going blind.* Frightened, I return to the hospital, to learn that I'm only severely dehydrated.

"Please, can't you order a colonoscopy?" I plead from the bed where I'm again hooked up to an IV. Dr. Harkness is once again on ER duty. "Can't *you* do it?"

He shakes his head. "I'm not a gastroenterologist."

"Then could I call the doctor, schedule an appointment myself?"

"He wouldn't see you. The order has to come from me or Dr. Fields. It's still too soon. You have to wait."

Wait. For what? What he must mean, I think, is that I'm not sick enough, not frail enough, not emaciated enough. Why can't he see I need help now?

County Hospital, November 23

If you are infected you can spread the disease to others. However, only people that are hospitalized or on antibiotics are likely to become ill. For safety precautions you may do the following to reduce the chance of spread to others: wash hands with soap and water, especially after using the restroom and before eating; clean surfaces in bathrooms, kitchens and other areas on a regular basis with household detergent or disinfectants.

CDC

Marc drops me off at what we think is the emergency room as he drives off to park the car. It's not the right entrance, however. Through slushy snow and bitter wind, I wander down the street, around the corner. After feeling better for close to ten days, able to eat small doses of food—convinced the *C. diff.* infection, or whatever it was, is cured—I awoke this morning with a temperature and severe bouts of diarrhea. Of course, I'm unable to schedule an appointment with Dr. Fields, this day before Thanksgiving. When I spoke by phone with her earlier, she suggested I go to County Hospital in Muskegon, about twenty minutes away, a hospital with better diagnostic services than Community Hospital. She returned the emergency page from her home, pots and pans clanking in the background. Small pellets of anger pinged behind my eyes, although I'd never let her know. Sick, I have lost control of my body. I am entirely dependent upon her.

Who is she?

I know nothing about her, not even where she attended medical school. After my previous doctor retired, I sought out Dr. Fields simply because she was a woman practicing at an all-women's clinic. I was sure that a woman doctor would be more nurturing, empathetic, understanding of my concerns. Is this lack of research on my part as irresponsible as not reading the warning labels on medication?

Today, on the phone, Dr. Fields told me to take aspirin for fever, Imodium for diarrhea.

I'd read on the Internet it was harmful to take Imodium, that it encourages *C. diff.* to bloom. But what do I know? I'm too scared and weak to think straight. I took an aspirin. I swallowed an Imodium caplet.

I'm a good patient.

The clerk who admits me at County Hospital is not interested in the fact that this is my fourth trip to an emergency room or that this mysterious infection vanished before recurring. *Just the symptoms, ma'am.* She writes up her form and points me down a corridor through a set of double doors that magically opens, as if I'm entering hell or Xanadu. Maybe both. By now, Marc has parked the car and caught up with me. We enter my curtained ER cubicle. I curl up under the covers, Marc on a plastic chair beside me.

"I'm Dr. Jones." A friendly young man in a white lab coat pulls back the curtain. "What seems to be the trouble?"

I give him the blow-by-blow with as many lurid details as I can remember. I make it sound as bad as possible. I want the works: every high-tech test performed *now*. I will refuse to leave the hospital without a diagnosis, a cure.

"We'll run some blood tests," he says, upbeat. "And a CAT scan, just to make sure."

A CAT scan! I'm thrilled. I want this superhuman machine peering beneath layers of skin, muscle, tissue, bone, into the core of every organ. Is my kidney acting as a kidney? Liver, a liver? Stomach? Intestines? Pancreas? Bladder? I barely know what else gently throbs beneath my skin's surface. I don't understand the purpose of a pancreas, I realize. I don't question my body. Who wants to know how a body functions? To visualize the inner workings is horrifying. I just assume that every part knows its job and performs dutifully in order to keep this organism known as "me" functioning.

But who am I, really? I always imagined myself in terms of my mind, what I think, as well as how I appear, on the outside. I have reddish hair and hazel eyes. I'm five feet, three inches. Before I got sick, I weighed about 115 pounds. I'm a liberal Democrat. I vote in every election. I teach. Isn't *this* me? Who wants to know more?

But this doctor could care less how I voted in the last election. He doesn't care whether I struggle with being Jewish or not. He wants to know when I last went to the bathroom, what I ate for dinner. "Does this hurt?" He probes my stomach. "This?" So now, wheeled into a giant doughnut of a CAT-scan machine, I imagine "me," who I am, differently. All of who I am is simply contained in a sack of skin. Without this body in some semblance of working order does the rest of me matter?

This isn't my first CAT scan. About two years ago, a routine physical turned up blood in my urine. Three sonograms, one CAT scan, and a clean urine sample later, nothing was found to cause the abnormality. However, the CAT scan showed a speck of "something" on the lower tip of my lung. "It's probably nothing," the doctor said. "These new machines are overly sensitive." But just to be sure, the doctor ordered another CAT scan.

Nothing was found then.

Nothing is found now.

"The CAT scan is negative." Dr. Jones proudly smiles, as if it's *his* body. "Everything looks perfect."

"So what *is* it, then?" I ask.

"Hepatitis A," he says, with confidence. "You have an elevated ALT level, and that's an indication of hep. A infection."

The nurse arrives with an IV, for fluids.

Dr. Fields's Office, November 28

"Hepatitis A?" Dr. Fields exclaims. "Where would you have gotten that? Nothing points to that."

"A slightly elevated . . ." My voice trails off.

I spent Thanksgiving weekend thankful for the hepatitis A diagnosis, the least serious of the hepatitis alphabet—no active recovery regimen, just let it run its course. "In a few weeks, you'll be fine," were Dr. Jones's last words as they rolled me from the emergency room in a wheelchair.

Marc, who has driven me here to Dr. Fields's office, and I glance at each other and shrug. "I guess I picked it up somewhere," I say lamely, my euphoria flattening as yeastily as it'd risen only a few days before.

Dr. Fields appears stymied, not the look you want to see on your doctor's face. "How often have you gone to the bathroom today?" she asks.

"Twice."

"Well *that's* good," she says, wanting to cheer us up—since I probably went about twenty-three times over the endless Thanksgiving weekend.

"But she's not eating," Marc says—Marc, who is usually shy and mild-mannered. *"That's the only reason."*

It's true: I've virtually stopped. I've lost over ten pounds since October 30.

"Well, let's get her on an iv, then," Dr. Fields says. "Maybe now it's time to call Dr. Bright for a colonoscopy. A *C. diff.* infection or Crohn's disease wouldn't show up on a CAT scan."

My dehydrated skin is the texture of leather: black-and-blue bruised leather, from all the ivs. The nurse, searching for a vein, is unable to penetrate it with a needle.

After talking to Dr. Bright, the gastroenterologist, Dr. Fields orders me back to County Hospital. Dr. Bright needs more lab tests before he'll perform the colonoscopy. Besides, maybe a nurse at the hospital will be able to hook me up to an iv.

County Hospital, November 28

I'm assigned a room in the main wing, even though I'm not scheduled to stay the night. My roommate is a suicide survivor under a twenty-four-hour watch. It's not clear why the two of us are paired in a room together, given such dissimilar symptoms. Except that the very randomness itself is symptomatic. But symptomatic of what—like whatever disease I have—is difficult to say.

Now, since Dr. Bright needs more lab-test results, of course I'm unable to provide a stool sample. I'm dried out. Nothing is left. So they feed me anything I want. I realize I'm famished, starving. I devour a chicken-salad sandwich on gooey white bread, an oatmeal cookie, chicken noodle soup, and stewed prunes, which I've never eaten before. There's a good reason. They taste like syrupy dirt. Pond water. Sludge at the bottom of a lake. Initially, all the food stays put in my system. The nurse suggests I walk around in order to speed things along. Up one corridor, down another. Marc accompanies me. Every room we pass is its own stage set or still life of tragedy. I wonder what's wrong with each patient. They probably wonder the same about me.

Later in the afternoon, Dr. Bright gets his specimen. After about a half-dozen useless attempts, the nurse finally plunges an iv into my leathery skin. For four hours I watch the iv bag drip. I sense the suicide patient on the other side of the curtain. She rustles the sheets. Apparently she overdosed. They pumped her stomach. Maybe *this* is the connection: we've both evacuated our skin.

Her young children visit later in the evening. The boy, breathless with drama, informs the nurse that *he* found his mother, called 911. The little girl pokes her head around the curtain to look at me. I stare back. I can't even smile, though I'd like to offer her encouragement, help her survive her mother. But who am I to speak?

On November 29, I receive the following e-mail from Dr. Bright's nurse:

colonoscopy and gastroscopy thurs. 12–1 at Community Hospital. register at 12:15. wednesday 11–30 clear liquid diet. wednesday at 5p. drink 1 and ½ oz. (3 tablespoons) of fleet phospho-soda mixed in 4 oz of water or ginger ale. throughout the evening you must drink at least 3 eight oz glasses of water or clear fruit juice. thursday at 7am drink 1 and ½ oz (3 tablespoons) of fleet phospho-soda mixed in 4 oz of water or ginger ale. follow this with one glass of water or fruit juice. then nothing else by mouth until procedure. Fleet phospho-soda is available without a prescription. purchase 3 oz bottle. call if you have questions.

I must be spotless in order for Dr. Bright to perform the colonoscopy the next day. The phospho-soda tastes, I'm sure, like nuclear waste. I gag with each swallow. My skin shivers sweat. Every ten minutes, or less, I am in the bathroom. By two in the morning, the black-and-white tiles on the bathroom floor seem to strobe. I don't feel the ground beneath my feet. I don't see my chest rise and fall with breath. I am all fluid, floating the nineteen steps between bedroom and bath. By six in the morning, I am polished stainless steel, scrubbed porcelain. Each cell of my body feels rinsed with astringent. My insides are scoured clean.

I am also desert-thirsty, pristine, parched. I feel light enough to float above the bed. The canary-yellow sheets waver like a flying carpet. Emptiness itself is a balm. It asks nothing of me, of my body.

I fantasize about lime popsicles.

Community Hospital, December 1

C. difficile is generally treated for 10 days with antibiotics prescribed by your healthcare provider. The drugs are effective and appear to have few side-effects.

CDC

I curl up under the covers of yet another hospital bed, now in the gastroenterology wing. My thin, freezing body is cocooned in a heated blanket, just as with previous visits to this hospital. All their blankets are baked in ovens with glass windows. I ask for a new one whenever the warmth ebbs. Finally, I'm wheeled in to the procedure area, where Dr. Bright waits for me. Yesterday I typed a two-page, single-spaced outline of the entire saga to read to him: so I won't forget anything; so he'll have a full history, all possible relevant information. Patiently, he waits for me to finish the document. "This time, we'll find out what it is," he promises.

"It's a *C. diff.* infection," he confirms, after I awake from the procedure with full-fledged, blesséd amnesia. I remember nothing since the nurse initiated the anesthetic drip. He prescribes Vancocin, a *good* antibiotic, to try once again to counteract the effects of the bad one, clindamycin. A ten-day supply of Vancocin, twenty-eight pills, 125 mg each, costs $370. One every four hours, a rigid schedule. Who knows what chaos will erupt if I miss a dose? 6:00 p.m. 10:00 p.m. 2:00 a.m. 6:00 a.m. 10:00 a.m. 2:00 p.m. I set the alarm. I stay on schedule.

On December 2, the day after the colonoscopy, Marc buys a copy of the *New York Times* that has an Associated Press article headlined, "Deadly Germ Is Becoming Wider Threat." The item, datelined Atlanta, the headquarters of the Centers for Disease Control, warns of *Clostridium difficile*, commonly seen in people taking antibiotics. The previous year, I learn, it caused one hundred deaths in eighteen months in a hospital in Quebec. Now, according to the CDC, four states (Pennsylvania, New Jersey, Ohio, and New Hampshire) show the same bacteria in healthy people who have *not* been admitted to hospitals, or even taken antibiotics. The bacteria, now resistant to certain antibiotics, work against colon bacteria. Therefore, when patients take certain antibiotics, particularly clindamycin, "competing bacteria die off and *C. difficile* multiplies exponentially." The CDC report focuses on thirty-three cases reported since 2003. Of these cases, one woman, fourteen weeks pregnant with twins, lost the fetuses and also died. The woman had been treated three months earlier with trimethoprim-sulfamethoxazole, for a urinary tract infection. Ten others among the thirty-three had taken clindamycin. However, eight of the thirty-three cases had not taken antibiotics within three months of the onset of symptoms. According to Dr. L. Clifford McDonald, an epidemiologist at the CDC, it's unclear what has caused this outbreak of *C. diff*. "In general," he cautioned, "if you have severe diarrhea, seek attention from a physician."

Marc buys a package of natural-fruit popsicles. I lie in bed, under the quilt, sucking on one. The winter night is still. The house, after the fluorescent lights and jangling equipment in the hospital, is quiet, dimly lit. The lime-green ice slowly melts on my tongue like an unleavened wafer, transubstantiated.

Hours remain seamless, one dissolving into another, one Turner Classic Movie into the next. Days revolve around black-and-white images, popsicles, and the Vancocin cycle. Is this purgatory? Will the popsicles cleanse or purge me? Severe symptoms subside, though my insides feel chafed. When I wash my face, for example, it hurts to lean against the sink. Rather than constant physical pain, however, I experience discomfort; or, more than discomfort, I fear my body will never again be normal. My skin feels dry, transparent. Not enough moisture even to sweat. My hair hangs brittle, bone dry. My lips and knuckles are raw, chapped. Or maybe it is my soul that is raw, transparent, chapped . . . my soul, waiting to be released.

If so, maybe the illness itself is purgatory. My past is catching up with me after all these years. This interior spiritual desert of a soul never blossomed into a lush, leafy oasis—instead, only miraged another new husband, another new location, another new identity—salvation always just around the next bend.

Maybe it took this loud bodily raucousness to stop me in my tracks. To get my attention. To clamor at me, telling me I've been looking for something beyond myself—rather than looking within myself. Now, must I prepare to accept that *this is* me? That whoever this sack of skin is, *is* me. Like it or not. Or, no, erase the "not." Just like it. I must just like *me*.

I never again hear from Dr. Fields. She never calls to ask how I'm doing. I'm not surprised. I find a new doctor, who orders my files from Dr. Fields's office. He tells me that the original lab tests came back normal: I never had a vaginal infection in the first place.

I write to Dr. Fields. I must be sure she knows about her erroneous diagnosis as well as about the potentially deadly prescription. "I want to make sure that you never prescribe this antibiotic to any of your other patients. After spending about ten minutes on the Internet it was clear, even to me, that clindamycin should *only be prescribed in a severe medical emergency.*"

Health insurance covers most of the costs, but the final tally tops $11,000.

Six months after the first symptoms, I still have periodic discomfort and have regained only five pounds of the twenty I lost.

Four years later, Fleet Phospho-Soda, the prescribed medication I ingested in preparation for the colonoscopy, is recalled by the FDA, for possibly causing phosphate nephropathy, or acute kidney injury.

And while I never discover the origin of that ghostly fluttering pain in my abdomen—the cause for my initial appointment with Dr. Fields—it never returns. If it does, I will not attempt to shoo it away. Perhaps I will even welcome and bless it as a signal from beyond, a sign of my heightened appreciation for my body, or at least as a reminder that things could be worse.

The *New* Pat Boone Show

What a crazy world we're living in, huh?

PAT BOONE

....

IN ONE WEEK I MUST FEEL well enough to attend a Pat Boone concert.

I spent this past month in bed, recovering from that *C. diff.* infection, leaving home only for trips to the doctor and the emergency room. Now, I hope, by December 9, I will be able to shower, wash my hair, dress in clothes other than sweats and pajamas. I must look my best for Pat Boone.

Nevertheless, one way or another, Marc, my partner, *will* pack me up in the car for the three-hour drive to the Macomb Center for the Performing Arts in Clinton Township to see him. More than a year has passed since I barged backstage, unannounced, after his concert in that megachurch in Holland, Michigan.

Now, however, Pat Boone has invited me backstage to meet with him after the concert. He invited me, along with Marc, to have "private time" with him.

I'm so touched to hear from you that I'm honestly having trouble writing this.

Sue to Pat Boone

I've barely eaten this past month because of the illness. I lost twenty pounds and look wasted. I *am* wasted. Even the sun shining through the window plunges me into sensory overload. Ditto when the phone rings. When I turn on a light. When the furnace kicks on. When the snowplow rumbles down the street. I can't read, either; even words are risky, exhausting.

My body is consumed only with itself, even as it also seems to be consuming itself. Every molecule not sloughed off as a result of the infection is in overdrive, keeping me—this organism known as "me"—breathing. Consequently, everything outside my body—light, noise, movement, words—is a distraction. Overwhelming.

My sole activity since falling ill is watching the Turner Classic Movie television channel. I'm able to tolerate only black-and-white films since, well, they don't make movies like they used to, back when smoking was good for you, alcohol even better. What a comfort to watch film noir death scenes, or at least actors trying their best to kill themselves the old-fashioned way. To say nothing of all the dead minks draped over socialites' shoulders (back when wearing dead animals was fashionable) in movies such as *A Night to Remember*, depicting the sinking of the *Titanic*. Which, by the way, struck the fatal iceberg on April 14, my birth date.

I mean, technically, I'm not dying, but since I feel as if I am, I'm oddly satisfied, almost comforted, watching film noir lovers blow smoke rings into each other's faces.

Night and day the old films spool, the action slow enough for my dull senses, my dehydrated eyes, to comprehend. Forties gangster movies aren't too strenuous, the high-speed chase scenes probably not careening over fifty miles an hour. Besides, they don't make gangsters like they used to, either, unambiguously dressed in black, uncomplicated, not a shred of motivation, no harking back to unhappy childhoods (brought to you in living color). Likewise, they don't make death like they used to, victims melodramatically writhing before swooning into a pool of gray blood. I can relate. *I* feel melodramatic, myself: seeing Pat Boone one more time is *my* last, dying wish. Even though, as I say, I'm not dying—at least not yet—and should fully recover.

Hour by hour I watch *Angels with Dirty Faces*; *Beware, My Lovely*; *Nobody Lives Forever*; *Dark Victory*; *All This, and Heaven, Too*. I barely distinguish the end of one film from the beginning of another. All the hours this past month blur. I eat a few spoonfuls of applesauce for breakfast. A few grains of rice for lunch, a few more for dinner. One-eighth of a piece of toast, dry. An anorexic fantasy come true, my stomach rejecting the tiniest onslaught of food. My skin feels transparent. Not enough moisture even to sweat.

I look forward to reading your books. Thank you for all the gifts. I feel blessed. And please let me know if you return to Michigan. I'd love to attend another concert . . . and maybe have the wonderful opportunity to meet you again.

Sue to Pat Boone

The only words I am able to read right now are Pat Boone's, the autographed copy of *The Miracle of Prayer*, which he sent me. And even though they *also* don't make religion like they used to—back when Christ was Christ and not Jerry Falwell or Pat Robertson or Mel Gibson or even, well, Pat Boone—I figure: *What the hell?* It's a way for time, for the illness, to pass more quickly while I wait to see Pat Boone. So I read page after page, chapter after chapter. I also pray—just in case—in order to be on the safe side. I follow Pat Boone's instructions, wanting to believe in miracles, the miracle of prayer: sudden wealth, cure from disease, a job promotion—you name it. "I'm telling you—and I'll amply prove it—that the power of genuine prayer can result in incredible, miraculous happenings that can only be explained in supernatural terms," Pat Boone writes in his book. "I just want you to understand that approaching an interested and loving Creator/God can be your best option, not your last resort."

God makes all good things happen, if you believe.

Yes, *if* I believe I'm getting well—*if* only I believe God will make me well—I *will* get better. I will. I will.

About a year after I handed Pat Boone that letter backstage, he responded. We've since exchanged several e-mails and letters. In one, he quotes from the Bible: "God works everything together for our good, to those who love Him and are called according to His purpose." The letter goes on to reassure me: "He picks up the pieces and fashions something good out of . . . horrific occurrences." I know Pat Boone refers to my childhood, but I want to believe that God (or Pat Boone) knows I need help *now* to recover from this illness.

In this weakened state, I want prayer, God, icons . . . the touch of Pat Boone's hand to make me better.

I grasp a marble in my atheistic fist while reading *The Miracle of Prayer*. It will anchor me to the ground so I won't float away, given my thinness, given the slenderness of my new, tender (un-believing) beliefs. Or perhaps I hold the marble as a totem: a ro-sary bead, a sign of existence, a medallion powerful enough to keep me alive until I see Pat Boone. *Please, God, let me get better. Please let me see Pat Boone after the concert.* The marble will help me! Its bluish-green surface resembles the earth in photographs from outer space. Where God lives!

Or is it all voodoo? Superstition? If I hold the marble in my left fist, I'll get better; if I hold it in my right, I'll be switched at birth and be Pat Boone's daughter.

‡ ‡ ‡

"We'll get there soon," a woman nicknamed Mom says to Marc and me.

The last note of the "Pat Boone Christmas Concert" fades into the frigid Michigan night. Mom, in a blue sweat suit, slowly taps her three-pronged cane along a sterile linoleum floor backstage at the Macomb Center. Her cropped gray hair frames her wiz-ened face, her moist mouth. Despite her name, I more envision her with crystals and tarot cards (or even shopping a blue-light special at K-Mart) than in a kitchen baking an apple pie. She glances up at me sideways, a glimpse from the corner of her eye. She knows I'm rushing her along, trying to hurry her, my footsteps almost in front of hers, even though I don't know the way to the green room. My main objective is simply to see Pat Boone before I collapse.

And while I wish I could say the weakness in my limbs is from the thought of seeing him, this is only partially true. Today, after all, is virtually the first time in five weeks I've been out of bed. So, alternatively, I want to grab Mom's cane for *me* to lean upon, as much as I want to kick the cane out from under her, take her down, trample her as I race along the passageways to find Pat Boone on my own. *Now.* I am anxious to see him. And even though he invited me backstage (via his assistant, via e-mail) after the concert, still, I worry he might slip from the theater before I find him.

We wander down one seemingly endless corridor after another. Photographs of entertainers who performed here over the years hang from walls, but no echo of past shows remains. No stomping feet. No clapping. No whistles. The photographed smiles are glassy, static, still. I pass rows of faces—some familiar, most not—following the white noise of fluorescent light, the dull tapping of Mom's rubber-tipped cane, lost in a maze of hallways through the underworld, much like the ones in the hospital.

Marc lags behind. He probably hopes to be lost in this maze, make a wrong turn, and end up, say, at a John Mayall and the Bluesbreakers concert, a group that recently performed here. Earlier this evening, during the show, Marc cringed as Pat Boone chided members of the audience to use the Christian greeting "Merry Christmas," as opposed to the religiously neutral "Happy Holidays." Later, when Pat Boone sang "Santa Claus Is Praying to Jesus," Marc slid down in his seat. Marc, a liberal Democrat like myself, would rather be almost anywhere else than here. Yet, while Marc is nominally here only to accompany me, surely even he knows that, although Pat Boone is a right-wing Christian, he's also, well, *Pat Boone* . . . and they don't make pop stars like they used to, either.

"'What a crazy world we're living in . . . '" Marc whispered during the concert, quoting Pat Boone's e-mail greeting to me.

"*Huh?*" I whispered back, adding the last word of Pat Boone's sentence—a tag line that's now a running gag between us. Well, it's a joke to Marc, but I myself am uncertain whether to take it ironically or not. Huh? Huh! Yes, the word that seemingly sums it all up, though I'm not altogether sure why. What exactly does the "huh?" reveal about Pat Boone?

Hi Sue!

What a crazy world we're living in, huh?

These lines begin Pat Boone's first e-mail to me. Literally, he must mean it *is* a crazy world in that, after all these years, I finally meet him only twenty minutes away from my house. He also invites me to write back to him, asks me to stay in touch. He signs his e-mail, "Warmly, Pat Boone."

But what is the subtext to the "crazy world"? What is the subtext to the "huh"?

Pat Boone sang his oldies during tonight's concert, even though it's a Christmas show: "Bernadine," "Moody River," "Love Letters in the Sand." He reprised "April Love," accompanied by his routine of finding a young girl to join him onstage. Just as during his concert in Holland, Michigan, he asked her for a kiss (a peck) on the cheek. Pat Boone also handed the girl a bouquet of flowers. She awkwardly held them, unsure what to do, caught with a stranger in the spotlight.

‡ ‡ ‡

"I hope you understand why I checked to make sure you were really invited backstage," Mom says as we continue our trek. "We can't just take anyone's word."

Earlier, in the lobby, I underwent an elaborate screening process, asked by the lobby manager, in her red jacket, to produce a copy of the e-mail from Pat Boone's assistant inviting me backstage. But because the lobby manager thought, perhaps, I faked the e-mail, she double-checked by cell phone with Pat Boone's travel manager. Marc and I finally got the "go ahead." Word came back via walkie-talkie informing us which door off the lobby Mom would unlock. This door—granting backstage access to heaven—or at least Pat Boone.

"You know," our guide to the green room adds, "if we didn't check credentials, everyone would try to get backstage to meet him."

In reality, Marc and I hovered by the backstage door alone. The sedate crowd peacefully filed from the auditorium out to the parking lots. So when Mom finally unlocked the door, Marc and I didn't push through crowds. Mom didn't shake her cane at throngs of fans. Only Marc and I waited, me squinting through the hairline crack between the double doors. So before Mom unlocked it, I spied her shuffling toward us.

"Have you met him yet?" I ask Mom.

She nods, her head hunched over her curved shoulders. "He's very nice. You'll like him."

Then, just as we round another corner, I catch a glimpse of him. He still wears his white-fringed sequined jacket, white pants, white boots, white silky shirt. White: Pat Boone's signature color. Back in junior high school, I found this unambiguous, good-guy white reassuring. Now, before I call a greeting, Marc and I are quickly ushered into the green room. "He'll be in to see you shortly," Mom says, shutting the door behind her, leaving Marc and me alone. I collapse on the couch.

Marc and I ate dinner at Ernie's Restaurant, about a mile away, before the concert. I, however, only tentatively forked a few mouthfuls of salmon, three swallows of baked potato. An elderly couple, in a booth behind us, settled in for dinner as well. We eavesdropped on their conversation with the waitress.

"We just came from the Pat Boone concert," the man says, referring to the matinee.

"Who's Pat Boone?" the teenage waitress asks.

"He was a singer before you were born," the man explains.

Marc leans forward in the booth. "'What a crazy world . . .'"

"*Huh?*" I say on cue.

‡ ‡ ‡

Pat Boone enters the green room, aglow in yellow corduroy slacks, a yellow shirt, an orange cashmere sweater. He wears a gold pinkie ring, a wedding band, a gold necklace. During the concert I was overwhelmed—after being in isolation for a month—by his white-white image, as well as by the scent of so many people, the band, the music, the applause. I closed my eyes. Leaned my head in my palm. Had trouble breathing. And now, as Pat Boone glides through the door, I am once again breathless. This is the most color I've absorbed all month. Gold. Yellow. Orange. A sunrise.

Marc and I stand up from the couch.

"Can I hug you?" Pat Boone asks, smiling.

When he enfolds my frail, ailing body, it feels like a laying on of hands.

Pat Boone will cure me.

"Would you like to sit here?" Marc nods toward the couch, beside me, where he'd been sitting.

Pat Boone shakes his head, pulling a chair directly in front of me. "This way I can see her better." Meaning me. As he settles onto the chair, he adds, "I hope you liked the concert." He explains he arrived in Michigan late last night from a previous show in North Carolina. "I was tired."

"You were wonderful," Marc and I assure him.

Pat Boone points to the velvet flower embroidered on my lavender jacket. "At home, hanging on my wall, I have a photograph of a flower growing up through concrete," he says. "Like you. Your childhood. You are like a flower growing up through concrete."

This is Pat Boone, too. Not just the religious conservative. But the April-love-love-letters-in-the-sand Pat Boone. The Pat Boone offering innocence. Redemption. Answers. Even in this crazy world we're living in, huh?

"You teach, don't you," he continues, more a statement than a question. "I wanted to teach. I graduated from Columbia University with a degree in English literature. I wanted to teach young people."

He is as I always envision: perfect hair, smile, teeth, wife, daughters, career, life. But I struggle to pay attention as he talks. I'm weak, dizzy. I'm just hoping not to pass out. Even as I lean toward him, smiling, an enormous sadness wells up inside me. I want to tell Pat Boone I've been ill. I want him to know I was worried I'd miss the concert. I'm equally sad that I look thin and frail. I'd wanted to be perfect for him, match his own seeming perfection. Instead, my skirt hangs loose. I notice a small rip in the flower on my jacket. My hair is limp, my face wan. My only hope is that he won't notice how sick I appear. I don't want to spoil this meeting after anticipating it for so long.

"On the day I graduated," Pat Boone continues, "I'd just left Gina Lollobrigida at the studio. I got out of a taxi in Central Park and lay back on the grass looking at the clouds, trying to decide what to do with my life. I already had the television show, hit records. Four daughters. But I still wasn't sure about a career. My father was in construction, but I knew I didn't want to do that. My mother was a nurse, but I hate the sight of blood."

Pat Boone laughs, adding, "Since I still had to fulfill contractual obligations, I stayed with the singing. But as a teacher, I'd have been a role model, setting an example for all those young lives."

"You do that with your singing," I say. "You set an example for *me*."

Pat Boone: an example of an ideal, or an idealized father? An ideal, or an idealized Christian? Entertainer?

Pat Boone has sold forty-five million records, or units, has had thirty-eight Top 40 hits over the course of his career. Right now, *Billboard Magazine* lists him as the number-ten rock recording artist in history. But more than success as an entertainer, he also started a volunteer organization for Cambodian refugees. He wrote the lyrics to the song "Exodus." The Israeli government appointed him Christian Ambassador of Tourism and gave him the Israel Cultural Award. He made it possible for more than two hundred thousand Jews to make *aliyah* to Israel.

Pat Boone sang "April Love" for Queen Elizabeth. Sang "Ain't That a Shame" to President Eisenhower. Sang "It's a Sin to Tell a Lie" to President Nixon.

Milked a cow on the *Tonight Show* with Johnny Carson.

In *Together*, Pat Boone writes, "[I] call [myself an] 'adopted Jew' because of the deep realization that everything we hold sacred as Christians has come directly out of biblical Judaism. I really feel that no Jew can feel more identification with Israel and all the historical biblical sites than a devout Christian; in fact, I've told . . . rabbis that I see Judaism as divided into four main branches—Orthodox, Conservative, Reformed, and Christian!"

Pat Boone: Christian? Jew? Who?

On the jacket of his newer, heavy-metal CD, *In a Metal Mood: No More Mr. Nice Guy*, Pat Boone sits astride a motorcycle in black leather and chains. Albeit he's a seventy-year-old man in black leather and chains—and *not* a chain strung with a cross.

Yet Pat Boone, either in black leather *or* his trademark white bucks, is still, well, *Pat Boone*. Isn't he?

"Oh, but I made some mistakes with my daughters," Pat Boone

is now saying. "I didn't mean to, of course. I love them very much. They always knew how much I loved them."

"You *always* loved them." I nod, confirming.

"Cherry wrote her book on her anorexia."

Cherry Boone is his eldest daughter. "It's a moving story," I say. "I read it."

"All the pressures of show business. It's difficult. Fifty years in the business."

I imagine Pat Boone gazing up at that blue sky in Central Park. Early spring. Fifty years ago *he* was early spring, a golden sheen in that one moment . . . alone by himself in the park, already a star, yes, but maybe not yet fully committed to *the* Pat Boone. *That* image. Maybe a trace of Charles Eugene Boone (his real name) remained, on that day he makes this decision about the rest of his life, this last moment *before* he's intrinsically, incontrovertibly *Pat Boone*.

Forever.

Whoever you are, I always loved you.

I wore my own pair of white bucks back in junior high school. No, I bought a pair of white bucks, but I only wore them inside my house. No. Only in my bedroom. I sat on my bed, legs straight, admiring the neatly tied shoes. The pristine leather. Spotless soles. Crisp laces. Perfect stitching. No one else ever touched them. Even I rarely brushed my fingers across them, not wanting to mar or stain the surface. The scent of new leather was sweeter than any gardenia corsage I ever received from a boyfriend. Before going outside, I rewrapped the shoes in tissue paper. In my closet was a locked drawer meant for valuables. I placed the shoes inside it. And turned the key.

Pat Boone's road manager enters the room after fifteen minutes.

The audience is over.

"Can I kiss you good-bye?" Pat Boone asks. "On the cheek."

I nod.

Marc snaps photos with his camera. In one, Pat Boone wraps his arm around my shoulders. In another, which the road manager shoots, Pat Boone drapes one arm around Marc, the other, me. We all stare at the camera. Marc appears determined: He *will* get through this. I seem dazed. *Pat Boone just kissed me.* But is it a kiss I only wanted back in junior high school? Who did he hug, kiss? Me, or a small, younger ghost of me?

And Pat Boone? Even now, months later, I'm not quite sure whom I see in the photograph. That smile. Yellow and orange clothes. The color of morning or sunset? Or maybe the photo is of only a face, that famous face, that dazzling young hopeful smile refusing to age, to fade. Still full of Pat Boonedom.

Or maybe *I* am the one full of Pat Boonedom. I was first riveted by him while watching *The Pat Boone Chevy Show* on our black-and-white Zenith television . . . before the Cuban Missile Crisis, before I donned love beads and bell-bottoms and demonstrated against the war in Vietnam, before the first man walked on the moon, before picking apricots on a kibbutz in Israel. Before marrying.

Pat Boone is innocent, all-American teenage summers at Palisades Park, Bermuda shorts and girls in shirtwaist dresses, corner drugstores, pearly nail polish, prom corsages, rain-scented lilacs, chenille bedspreads and chiffon scarves, jukebox rock and roll spilling across humid evenings, back when linoleum was better, more real, than wood. He is Ivory soap, grape popsicles, screened porches at the Jersey shore, bathing suits hung to dry, the smell of must and mildew tempered by sun and salt. He is a boardwalk Ferris wheel, its spinning lights filling dark spaces between stars. He remains all the things that, as you age, you miss—the memory of this past smelling sweeter than honeysuckle on the Fourth of July.

Did those Pat Boone summers really exist—or only in memory? Memory, its own accurate reality, still leaves you sick with longing for Pat Boonedom: a hopeful antidote for time spooling forward into the present, into the future—nostalgia more real, more intense than the past itself.

If only Pat Boone could make the past like he used to. If only . . . since they don't make the future like they used too, either. All you have is one snapshot moment, when all of time coalesces.

Like this: You stare at photographs of Pat Boone's family in his book *Together*. You trace a finger across indelible family portraits of them on their bicycle built for six. Photographs of four generations of Boones, a family all together . . . whereas you, yourself, have no children, two divorced husbands, two dead cats, estranged relatives. Whereas you still feel as if you've never been anyone's daughter. Pat Boone who, in his books about God and religion, in his teachings, provides answers to existence. Whereas you have no answers. None.

And no white bucks any longer either. You now realize you don't know what happened to the pair you bought in junior high. Just lost—like so much else along the way.

Except for this longing, a pale throb of memory, a hum just below the surface of all the years since you first saw his image, first heard him sing.

‡ ‡ ‡

Pat Boone and his manager leave the green room. By the time Marc and I collect our coats and enter the corridor, they're gone. Vanished. Without a trace. Perhaps taken up in the Rapture, Marc might joke. I glance around. Which hallway back to the lobby? No one to ask. No Pat Boone. No sign from God pointing the way.

Huh?

Pat Boone hugged me. Yet my ailing body feels no different. So, no, not a laying on of hands, after all. Yet, *yet*—he noticed the embroidered flower on my jacket. Decades after my teenage crush, he touched me. Talked to me. It *is* a crazy world in which I've finally met Pat Boone after all these years. And crazy that I'm ill when the dream comes true. Or ironic, huh?

It is this *almost*-ironic, *almost*-earnest, *almost*-heartfelt "huh?" that saves Pat Boone. He sings the soulful "Moody River," after all. He sings the jazzy "Tutti Frutti." But Pat Boone's river is never too moody. His *tutti frutti* isn't too down and dirty. Pat Boone is neither too tutti nor too frutti. He's not too "au rutti," either, as if I know what "au rutti" even means.

Pat Boone *is* pure "huh?" with a question mark.

The joys were often sweeter because they came by surprise; the wounds, though they hurt like crazy, were also surprises, usually not preceded by dread and apprehension; and most of the fun and laughs were sweeter because they jumped up and grabbed us, with little or no preview. Isn't your life like that? Isn't the most precious escape the one that comes when there seems to be no hope and you are already resigned to your fate?

Pat Boone, *Together*

Huh?

Once Pat Boone's music, his lyrics, his voice, his smile offered hope, the promise of a safe, bleached suburbia for all those bobby-soxer Christian girls. Wannabe Christian girls, too.

Pat Boone is hopeful *for* me. It is his own never-ending hope that I love.

And if Pat Boone considers himself a Christian Jew, then I can be an unbelieving believer, right? For here I am backstage in a green room with the father I always wanted, for the very first time.

Boone *ex machina.*

It *is* a crazy world, huh?

Oh, Jesus, *yes.*

My Sorted Past

MY PARENTS AND I STROLL ACROSS shaved lawns at Grossinger's, a resort in the Catskill Mountains' Borscht Belt. Warmth from the tennis courts, the golf course, and the post–Labor Day blank hotel windows rises and shimmers before dispersing into autumn. I notice a lone couple on chaise lounges as we approach the silent swimming pool. "Look," I whisper to my parents. "Elizabeth Taylor and Eddie Fisher."

My mother scrounges in her bag for a piece of paper. All she finds is a square white card, a reminder for my upcoming orthodontist's appointment. I flip it over. The back is blank. Perfect.

My parents stand behind me as I hand the card and a blue ball-point pen to Elizabeth Taylor. Her perfume, in my unimaginative teenage mind, must be Chanel No. 5. A pastel chiffon scarf cups her black hair. Her eyes *are* violet . . . or maybe simply deep with loss and desire. Pink lipstick. Although she doesn't quite smile, she doesn't seem annoyed at the intrusion. She props the card on her tortoiseshell purse with a silver clasp. She clicks open the pen and scrawls her name, the "E" in Elizabeth and the "y" in Taylor fancy flourishes in her well-rehearsed autograph. Her diamond ring reflects her starry life. She passes purse, card, and pen to Eddie Fisher, who signs below her. His smile is broader, more eager, though his autograph is smaller than hers, humbler.

I recall from reading movie magazines that Eddie Fisher's first job at Grossinger's was as a boat boy on the lake. He later returned as a singing sensation. He married Debbie Reynolds here at Grossinger's. Only recently Eddie Fisher married Elizabeth Taylor (Michael Todd, her third husband, died in a plane crash), after their sordid affair, after he abandoned Debbie Reynolds, after Elizabeth Taylor converted to Judaism.

My mother once worked as a secretary for Michael Todd, but she doesn't mention this tenuous connection.

Other than to ask for the autograph, I say nothing further. Yet I wish I could recline in the empty lounge beside her, pretend to be her child, a famous Hollywood daughter. I slip the card in my pocket so I won't lose or smudge it. I envision bringing it to school. My friends will *ooh* and *aah* as if Elizabeth Taylor sprinkled stardust on me. As if fame can be conferred upon all who, even momentarily, enter its secret violet circle.

My parents and I continue across the stone patio, heading toward the parking lot. I glance back. Elizabeth Taylor and Eddie Fisher haven't moved. They pose in their lounges, not speaking, not holding hands. Perhaps she pauses on this still autumn day to sort out her past as she learns the new role of sedate widow . . . or recently converted Jewish wife.

In this silence, you would never suspect her swirling life. She seems almost lonely. Based on the movie magazines, surely I know the *real* her, the real woman's moods and thoughts.

How can she be lonely?

Soon she will wing back to Hollywood, whereas I will remain a whisper in the presence of fame, ebbing as quickly as the sound of the click of a ballpoint pen.

Years later, now an adult, I receive a phone call one evening out of the blue (or perhaps violet) from an independent Hollywood producer. She says she discovered me—well, not the *actual* me sitting at a drugstore lunch counter at Hollywood and Vine, but at least my memoir—in the Beverly Hills public library. She wants to purchase the movie rights.

To prepare for the interview with the screenwriter, I search through boxes stuffed with old photographs. She wants to see photos from the years when I acted out a sexual addiction—my misguided search for love—the focus of the movie. Photos capture time. *Look: this is the lonely and confused girl I once was, right here. Look: here's a wedding photo, back when I wanted to believe I could be an ordinary, normal wife.* Here I am, in all these photos, as if I'm holding many variations of "me" in my hand.

In the midst of sorting photographs, I discover the square white card in a leather keepsake album. I trace a fingertip across those familiar autographs. I easily lift the card off the page, the old glue cracking. On the flip side is the appointment for the orthodontist.

Richard A. Lowy, D.D.S.
302 Main St., Chatham, New Jersey
MErcury 5–2303
If unable to keep this appointment please give due notice.

A nurse scrawled my name in a blank space, along with the date of the appointment: "Oct. 3, 11 o'clock."

MErcury: Those old, evocative telephone exchanges.

In the movie *Butterfield 8*, Elizabeth Taylor plays the role of Gloria, who, according to the movie's promotion, is *"part model, part call-girl, and all man-trap.*

"This is Danny . . . who knew that no one man owned Gloria!

"This is Liggett . . . who called Gloria whenever his wife was away!

"The glamour girl who wakes up ashamed! The most desirable woman in town and the easiest to find . . . just call B Utterfield 8.

"She must hold many men in her arms to find the one man she could LOVE!"

These could (almost) be advertisements for my own movie, my own life—minus the exclamation marks, minus the "glamour"—but full of the shame.

The screenplay is completed. The actors are cast. A date is set to begin production. I fly to Vancouver, British Columbia, to visit the set.

"A photograph!" I say, on cue, holding up a small, digital camera.

I recite my two words of dialogue as I emerge from a group of extras, partygoers. In the scene, the actors playing my father, mother, husband, and me gather together, smiling, as I snap the picture.

The scene depicts my parents' anniversary party, and Grant, the director, asked if I'd like a cameo. The action takes place not on a sound stage, but in the dining room of a real family's home, rented by the production company, to represent my parents' house. This McMansion, though, is nothing like any place my family ever lived.

This photograph that I, playing the role of photographer, snap, portrays how my family always appeared perfect and loving in public. It was a façade, however, masking the *real* family, one in which my father misloved me in private, when I was a child.

The actress playing my mother flubs her line.

I step forward and, again, say, "A photograph!" I press the shutter.

This time, the actor playing my father forgets to smile. Also, one of the extras, perhaps wanting to be noticed in the crowd, gyrates her arms. "No dancing," Grant instructs. The actors and I, as well as the *real* cameraman filming the scene, set up for take three.

Earlier I sat in the hair-and-makeup trailer beside Sally Pressman, the actress portraying me. Eye shadow, liner, mascara, lip gloss, powder, blush. Staring into the mirror, I watched my transformation. Yet there's only so much that makeup can fix. I momentarily imagined I was Sally, a television star, with people waiting on me, enhancing my appearance, always surrounded, as we are now, by trailers for the cast, the crew, the production office, as well as trucks carrying cameras, lighting, sound equipment, props, and a catering service.

In my real life, I sit for hours in a room in my house with messy hair, wrinkled sweats, alone with a laptop computer.

Now I'm almost afraid to breathe. I don't want to muss my hair or smudge my makeup. At least I haven't flubbed my line. Even though my dialogue consists of only two words, I'm nervous I won't speak with the correct inflection. Is it "a photograph?" or "a photograph!"? I decide the latter, though no one coaches me. I'm equally fearful that I'll appear too serious. I'm supposed to smile, which is difficult, having dreaded my real parents' *real* anniversary party years ago, where I also pretended we were a happy family.

Or suppose my smile looks like a grin, since those braces I once wore didn't correct my overbite. I want a smile as dainty as Elizabeth Taylor's.

My previous acting experience consists of the time in second grade when I was supposed to star as Little Red Riding Hood. On opening night I stepped from the wings to walk through the dark, cardboard-cutout forest. I wore a cape with matching hood sewn by my mother and carried a wicker basket with food for my sick grandmother. In reality (whatever that is), the basket must have been empty. Then, too, I pretended to be a happy little girl, just as instructed during rehearsals.

I *was* happy, at first. The starched cotton hood felt like a helmet, protection. I skipped from tree to cutout tree, believing that my magical cape was sewn with lightning and fire. Maybe, despite the script, I even believed it would protect me from the big, bad wolf.

Suddenly, a rustle.

Is that what I heard? What disturbed me?

Perhaps I sensed the wolf prowling the path behind me, gaining on me. Perhaps I glimpsed him from the corner of my eye—or maybe he appeared only in my mind's eye—a furry, humid beast. I reached for the bow under my chin to tighten it, to assure myself nothing had slipped out of place, that my otherwise bare throat was protected. I was supposed to pretend not to even anticipate the wolf before he approached me.

I couldn't.

In a breath, I forgot all the stage directions as well as my lines. Instead of waiting for the wolf, I crouched behind a tree, hiding. The wolf, cunning enough not to eat Little Red Riding Hood in public, was simply supposed to ask where my grandmother lived, was supposed to rush to her house before my arrival, eat the grandmother, don her clothes, wait for Little Red Riding Hood, then eat her, too.

I pulled the hood low over my face. I tugged the cloak around my body as if it could confer safety, invisibility, invincibility. The scent of glue and paste and waxy crayons rose from the floorboards of the makeshift stage, but it was as if I inhaled dank leaves and tangled vines.

I ran from the stage, crying.

I ruined the play, of course. Mortified, I refused to return to school for six months . . . even though the real wolf lived inside my own house.

"A photograph!" I say.

I wish real life had retakes.

I wish I could rewind my life back to the second-grade stage of *Little Red Riding Hood*. Then I could redo not just that scene, but the whole story. Instead of hiding from the wolf, I could lie in wait.

It takes less than an hour to read the entire script for the TV movie—105 double-spaced pages with wide margins, including stage directions. Before filming began, I wondered how the whole story could be conveyed so quickly. Even the shoot will last just three weeks, while the movie itself will run only two hours, including commercials. Now, watching the anniversary scene, I understand how, as with the snap of a camera ("A photograph!"), the movie condenses long paragraphs I wrote in the book into a moment of action.

Sally, then, will recover from my childhood and sort out my past in either three weeks or two hours, depending . . . whereas in the book it takes several hundred pages and, in reality, took years.

Cast and crew move to a new location, another house rented by the production company. It represents my home. I sit on a black canvas director's chair, my name inserted into a plastic sleeve on its back. I scan the salmon-colored schedule sheet. This sheet lists each scene location as well as a one-line description of the action. The scene currently being shot bears the notation "the camera follows Sue's cheating path."

Sally prepares to leave the house to meet a man, an illicit lover, scant minutes after her husband departs for work. She applies perfume to her wrists, gloss to her lips, and walks downstairs. After she picks up the car keys to walk out the door, the camera, situated behind her, follows the back of her head before panning down to her legs.

Except, in the mirage of movies, they're *not* Sally's legs. A body double is used in order to give Sally time to rest.

In the monitor I watch the feet that resemble Sally's, in high heels, walking toward the door. . . . *My own real feet once, in midnight-blue velvet slippers with metallic stars sprinkled across the toes, charmed shoes to cast a spell on those illicit men, to conjure sex into love. . . .*

The camera, in the second half of the scene, tracks the real Sally—not her body double—hair messy, now sneaking back home from the motel. . . . *Kicking off those starry shoes, I stepped back inside my real house. I carried them, as if the shoes had lost their sorcery . . . or my cheating feet had lost their way.*

Except in real life, testing the waters of recovery, I also wore those midnight-blue shoes to my first meeting of Sex Addicts Anonymous. It was as if, while *I* wanted to recover, my feet did not. The shoes themselves seemed to hold out hope they could lead me along an enchanted path—wandering toward some impossible love—or at least one last fling. I slithered onto a metal folding chair in a church basement. I crossed my legs, swinging a foot back and forth to attract the attention of the guy sitting beside me. My shoe sparkled starshine.

Love the shoes, he said, inviting me out for coffee after the meeting.

Ashamed, I never wore them again.

The director calls out, "Sue's on the set. Sally's on the set."

I am not, in fact, on the set. I am outside the range of the camera, watching. At times, they call Sally "Sue"; more than once I respond.

It is Sally who emerges from a dressing room in the lower level of the house. She climbs the stairs past the living room up to the bedroom. She wears a bodysuit, a terrycloth bathrobe over it. The upcoming sex scene will be a closed set to protect the actors' privacy. A few minutes later, the male actor (a robe also covering his bodysuit), with whom I have an affair, appears.

I watch him follow Sally (or me?) up the stairs.

I imagine the bodysuits to be constructed of thin rubber, though I never see them. They must be molded tight against the skin—both disguise and protection.

In real life, when I met men, I climbed stairs—to apartments or motel rooms—without protection or body double. When I was a college student in Boston, a lover, old enough to be my father, gave me a maroon cashmere scarf—armor as flimsy as a red cotton hood. For years after the affair ended, I hid the scarf in a lavender box, a jumble of mementos from men. The souvenirs lasted longer than those random lovers: all that remained of the affairs, of the men.

Later in the movie, Sally will retrieve a facsimile maroon scarf from a facsimile treasure chest and press it to *her* face—an addict seeking the scent of a man—a temporary high. In the salmon-colored, one-liner scene notes, it says, "Sue's treasure chest reveals her sorted past."

Someone forgets a pair of headphones on the couch in the almost-deserted living room. Even without slipping them over my ears, I hear the disembodied voices of the actors and crew upstairs in the bedroom, planning the sex scene.

Grant's voice instructs Sally and the male actor how to pose in bed. They whisper to each other. Sheets rustle.

Through the headphones, I eavesdrop on my life.

Is this me? Who was I back then, when I lived these events? Who was I when I wrote the book and interpreted my own life? Who am I now, watching and listening to someone else define me? Who is *that* me? *This* me?

All the scenes during my three-day visit to the set show me struggling with myself, my marriage, my addiction. Grant told me they'd filmed the scenes of Sally in recovery at the beginning of the shoot.

About an hour later, the actor playing the dangerous man slinks down the stairs as if he really had committed adultery. He is sweaty. His hair is messy. He looks done in.

I feel done in.

Upstairs, the set once again open, I watch Sally calling her (my?) husband, long distance, after her (my?) lover has left. She sits on the floor in a robe, a bottle of wine beside her. As if the sex scene has unnerved her, Sally struggles to remember her lines—for the first time since I arrived on set. She props the script by the nightstand, hidden from the camera. She speaks the typed words that plead with my husband to never stop loving her, pleading her own love, too: lying and not. Sincere and not. From guilt, from fear, she promises an impossibly better marriage. Scripted words *I* once spoke . . . memorized lines I imagined a wife should say even as, in the quicksand denial of addiction, I didn't know the definition of love, of husband, of wife.

It's not true that my only other acting experience was as Little Red Riding Hood.

In real life, I convinced a cuckolded husband that I loved him. Lost and confused, I convinced dangerous men—as well as myself—that I loved them as well. It was guerrilla theater. It was psychodrama. It was theater of the absurd. Even, at times, black comedy. What it wasn't, was pretty.

A paperback edition of my book is slated for publication, to coincide with the movie. For the new cover, I send my editor an old photograph of myself taken beside a boardwalk at the New Jersey shore. It represents the way I've always envisioned the part of me that's an addict. I wear a black-leather jacket. My fist clamps a hip. I look cool, detached, seductive. I lean against a wood pillar. Carved into it are the words:

Love

Is

Here

Every

Day!

The photo is dark and grainy. My editor explains that the art department can't sharpen it up. It won't work for the cover.

Grant had taken a photo of Sally posed against a similar background, with the same slogan. The publisher uses that image on the cover instead.

It's unnerving at first. Later I grow comfortable with this doppelgänger.

After all, there are—have been—so many other selves, real and imagined. For years, I never even knew to label myself a sex addict. I merely thought of my life as an out-of-control mess, one failed dress rehearsal after another, as I tried out various identities, hoping to find one that would fit. I was convinced that eventually I'd lose everything: friends, husband, job, house. I envisioned myself as one of those ladies, all my worldly possessions in two paper bags. I would live in a refrigerator carton over a subway grate in New York City.

At the same time (never mind the contradiction), I *also* fantasized that, eventually, one of the illicit men *would* fall in love with me. We'd melodramatically run off together into the happily-ever-after (faux) sunset.

No version—not real life, not the book, not the screenplay, not even the Hollywood movie—manages to bring *that* ending to life. Who I am, now, is a woman thankful for more realistic endings.

The premiere of the movie is scheduled for April 19. I haven't seen the final cut. I'm a wreck during the weeks leading up to it.

Even though the book I wrote reveals more secrets than the movie, still, only people who really want to know about my experience read it. Plus, a reader imagines scenes as she wishes. For the movie, however, anyone casually channel surfing might suddenly land smack in the middle of my life. You will see *this and this and this* on the television screen. I fear my secrets are more naked, more exposed on a TV screen in living color.

Besides, you can't possibly know when any one person might be reading your book. But now it's exactly 9:00 p.m., April 19. Here is your life on TV!

Another part of me, however, looks forward to the movie, as if it will provide answers, shed light on my life. After all, I haven't yet seen my recovery.

My first reaction to the movie is to be dumbstruck by the music. A soundtrack!

In real life, my own background music tracked my moods and phases. As a child—listening to the "Terry Theme" from Charlie Chaplin's movie *Limelight*—I fantasized being a lost ballerina saved by a tramp. One Pat Boone song after another enhanced my teenage dreams. Jim Morrison and The Doors pounded my hard-core sex addict years. Frank Sinatra, old enough to be my father and the favorite singer of the married maroon-scarf man, crooned "The Lady Is a Tramp" and "Strangers in the Night." More recently, postrecovery, I endlessly played Elton John's "I'm Still Standing."

The party scene rolls onto the screen.

A photograph!

I'm not as pretty as Sally Pressman . . . or Elizabeth Taylor. I want to look like a movie star. I want to share their beauty. I share their Jewishness, so why not? But maybe that's not really me, anyway, snapping the photo. How can it be me when I'm *here*, sitting in a room in my house in Michigan? I feel as if I'm having an out-of-body experience. I'm disguised as a photographer. Sally is disguised as me. Or she is me. She cries when I would have cried. She feels lost when I'm lost.

After the movie is over, I receive an e-mail at my own e-mail address but with the salutation "Dear Sally Pressman." I reply that I am, in fact, *me*—which is essentially what I myself have been struggling to articulate for years. Or articulate who I've been struggling to be.

Sally hands me her copy of my book to autograph, right before I leave the set in Vancouver. She'd scrawled stars and check marks in the margins to note certain passages. Some sentences are underlined, others highlighted. I sign my name on the title page, with a blue pen, along with a little message.

I regret that I never asked Sally for *her* autograph. But what would she have signed for me? A loop of celluloid? My copy of the salmon-colored schedule of scenes? Perhaps she could have signed her name beside the line about Sue's sorted past.

Of course the word "sorted" was meant to be "sordid." But I like the mistake. In the movie, in my book, in my flesh-and-blood life, I've sorted through selves, as if through old photographs, in order to discover one image that's the one authentic me. How many costumes and masks did I change to wander through one small life?

A few weeks after the movie airs, toward the end of May, I'm in a local health food store purchasing a package of gingersnaps and a vial of lavender oil. I hand the woman my Visa card. She glances at the name. She asks if I'm the writer, the one in the TV movie? I nod. She gets so flustered she has trouble placing my items in the bag. She says she can hardly wait to tell her daughter that she met me. I sign my name on the Visa slip with an extra flourish, hand it back to her, and tell her that my life will be rebroadcast over the upcoming holiday weekend.

GENTLE READER,

Now, as the end draws near, can enlightenment finally descend upon my sordid and sorted past, as seen on TV, starring a Jewish actress in the story of my lost life?

If so, praise Be to Christ, God, Yahweh, Buddha, Allah, Vishnu, Shiva, Jehovah, Elohim, Zeus, Jove, Zoroaster, and the Whale who ate Jonah!

But just in case this actress impersonating me isn't enough, *let us not forget* that Pat Boone hugged this little gefilte. No, not, admittedly, like a laying on of hands. But certainly like a Good Father, a Father who praises his precious round gefilte, a Father who sees his daughter not, in fact, as a gefilte, but as a girl, a flower pushing aside concrete . . . as the good, blossoming Jewish soul she (finally) is, or will now (almost, or at last) grow up to be.

What are the odds that I would have an audience with Pat Boone, who calls himself an "adopted Jew"—while *I* wanted to be adopted by him? What are the odds that *he*, this father of four, would be the one to finally see me? And who would have thought that Pat Boone and I would both glow, as if together, in the limelight . . . even though, for me, *that* role lasted only a moment . . . while the role of being me goes on, and on.

S.W.S.

An Argument for the Existence of
Free Will and/or Pat Boone's Induction
into the Rock and Roll Hall of Fame

CALL ME SUE.

Byline: Girl Reporter.

Daily Planet.

Dateline: Metropolis.

In the a.m. (on one day in the past, present, or future) approached by Male Caucasian Editor, Perry White, smoking a stogie.

SECRET ASSIGNMENT!

COVERT OPERATION!!

INTERNAL and/or EXTERNAL INVESTIGATION!!!

SUE BAD-HABITS GIRL REPORTER lights a Chesterfield. Takes a drag. Exhales. Pulls typed copy of current article out of her Underwood typewriter: "Ever-Changing Daily Forecast for Metropolis, U. S. A.: gray, dark, overcast, cloudy, murky, unknown. Or: sunny, smiley faces, happy halos of light." Likes to give citizenry options. Better than writing obits.

Editor White leans forward to whisper details of Secret Assignment. SUE ON-THE-BALL GIRL REPORTER glances around. Eavesdroppers?

Clark Kent, across room, pounds typewriter keys. Pauses. Leans back in chair. Surreptitiously removes glasses. Wipes them on handkerchief with peacock-blue border. Slides glasses back on. Gazes out window. A bird, maybe a pigeon, flies past. The drone of an airplane rattles glass.

It's a bird. It's a plane . . .

Perry White, slipping a Top Secret file folder onto SUE TRUST-WORTHY GIRL REPORTER's desk, cryptically says, "Unknown Forces at work who, in the future, will prevent Pat Boone from being inducted into Rock and Roll Hall of Fame. Discover identity of Unknown Forces. Be prepared for possible Obliteration of Enemy."

Lois Lane strolls into office. Dreamy look on dreamy face. Instead of her usual black pumps, wears bobby socks and white buck shoes. Clutches a copy of Pat Boone's book *'Twixt Twelve and Twenty*. Clark Kent's gaze pierces the cover. The laser intensity could bore holes. He scowls.

SUE OBSERVANT GIRL REPORTER considers changing weather forecast: Lightning, thunder, mayhem, nuclear winter.

Editor White blows smoke rings. Gives Sue meaningful look.

Sue gives him her SUE GIRL-REPORTER-ON-THE-JOB look. Stubs out Chesterfield in ashtray. Peeks inside Top Secret file folder.

It's a . . .

. . . comic book?!?! . . . a DC National, May 1959 edition, which raises the dark specter of conspiracy!? On the cover: *Superman's Girl Friend Lois Lane* "featuring 'Pat Boone in Superman's Mystery Song!'" On the left-hand side, Superman, red cape swirling, swoops into the scene where Lois Lane sings while playing a piano. Pat Boone, beside her, strums a guitar. (Does he play a guitar in real life? SUE FACTUAL GIRL REPORTER REQUESTS A FACT CHECKER.) Superman realizes he must use all of his superpowers to stop the song from becoming popular.

Why?, SUE EVER-INQUISITIVE GIRL REPORTER asks herself. Is Superman orchestrating the sabotage of Pat Boone's induction into the Rock and Roll Hall of Fame?! What's his beef? Jealousy? Under the influence of liberals? SUE PARANOID GIRL REPORTER turns comic book over so no one can see the lead story line.

"Why the Pat Boone book?" SUE SOUNDING-INNOCENT GIRL REPORTER asks Lois Lane.

Lois Lane sits at her desk. Removes plastic cover from typewriter. Places book beside it. Trails her fingers across Pat Boone's image. "Didn't you see the billboard downtown? '*One Day Only. Pat Boone at the Rialto.*'"

Pat Boone right here in Metropolis!?
Sue sticks a No. 2 yellow Ticonderoga pencil behind ear. Palms sweat. Eyes narrow. Takes a deep breath. SUE OLFACTORY-SENSES-ON-HIGH-ALERT GIRL REPORTER smells a rat.

What are the odds that *four* items involving Pat Boone converge in Metropolis at the same time?

1) GIRL REPORTER is instructed to conduct an internal-external covert operation–investigation into why Pat Boone won't be inducted into Rock and Roll Hall of Fame in the future.
2) Lois Lane enters *Daily Planet* holding Pat Boone's best-selling book.
3) Clark Kent scowls at it.
4) Pat Boone just so happens to be here, *today.*

A coincidence? SUE CYNICAL GIRL REPORTER doesn't think so.

Lois Lane (who in 2014 will be known as LoLa on *Entertainment Tonight*) sighs. She says, "I want Pat Boone's autograph on the book! I've worn out the grooves on all my Pat Boone albums. I have every product endorsed by him. The Pat Boone Toothbrush. The Pat Boone Transistor Radio. The Pat Boone Jewel Box. The Pat Boone Pen and Pencil Set. The Pat Boone Portable Record Player. The Pat Boone White Bucks (of course). The Pat Boone Secret Decoder Ring. The Pat Boone Acne Cream. The Pat Boone Bomb Shelter. The Pat Boone personally autographed New King James version of the Holy Bible. Almost as if he wrote it *himself*!!"

Clark Kent worriedly runs his fingers through his jet-black hair.

"And his new hit is sweeping the country," Lois Lane exclaims.

"Won't Superman be jealous?" Clark Kent asks.

"Why should he? I just like Pat Boone's music. Besides, Superman flies like a bird above jealousy."

SUE GIRL REPORTER EXTRAORDINAIRE, in order to get to bottom of conspiracy, lifts receiver on her black rotary phone. Works her sources. Calls the Rialto. Tracks down Gerry Smith, Pat Boone's road manager. Lands an interview! Yes, Pat Boone is free to meet with SUE GO-GET-'EM GIRL REPORTER at 3:00 p.m. at the *Daily Planet!*

In preparation, SUE INVESTIGATIVE GIRL REPORTER dials the to-be-used-only-in-emergency outside telephone line that connects to the future. Calls Sarah Palin. Members of the conservative Tea Party. Right-to-lifers. Mike Huckabee. Glenn Beck. Rick Santorum. For opposing viewpoint calls gay, bisexual, lesbian, and transgender movement. Editors of *Ms.* magazine. Christian theologians. Rabbis. Future incarnations of Fats Domino, Little Richard, Mick Jagger. Director of the Rock and Roll Hall of Fame not yet built in Cleveland. Anonymous sources. Deep Throat. Foes. Fans.

Discovers that, in the year 2014, when Pat Boone will have been snubbed by the Rock and Roll Hall of Fame for the umpteenth time, you either

1) love Pat Boone;
2) are nostalgic for Pat Boone;
3) hate Pat Boone;
4) never heard of Pat Boone.

2:55 p.m.

Lois Lane powders nose. Clark Kent's scowl deepens. Perry White—still a Caucasian Male Editor—rushes from private office, two stogies in his mouth, waving a third. "Pat Boone's besieged by fans! Downtown is gridlock! He'll never make it here!"

"Call 911!"

Clark Kent excuses himself. Rushes to the restroom. Comic book readers everywhere witness transformation. Clark Kent strips off his shirt. His pants. Beneath is his little peacock-blue-tights number, the insignia "S," in red, on the chest. Putting aside personal feelings of jealousy toward Lois Lane's feelings toward Pat Boone, he rises, as it were, to the occasion.

It's SUPERMAN*!!!*

Now, across town, THE MAN OF STEEL zooms, faster than a speeding gefilte, above throngs of adoring fans until his laser eyesight pinpoints Pat Boone.

Superman swoops the teen idol up in his arms to deliver him to the *Daily Planet* office. Gently cradles a smiling Pat Boone against his manly chest. Darting around skyscrapers, they careen high above Metropolis. Pat Boone fails to notice future urban decay about to blight cities . . . fails to notice all-American boys and girls thinking about their future alter egos selling crack cocaine in the alley behind the Rialto. Today, Pat Boone's white buck shoes remain spotless, like always, in Pat Boone's world, spit-polished to perfection.

2:59 and 55 seconds.

Pat Boone strolls into the *Daily Planet*. Five seconds later Clark Kent "returns" from the men's room, a thin line of sweat above his lip. He approaches Pat Boone, holds out his hand, and says, "The name is Kent. Clark Kent."

A thought bubble appears over SUE EXPERT-AT-MOVIE-ALLUSIONS GIRL REPORTER's head: "Well, if that's not a rip-off, I don't know what is." She eyes Clark Kent suspiciously.

SUE INTREPID GIRL REPORTER clears throat and opens reporter pad. Pat Boone sits beside Sue's desk.

"Just for the record: Your real name is Charles Eugene Boone, right?"

Pat Boone flashes his pearlies and chuckles. "So true. So true. My parents expected—wanted—a girl, so had picked out the name Patricia before I was born. Boy, did I surprise them, haha. But they called me Pat anyway. And it stuck."

SUE ON-THE-HUNT-FOR-TRUTH GIRL REPORTER licks the tip of her No. 2 pencil: "But that must've seemed, well, *strange*. You ever *feel* like a Pat-ricia? Haha."

"Not with a wife and four girls."

Lois Lane swoons. Her dreamy eyes in her dreamy face dreamily gaze at Pat Boone.

Clark Kent dreamily gazes at Lois Lane dreamily gazing at Pat Boone.

SUE JUST-THE-FACTS GIRL REPORTER: "Review your accomplishments for our readers who will one day influence the vote on your induction into the Rock and Roll Hall of Fame! What's your biggest hit?"

"'Love Letters in the Sand.' Five million copies. It was on the singles chart for over six months. I also set an all-time record, which has never been broken, of 220 consecutive weeks on the *Billboard* hit singles chart!"

"Impressive! And your hit TV show?"

"I'm the youngest entertainer to host my own TV show. But that almost fell through. Initially, Chesterfield cigarettes wanted to be the sponsor. But I could never be endorsed by something harmful to our young people. Schlitz beer offered next, but I turned them down, too. Thank goodness Chevy came along."

Sue surreptitiously slides her pack of Chesterfields into her desk drawer.

"Moving on: Would you care to comment on the future Rock and Roll Hall of Fame induction snub that's going to piss you off in a couple of decades or so?"

"Well, I would *never* say the word 'piss' in front of a girl. But you better believe it."

SUE NOT-PULLING-ANY-PUNCHES GIRL REPORTER asks, "How would you respond to this statement: African American musicians feel as if you ripped off their music with your hits such as 'Tutti Frutti' and 'Ain't That a Shame'?"

"Yeah, ain't *that* a shame?!" Pat Boone sighs, smiles, and shakes his head. "The funny thing about that song? There I was, having graduated magna cum laude from Columbia University in *English.* And I had to say the word 'ain't.' I *tried* to fit 'isn't' into the rhythm, but it just didn't sound right."

"But to return to the charges . . ."

"Yes, yes. All nonsense. Untrue. Here's the truth, as I will one day write in my 2006 book, *Pat Boone's America, 50 Years: A Pop Culture Journey through the Last Five Decades.* Might as well get started early on publicity."

Pat Boone then quotes himself from his not-yet-written book while SUE TOP-NOTCH GIRL REPORTER scribbles furiously.

"If there was a master scheme (as it's been cartooned by agenda-driven 'researchers') to create a thoroughly palatable white star, and then get him recording the biggest selling releases from black stars (to exploit them monetarily while obscuring their identities) it sure didn't track that way in practice. Coming from the early to mid-1950s record business model, more than ever before or since, recording your own 'covers' of other people's charted releases was simply standard operating procedure."

"So you deny the charges." SUE SPEEDY GIRL REPORTER writes . . . *almost* faster than a speeding bullet.

Pat Boone no longer smiles. Dark forces gather behind his smooth white forehead . . . or it's as if a line of dust settles in the cracks of his trademark white buck shoes.

"I mean, don't you think that accusation will hurt you in terms of not being inducted into the Rock and Roll Hall of Fame in the future? To say nothing of the, well, Christian proselytizing? And your friendship with *Sarah Palin.* Opposition to gay marriage. No abortion for anyone under any circumstances. . . ."

He leans close to Sue. "It's a conspiracy," he whispers. "What about *liberal* proselytizers. Jane Fonda. The Dixie Chicks."

SUE ALL-KNOWING GIRL REPORTER knows that Jane Fonda and the Dixie Chicks received their fair share of flack as well. But she doesn't want Pat Boone to get distracted. "Perpetrated by . . . ?"

About to speak, Pat Boone's words are truncated by a low rumble of thunder. Storm clouds churn over Metropolis. Clark Kent stands from his desk to look out the window. Comic book readers everywhere hear him contemplating the fact that if a major thunderstorm hits, he'll have to become a quick-change artist again. He feels almost like a cross-dresser, like a member of the nonexistent group "White Male Superheroes in Business Suits Cross-Dressing Society" (WAMS-SHOD for short), but that thought bubble is cut from the final edit of the comic strip.

The storm CRAASSSHHHS. Rain SSLLASSSHS.

Clark Kent once again excuses himself, offering to go to the coffee shop on the corner for refreshments. "Sugar with your coffee?" he asks. "Cream?"

"Oh, just a nice cold glass of milk for me," Pat Boone chuckles. But his chuckle isn't as hearty as when he arrived.

Either the storm or the relentless questions visibly affect Pat Boone's mood.

As if he himself is outside in the storm, his white skin seems to ossify. His brown eyes darken to the color of the bottom of a rain puddle on asphalt as if he sees into the future, envisioning his own presence in it.

"The conspiracy?" SUE CONSPIRACY-BUFF GIRL REPORTER asks again, drawing him back to the conversation.

"Yes, yes, I know," Pat Boone says. "Which is why I will write that book in 2006. To explain . . ."

"Explain?"

"Or *question*," he says earnestly. "Where's the America I used to know? It seems like it was here just a moment ago. What happened to it? Where did it go? *And who took it away from me?*" [Intrepid Reporter's emphasis.] "Because even though so many of us are committed to God-fearing, family values of the true

American spirit, the truth is that our nation has drifted so far off course and downstream, we hardly recognize it anymore."

"So those who, you claim, will allegedly one day drive us off course are the ones who will prevent you from being inducted?"

Pat Boone shrugs, lost.

"Let me help you out here," SUE RELENTLESS GIRL REPORTER says. "Listen to this quote from the New Yorker that will appear in June 2010. It's about that trip you will take to Israel with presidential hopeful Mike Huckabee. The one where he says that he's 'crazy about Israel,' where he proclaims, 'I worship a Jew.'"

"All God-fearing good Christians do."

"But Huckabee will say it wearing Ray-Bans and a polka-dot shirt with gold cufflinks in the shape of Arkansas! What kind of fashion statement . . ."

Pat Boone pleads, "On that trip I will sing my heart out on 'Thanks for Just Being You.'"

"I know. I know. And maybe if we could just redo future history, and you could just stick to singing 'April Love' all the way to the Pearly Gates." SUE EMPATHETIC GIRL REPORTER pauses to give her words a chance to sink in. "But here's what that article will quote you as rhapping (as in 'rhapsodizing') in the middle of your song 'Thanks for Just Being You':

"Honey, our little girl surprised me today. She said, 'Daddy, I know I'm gonna grow up to be a wife and a mommy someday. I know what a mommy is, but what's a wife, really?'

"A wife is the one that feeds and waters and cleans up after that family pet she didn't want." There was a wave of knowing murmurs from the believers. "A patient soul that picks up my dirty socks and underwear and handkerchiefs and washes them and puts them back in the drawer so she can do the whole thing again, next week. . . . A good wife is simply a gift from God."

"See, my point here," SUE DOGGED-TOUGH-AS-NAILS GIRL RE-PORTER exclaims, "is that's the *kind* of thing that, frankly, makes it difficult for *women* to support your induction. You want *your* America back. But what *is* or *will be* your America? What about Americans living in ghettos? The homeless? The unemployed? Kids shot in drive-by shootings? Gays unable to marry? Women who're underpaid?" SUE UNDERPAID GIRL REPORTER glances toward Editor White's office.

"Women have always been my biggest fans," Pat Boone defends. He nods toward Lois Lane, whose expression hasn't changed since she first laid eyes on him. She begins to hum, however, sounding as if she's making up a song. "To say nothing of *you*, lest you forget." His gaze arrows back to Sue.

SUE USUALLY VERBOSE GIRL REPORTER can't think of a thing to say, unable to explain the Theory of Contradictions to Pat Boone, especially that things won't always be so, well, black and white, or simplistic, in the future.

Meanwhile, in another part of town, Superman is ZOOMZOOM-ZOOMING into the eye of the storm. GROWWRR! CRRASH! BOOOM-MM! Neon signs across Metropolis short-circuit. Steam from subway grates roils into the atmosphere, almost obscuring our own SUPERHERO member of WAMS-SHOD. The scene is turning into a "Superman-Meets-Batman-in-Gotham City, Girls-and-Boys," nightmare. CRAAACKK! Lids of garbage cans clank in alleys. RIIIPPPP. American flags are stripped from flagpoles. Superman SOARSOARSOARS to a car wreck, plucking out a little girl clutching a Pat Boone album from a smashed-in rear seat. Superman whooshes across town, his cape seemingly rigid in the stiff breeze, one step ahead of a black coroner's van with white lettering.

Back at the *Daily Planet* . . .

"The breakdown of family life and traditional moral values is front-page news" (in the *Daily Planet*?!) "nearly every day," Pat Boone says, as if gazing into a crystal ball shaped like a white buck shoe. "Could this really be my America?"

"What *is* America?" SUE POLITICALLY CORRECT GIRL REPORTER questions. "Isn't there room for everything, for all of us? Republicans. Democrats. Believers. Nonbelievers. Straights. Gays. Superheroes. Gothamites. Gefiltes. Whitefish. . . ."

Pat Boone shivers. "*Back now*, today, it's all so clear: You either love Elvis Presley or you love Pat Boone. White bucks versus blue suede shoes."

"Why's it *always* about the shoes?" SUE FASHIONISTA GIRL REPORTER asks.

Lois Lane, now going by LoLa, starts to sing, but it's difficult to make out the lyrics.

"The good white-buck girls all love *me*," Pat Boone continues. "The clean-cut girls who don't cuss or smoke or engage in sexual activities before marriage. The girls who *pray*."

"You think that not one of your fans ever got into trouble or had sex before marriage????"

Tears well up in Pat Boone's eyes. "No, no," he sighs. "I refuse to believe that any of *my* fans . . ."

"But I, Sue, Girl Reporter, swear like a sailor."

"I'll pray for you."

A confused expression forms on Pat Boone's face—the kind of expression you might have, say, if, in a moment of extreme existential turmoil, you contemplated Lawrence Welk's inner life.

"I have it!" LoLa jumps up from her chair. She begins to sing the song straight out of the comic book. It's a tribute to her boyfriend Superman. Pat Boone joins her. As they harmonize, the cover of the comic book seethes and squirms with life. (Comic books have the right-to-life, too.)

CRAAACK! SOCCKKK! BOOOOM! POW! CRRASHH!

Superman must thwart their efforts at singing the song about him. He darts to the shore of a conveniently located lake whose beach, composed of silica sand, he converts to a soundproof plastic dome that he drops over Pat Boone and Lois Lane so no one can hear them sing.

"Another country heard from," SUE KEEPING-IT-REAL GIRL RE-PORTER reports. "Why keep the song secret?" she asks Superman.

"I wrote the lyrics," Superman says.

"Don't tell me *you* want to be inducted into the Rock and Roll Hall of Fame, too? What, a 'one-hit wonder' category?"

Superman shakes his slick black hair. As if he uses steel-hard product, not one strand falls out of place.

The lyrics, an anthem to Superman's power to keep Metropolis (or the entire USA) safe from villains and tyranny, are revealed only to comic book readers, thus remaining a mystery to the world at large. "Unwittingly, in the nine lines of the song, I reveal my true identity," says a thought bubble floating over Superman's head. "The first letter of each word in each line spells out 'Clark Kent.' Now I have to prevent it from ever being sung aloud."

LoLa, now Lois Lane again, and Pat Boone gesture to Superman to lift the plastic dome, agreeing never to sing the song, though they—not being comic book aficionados—haven't cracked the secret code.

"But suppose *that's* the song that could finally propel me into the Rock and Roll Hall of Fame?" Pat Boone opines.

"It sounds like a theme song for the Republican party," SUE JUDICIOUS GIRL REPORTER judiciously observes.

"Republicans are people, too," Pat Boone exhorts.

Tell me about it. "Of course they are."

Pat Boone tells Sue about how the South African government allowed a mixed-race audience for his concert at his insistence.

He cleared the way for black performers, including Little Richard and Fats Domino, and also threatened to quit his TV show when his sponsors forbade him to have Harry Belafonte as a guest.

SUE GETTING-TO-THE-NITTY-GRITTY GIRL REPORTER scribbles as fast as she can.

"And, I bet you didn't know that my daughter Cherry was married by a Christian *and a Jew.*" Pat Boone, feeling his oats again, smiles and winks. "Our minister, Jack Hayford, married Cherry and Dan at Church on the Way, and then Rabbi Hillel Silverman of Temple Sinai in Los Angeles prayed over and blessed them at the reception, which was held at Bel Air Country Club."

Pat Boone stares into Sue's eyes. "Any relation?" He chuckles, as the remnants of the storm now gust away from Metropolis.

GIRL REPORTER AND FUTURE HIPPIE SUE is unmoved. "Let's just stick to the music, shall we? What should I say to readers of the *Daily Planet* about your noninduction into the Rock and Roll Hall of Fame, even though the first class of inductees (which includes Fats Domino and Little Richard) won't take place for twenty-seven more years?"

"How about this," Pat Boone says:

Even though their political feelings have more in common with Pat Boone than with, say, Mick Jagger, mainstream Americans who listen to popular music from the more edgy, rugged end of the spectrum tend to assume that their political feelings must be unlike those of conservative "squares" like Boone. Thus the professing liberals behind things like MTV's Rock the Vote seem hopeful about moving election outcomes in their favor essentially by enlisting music fans to vote reflexively against things square.

No wonder the trendy-haired, ear-studded Hollywood types who decide about "induction" into the Rock and Roll Hall of Fame (it's no grassroots process, kids!) prefer to keep a known conservative like Pat Boone strangely out of it."

CONSPIRACY! Rigged by trendy-haired ear-studders. SUE READY-TO-MOVE-MOUNTAINS-FACT-CHECKER GIRL REPORTER decides to nail this down once and for all.

POP BOOM BLAM!!

CRRRAAACCCKKK!!!

Suddenly, all the typewriters in the newsroom evolve into Apple computers. All the reporters' desks turn into cubicles. The newsroom is transformed from the clack of typewriter keys to the soft tap-tapping of computer keys. Black rotary telephones shrink into BlackBerries. And before you know it, SUE LEAVE-NO-STONE-UNTURNED GIRL REPORTER is Googling the "Rock and Roll Hall of Fame" on the World Wide Web. She clicks to the link on "Induction Process," prints out the requirements, and hands a copy to Pat Boone.

Scanning it, Pat Boone exclaims, "'Twenty-five years since my first release'? Check."

"'An impact on rock and roll'? Check!"

"'Superior style and technique'? 'Musical excellence'? Check and check!"

"'Length and depth of career and body of work'? Check!"

Pat Boone reads aloud, "The Foundation's nominating committee, composed of rock and roll historians, selects nominees each year in the Performer category. Ballots are then sent to an international voting body of more than 500 rock experts. Those performers who receive the highest number of votes—and more than 50% of the vote—are inducted. The Foundation generally inducts five to seven performers each year."

SUE MOMENTARILY STYMIED GIRL REPORTER and Pat Boone stare at each other.

"Numbers of votes," Pat Boone admonishes. "No check."

He crumples the printout and tosses it into the paper shredder.

GROOWWL!! CLAAANK!!!

"I'm listed, according to *Billboard,* as number ten all-time recording artist. Forty-five million records. One hundred thirty albums. Thirty-eight Top 10 hits, gold and platinum. *What more can I do?*"

SUE SYMPATHETIC GIRL REPORTER both nods and shrugs. Not that she believes, philosophically, in what Pat Boone believes, but she believes in *him*, in his sincerity and commitment to wanting his own America back, the America he believes in, even though—outside of comic books and black-and-white TV sitcoms—his America never quite existed, even though he believes it did.

Nevertheless, Pat Boone is right: It should be only about the music.

"I devoted my whole life to music," he says. "To doing good work. To trying to make a difference. To helping shape young lives."

He places his palms together as if in prayer.

SUE NEWLY MINTED CHEERLEADER GIRL REPORTER says, "You made a difference to Lois Lane and, well, *me*. And after all, your recording career will ultimately include everything from *Pat Boone Sings the New Songs of the Jesus People* to *In a Metal Mood: No More Mr. Nice Guy*. To say nothing of 'Tutti Frutti.'"

"Au rutti," he whispers reverentially.

"Au rutti, indeed!" SUE GETTING-WITH-THE-PROGRAM GIRL REPORTER says. "Let's look at this objectively. Little Richard and Fats Domino know the truth—how you really helped their careers. Plus, *after fifty years you still have fans!* How many other musicians have lasted this long in the business?"

"I've been very blessed." Pat Boone nods.

"Maybe *that's* more important than the Rock and Roll Hall of Fame, anyway?" SUE NO-LONGER-CYNICAL GIRL REPORTER pleads.

As if he doesn't hear her, Pat Boone says, "Sure, I never pierced my ears or did drugs, but *I wore black leather, too.*"

"Well, *if it's that important*—we could try to start a groundswell of support! The *Daily Planet* could publish editorials! We could start a petition campaign on Facebook! DC Comics could publish a special issue: SUPERMAN AND PAT BOONE VS. MICK JAGGER AND THE ROCK AND ROLL HALL OF FAME!"

Clark Kent and Lois Lane glance at Pat Boone and SUE OUTSIDE-AGITATOR GIRL REPORTER. Thousands of readers of comic books now know that Superman *not only* scooped sand from the shores of the lake but also took a quick baptismal dip in the cleansing waters, thus converting into a BORN-AGAIN SUPER-HERO!! Now, fully on the side of Pat Boone's FAIR AND BALANCED induction into the Rock and Roll Hall of Fame, Clark Kent aka Superman prepares for a quick change in order to CLACCK POP BOOOOM through the Rock and Roll Hall of Fame in Cleveland and smash the building to smithereens.

"You think?" Pat Boone asks, his voice quavering with hope.

SUE SUCCUMBING GIRL REPORTER nods.

"But if I fail to be inducted yet again, I might begin to look like a fool . . ."

A FOOL???!!!

YOOOWWZZZAAAAA!!!!

SUE CRACK-INVESTIGATIVE GIRL REPORTER cracks the case!!!

!!!!NEWS FLASH!!!!::::

The wire services *light up your life.* BEEP BEEP. TYPO! Correction: the wire services light up *with* life!

Dateline Metropolis: SOMEONE UPSTAIRS, WHO SHALL REMAIN NAMELESS, CONFUSED THE ROCK AND ROLL HALL OF FAME WITH THE PAT BOONE SONG "FOOLS HALL OF FAME" *and he's been inducted into the wrong hall??!!*

Is it all a case of mistaken identity? Is Pat Boone's publicity shot hung in the incorrect edifice?

SUE EXHAUSTED GIRL REPORTER's success at unraveling the mystery feels hollow, however. Maybe this explanation is sufficient for the masses who rely on comic books and FOX-TV for their news, but surely it's more complicated than a case of mistaken identity.

SUE CONFUSED GIRL REPORTER debates, not for the first time, the pros and cons of real people talking to fictional characters as well as real people who are fictionalized on pieces of comic-strip paper. Besides, she herself struggles with double-identity issues, having contracted this condition by existing, as it were, both inside *and* outside the pages of the comic book. SUE BLOOD-HOUND GIRL REPORTER now, for the first time, considers the danger, when all is said and done, of such an existence. Would individual lives—and even the universe—be clarified by choosing one or the other? She flips through the DC comic looking at images of the young, innocent, future-before-him Pat Boone, fans swooning after his performance at the Rialto.

SUE ABLE-TO-PREDICT-THE-FUTURE GIRL REPORTER now realizes that the exact moment he, Pat Boone, steps from the pages of the comic book—once he has *free will*—once he's able to speak his own mind, no longer controlled, as it were, by Jerome "Jerry" Siegel, then the proverbial #%&**# will hit the fan.

Siegel, creator and main writer of Superman comics, the son of Jewish immigrants from Lithuania no less, knows, after all, a thing or two about changing identities. He was also known, at times, by his less-Jewish-sounding pseudonyms Joe Carter and Jerry Ess and *was*, ironically, *POSTHUMOUSLY* inducted into the Will Eisner Comic Book Hall of Fame in 1992 and the Jack Kirby Hall of Fame in 1993. *But only posthumously.* So maybe he also knows a thing or two about hall of fame conspiracies and snubs?!

In short, the only solution for Pat Boone to be inducted into the Rock and Roll Hall of Fame is to cloak his true, conservative Christian identity by remaining inside the pages of the comic book, consorting with ever-popular superheroes, where the future is knowable, where GOOD DEFEATS EVIL, or where Siegel and Superman will predictably map out his future. A future where it *always* remains the 1950s, *always* celebrates Pat Boone's red-white-and-true-blue America. Where Pat Boone won't get embroiled with hippies, the British invasion, hard rockers . . . where he'll never even meet Sarah Palin or be clutched to the heaving chests of the Birthers, the Tea Partiers, etc., etc., etc.

But Pat Boone, as if reading SUE WHO-WEARS-HER-HEART-ON-HER-SLEEVE GIRL REPORTER's mind, looks determined. "I yam what I yam," he proclaims.

Aren't we all?

Aren't we all just superheroes but afraid to dash into the first phone booth we find, strip off our ordinary clothes, reveal our true, human selves, and speed-dial heaven? I mean, just try to even find a phone booth anymore.

Pat Boone stands as if to make a move, to step outside the comfy confines of the comic book. Sue, despite having looked up to, and needing, Pat Boone for years, now feels as if *she* is the one who needs to lend a helping hand to Pat Boone, to grasp *his* hand, pull him back inside the comic book, where time, blessedly, stands still, where no one ages or changes.

"I want to matter," Pat Boone confesses, putting one foot outside the margins of the comic book . . . *and* right on a banana peel.

SUE, whose role as GIRL REPORTER dwindles to an end, solemnly turns to the final page.

Encore

AFTER THE ELECTION OF BARACK OBAMA as president, I dream I'm wandering a beach in Florida with Pat Boone. We reach a swampy inlet of water that we must cross in order to continue on. I'm not wearing shoes and worry I'll be bitten by an alligator. Pat lifts me, safely carrying me to the opposite shore.

"I've been in love with you since junior high school, you know," I say to him when he sets me down.

He nods. "I haven't known you, though."

"The Republicans lost the election because they lost their way trying to keep Terri Schiavo alive." I refer to politicians who sued to keep this brain-dead woman on life support, against her husband's wishes. I didn't watch the Republican convention, but I read on the Internet that Pat Boone attended it.

"But what did you expect them to do?" he says. "Just let her die?"

The Florida sun reflects off sand and water. I look up at him, though it's difficult to see his features in this dazzling halo.

"What would you do to keep *me* alive?" I whisper.

For you, he says, *I would iron the night.*

IN THE AMERICAN LIVES SERIES

To order or obtain more information on these or other University of Nebraska Press titles, visit www.nebraskapress.unl.edu.